AF598908

THE STENCIL GRAFFITI MANUAL

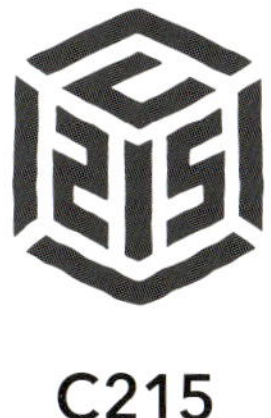

C215

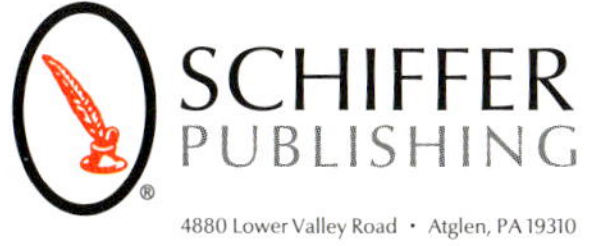

"Emptied emptiness is full
Emptiness filled with its emptiness is emptiness
Emptiness filled with its fullness is emptiness
Fullness emptied of its fullness is fullness

Ghérasim Luca, *Other Secrets of Emptiness and Fullness*"

CONTENTS

INTRODUCTION

The first time a stencil slammed into me was in 2004, on the corner of an alley in Barcelona. It was a stencil by the American artists Faile, representing a monkey painted in black, with a whole slew of texts imitating a vintage-style advertisement, on a white acrylic background. The detail, the delicacy of the painting and the stylistic discrepancy with what we commonly saw painted in the streets at the time struck me intensely. I approached it by asking myself: "How is it done? What *is* this?" My curiosity for stenciling was born. Four years of observing this new art scene followed, which led me to become a professional stencil artist in 2007.

Fifteen years after that first shock in Barcelona, I have accumulated experience that I'll share here by presenting the possibilities of this art. I am often asked to publish tutorials, run workshops or give courses to teach my processes, which I always refused to do. I have never wanted to prescribe a process to others or risk strangling their creativity. However, the public often has an extremely limited view of stenciling, trying to reproduce the existing rather than trying new directions. With this book, I don't want to teach my own way of stenciling, but all the possibilities of this art, so that everyone can forge their own style.

The book that you are holding in your hands is therefore a manual, an inventory of techniques to be appropriated in order to get yourself started in the art, or to help you develop stenciling's potential. Stencils have no limits and can be adapted to all styles.

Many artists agreed to take part in the interviews. Throughout these pages, they share with you their expertise and their passion for stenciling. This multi-voiced manual is not only the fruit of my experience, but also, and above all, of the meetings and links forged over time with other artists in this field.

Faile,
Fashion Chimp.

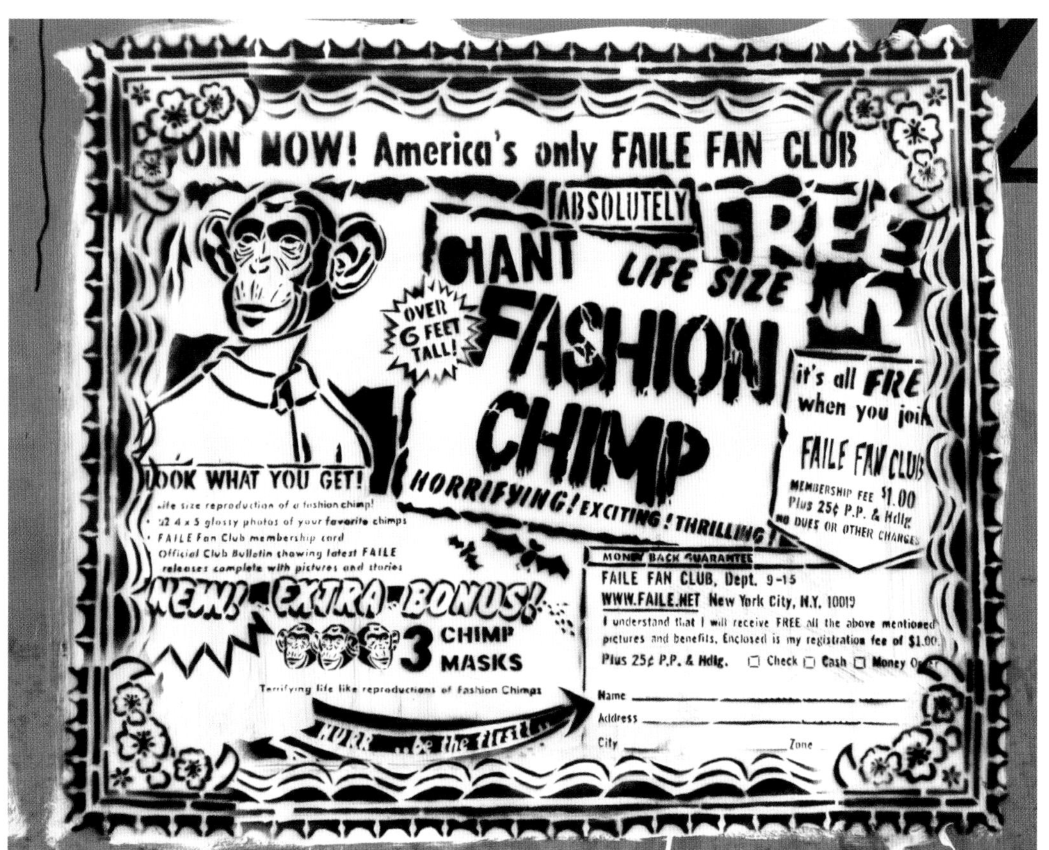

In honor of the "Je suis Charlie" movement generated by the Paris attacks of January 7, 2015, I distributed several hundred stencils so that everyone could make this message their own.

WHY STENCILS?

The tool called a stencil consists of a template that covers a surface and through which one paints. When it is removed, it reveals a negative print. An interesting thing about the term "stencil" is that it designates a tool, a process and the work resulting from its use, and this is the case not just in English but in many languages. So when we talk about a stencil, do we mean the tool or the works that result from it? Some consider that the art of stenciling lies in the creation of this tool, others in its application. But the two seem inseparable to me. An unpainted stencil is just a cutout, which becomes a stencil only once this cutout is painted. Indeed, the art of stenciling, and its corollary the talent of a stencil artist, does not depend solely on the appreciation of the tool or on its use.

To create a stencil is to launch into a project, because its drawing or its pattern has to be defined even before the creation of the painted work. It is a cerebral art, one where it's a question of anticipating the result well before its execution.

Stencils are used for three main qualities.

- They make it possible to reduce the line of the spray can and to draw more precisely than any tip—or cap—allows, because the fineness of the stencil cut determines the fineness of the line.
- They offer the possibility of unlimited duplication of a message or a pattern.

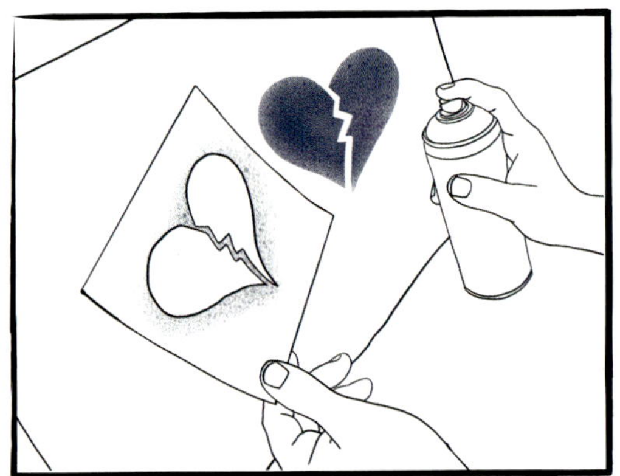

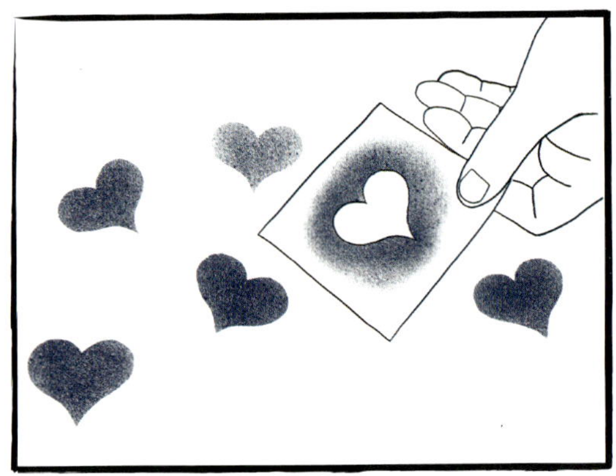

- They allow you to paint a predefined pattern rapidly.

The person who paints with a stencil is not necessarily its author, which will be the case if you use the stencils I provide for you at the end of the book (see p. 144). This fact can give rise to a "viral" phenomenon—the same stencil can be reproduced by hundreds of people all over the world—which poses the following question: Who is the artist, the creator of the stencil or the one who (more or less skillfully) used it? I love this complexity in the art of stenciling and in the making of these tools.

However, stencils have their limits. They take quite a while to make. Also, when the painting is large, you might wonder if it's not simpler and faster to do it freehand. However, whatever the size, some graphic renderings lend themselves better to stencil painting. Stenciling's binary dimension of voids and solids produces a certain highly contrasted aesthetic that's difficult to deny. There is a stencil state of mind, in the content as well as in the form.

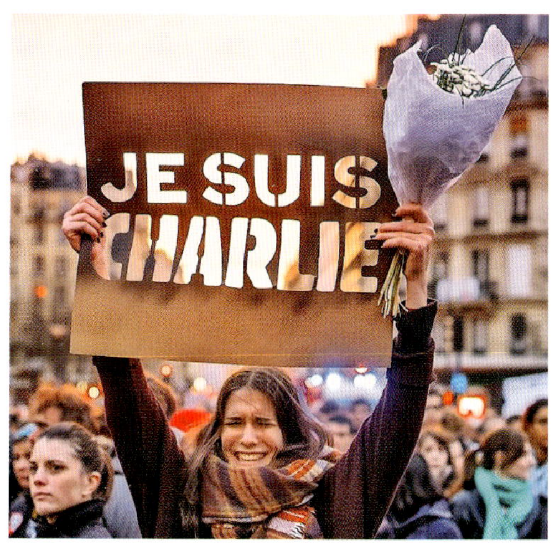
JE SUIS
CHARLIE

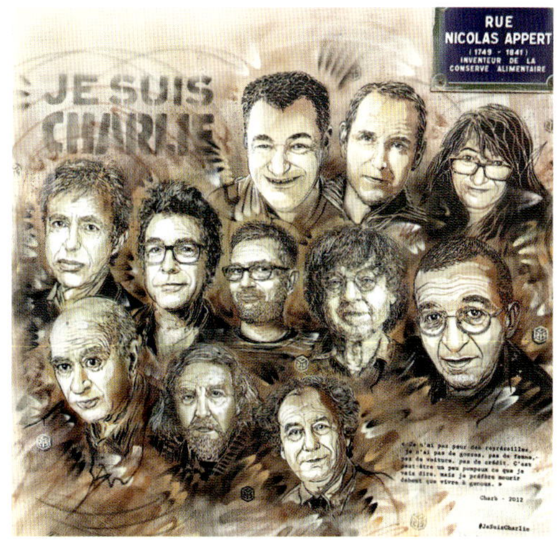
RUE
NICOLAS APPERT
(1749 - 1841)
INVENTEUR DE LA
CONSERVE ALIMENTAIRE
JE SUIS
CHARLIE

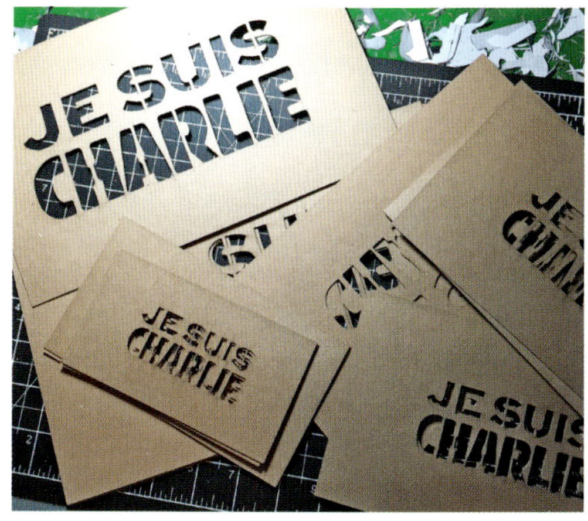
JE SUIS
CHARLIE
JE SUIS
CHARLIE
JE SUIS
CHARLIE

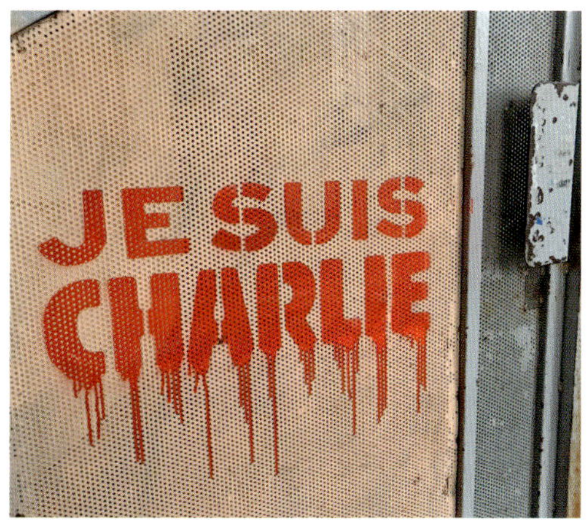
JE SUIS
CHARLIE

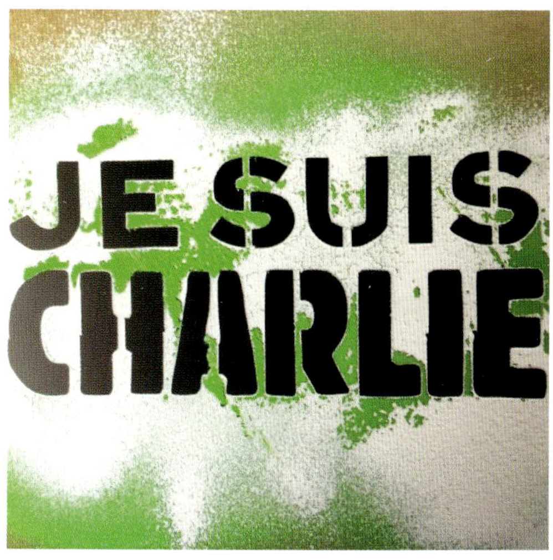
JE SUIS
CHARLIE

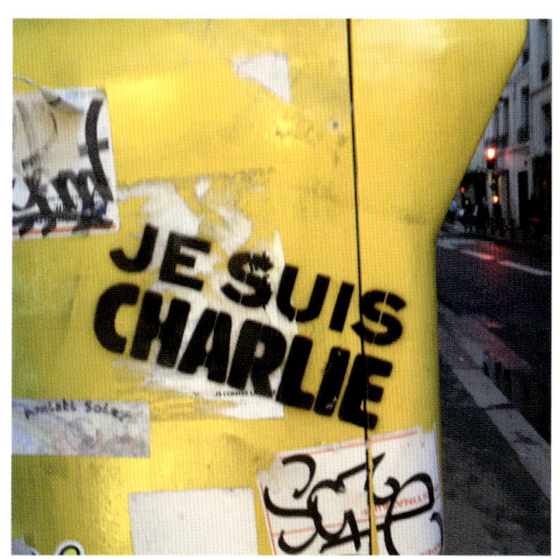
JE SUIS
CHARLIE

Variations of the same stencil:

1. Roubaix, France, 2017.

2. Roof of the Eyrolles Editions building, Paris, 2019.

3. Ivry, France, 2018.

4. Moscow, 2019.

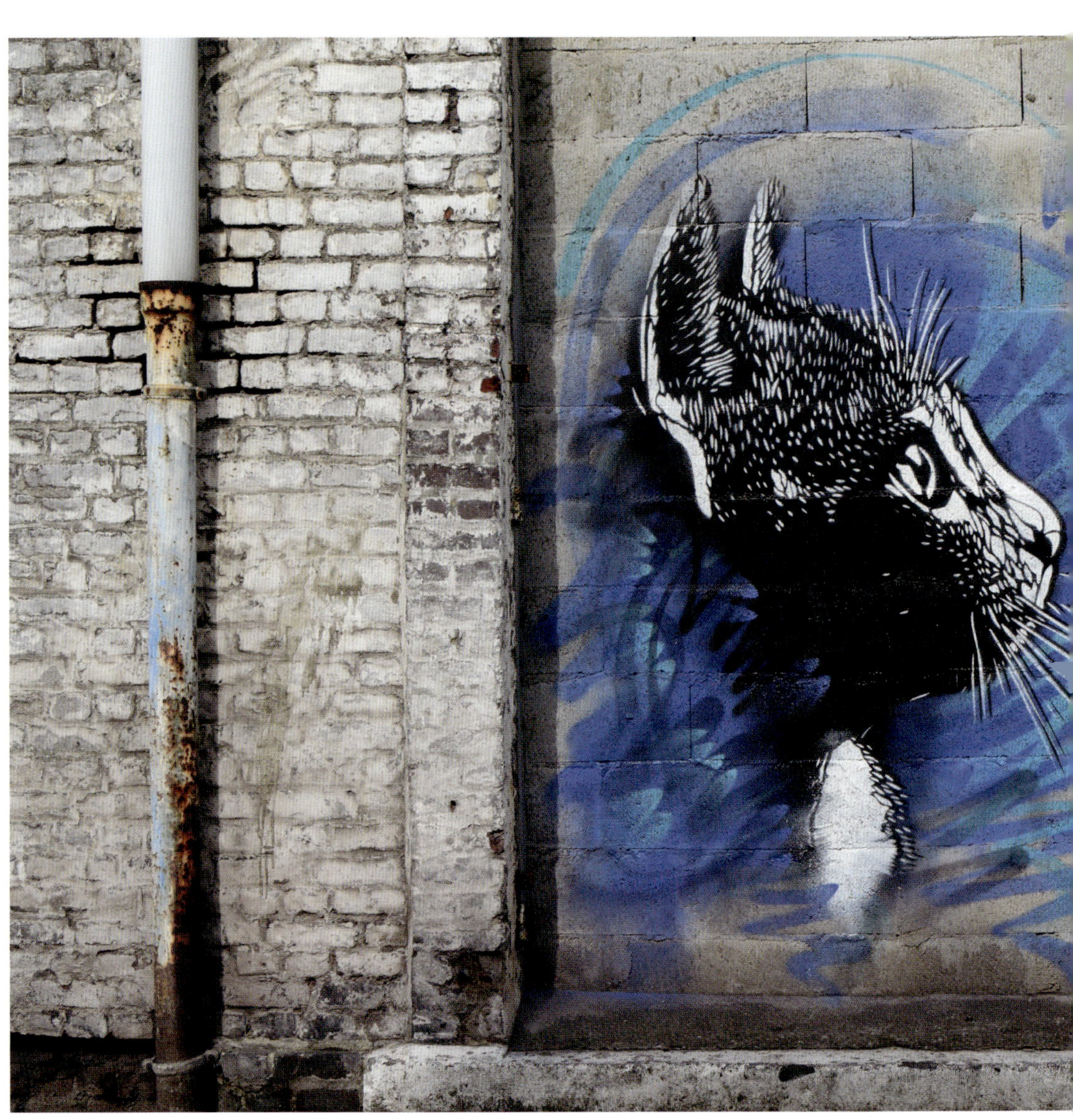

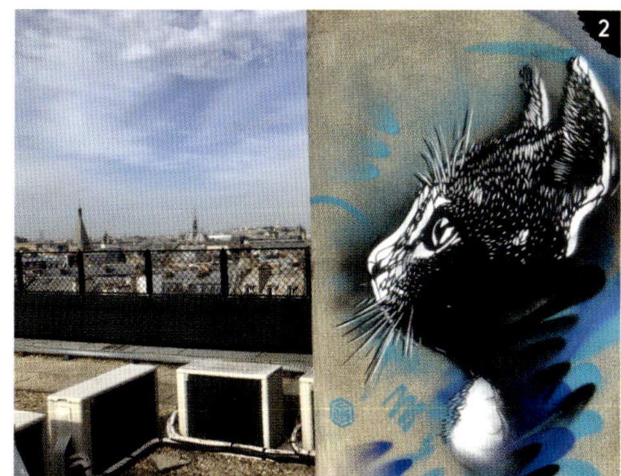
2

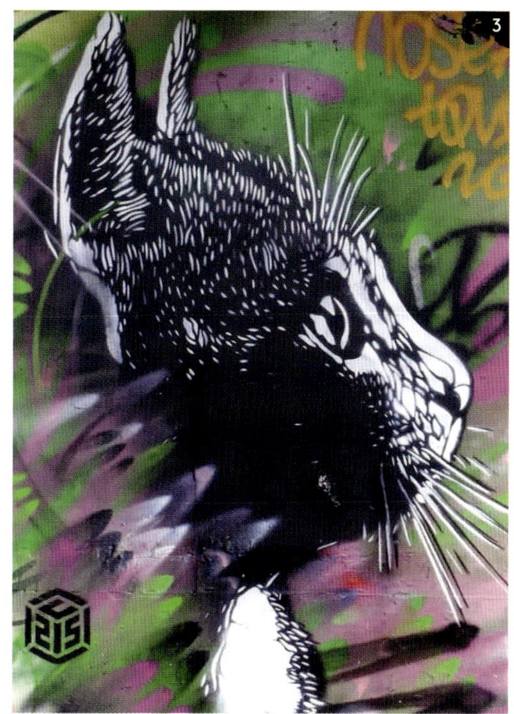
3

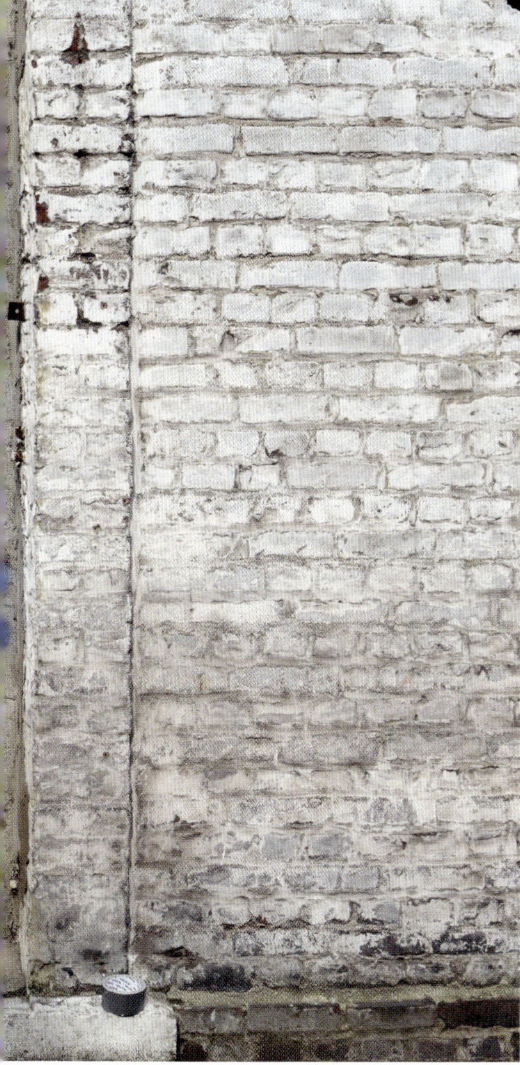
1

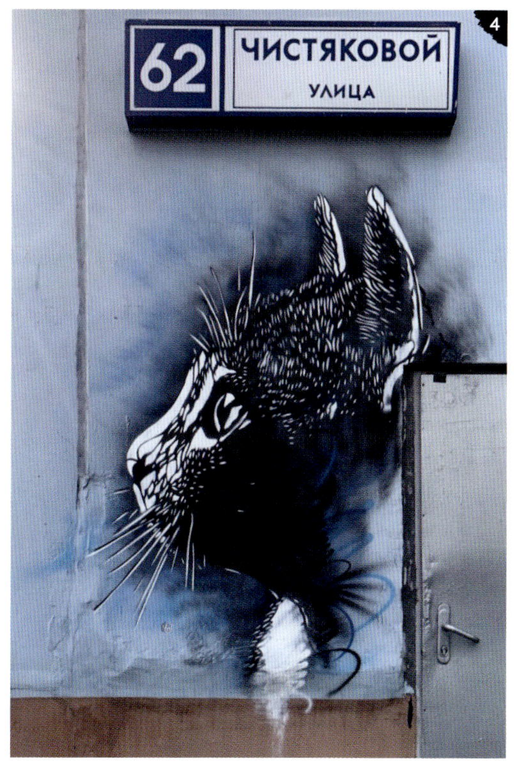
4
62
ЧИСТЯКОВОЙ
УЛИЦА

THE HISTORY OF STENCILS

Stenciling is an ancient technique. In France, the Chauvet-Pont d'Arc cave houses frescoes more than 30,000 years old showing hands painted in negative. Used as stencils, the hands masked the wall of the cave, onto which wet pigments were projected. Once removed, they revealed their form. We find here a perfect example of the entire stencil technique: one masks a support, one projects or applies paint, one removes the masking and the work appears.

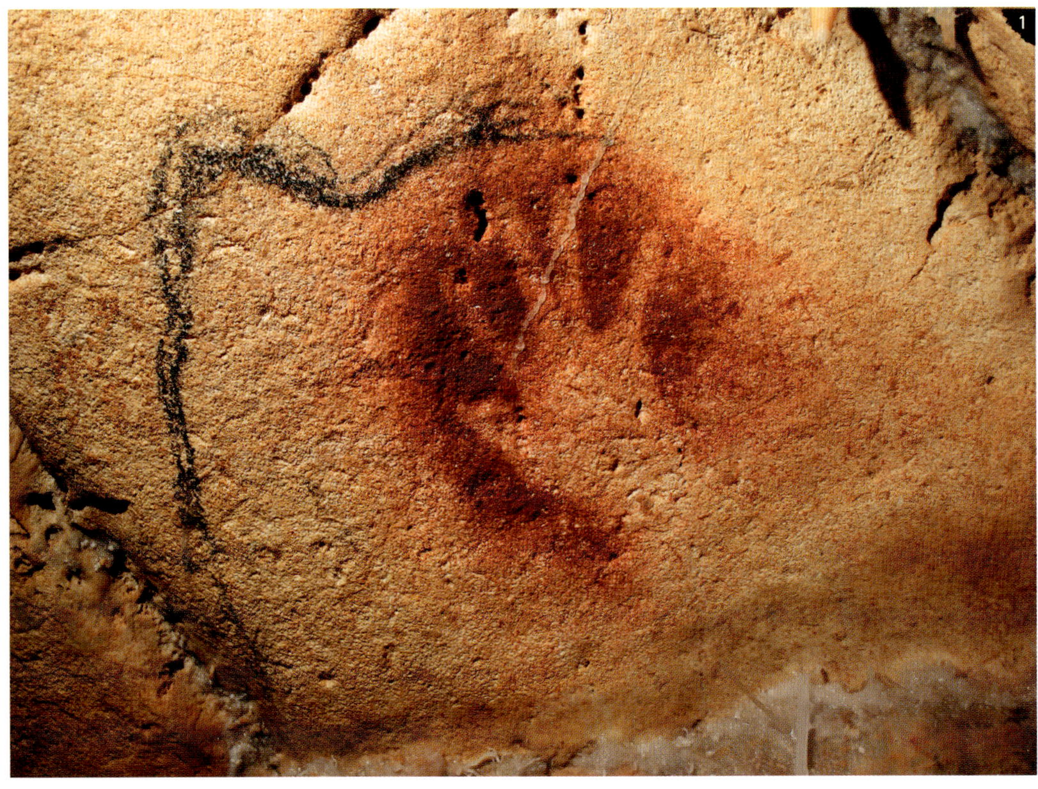
1

1. Red negative handprint and partial black outline of a mammoth. Detail of a work on the cave walls of Chauvet-Pont d'Arc, Ardèche, France. The artist projected pigments onto their hand placed on the wall, then removed it.

2. Stenciled portrait of Mussolini on the walls in the streets of Rome around 1943.

3. Poster of the National School of Fine Arts, Paris, 1968. The same stencil is repeated with both light and dark paint.

In ancient Egypt, stonemasons would copy their charcoal patterns onto the stone, which they then carved. In the Renaissance, the drawn designs were enlarged and pierced with small holes along the drawn lines. Artists applied these papers to the wall following the grid, then stamped them, and the sketch was then reproduced on a larger scale. The same process was used to copy a tapestry pattern from one weaving to another.

The modern age also saw the development of stencil colorization by zone, as in the images of Epinal.

In the contemporary era, some artists used industrial marking letters made with stencils in their works, such as the cubist Albert Gleizes. During the twentieth century, the stencil was the propaganda tool par excellence, and it's not accidental that the first portrait painted entirely with stencil was, according to the artist Blek le Rat, that of Mussolini, seen in the streets of Rome during the 1940s.

The stencil saw prodigious growth with the appearance and then the widespread use, starting at the end of the 1960s, of the aerosol can, which allows paint to be projected onto the stencil quickly and cheaply. Used in a militant and propagandist spirit, the stencils of the Paris protests of May 1968 and then those of the punk rock years beginning in the 1970s expressed the aesthetics that gave birth to what we today call stencil art. Today stenciling is no longer considered an intermediate step or second-rate art; it has become an art form in its own right, with artists competing in ingenuity, originality and audacity to achieve ever more stunning works with this tool.

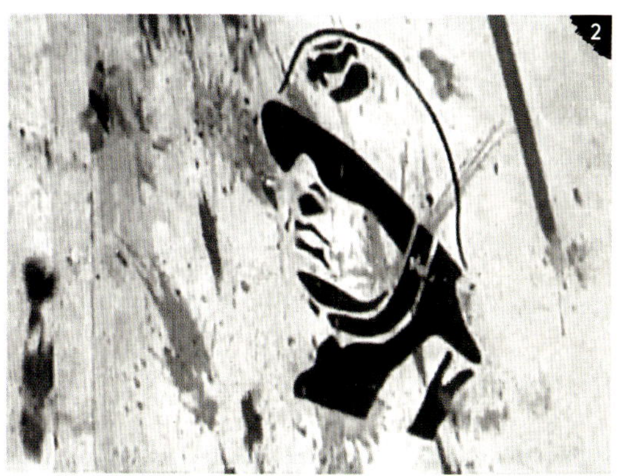

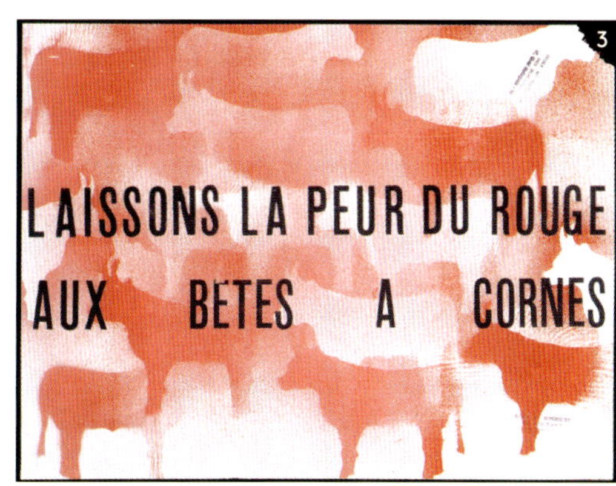

MATERIALS AND TOOLS

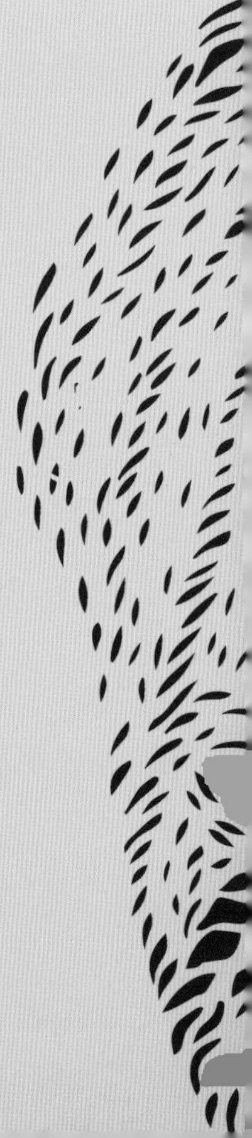

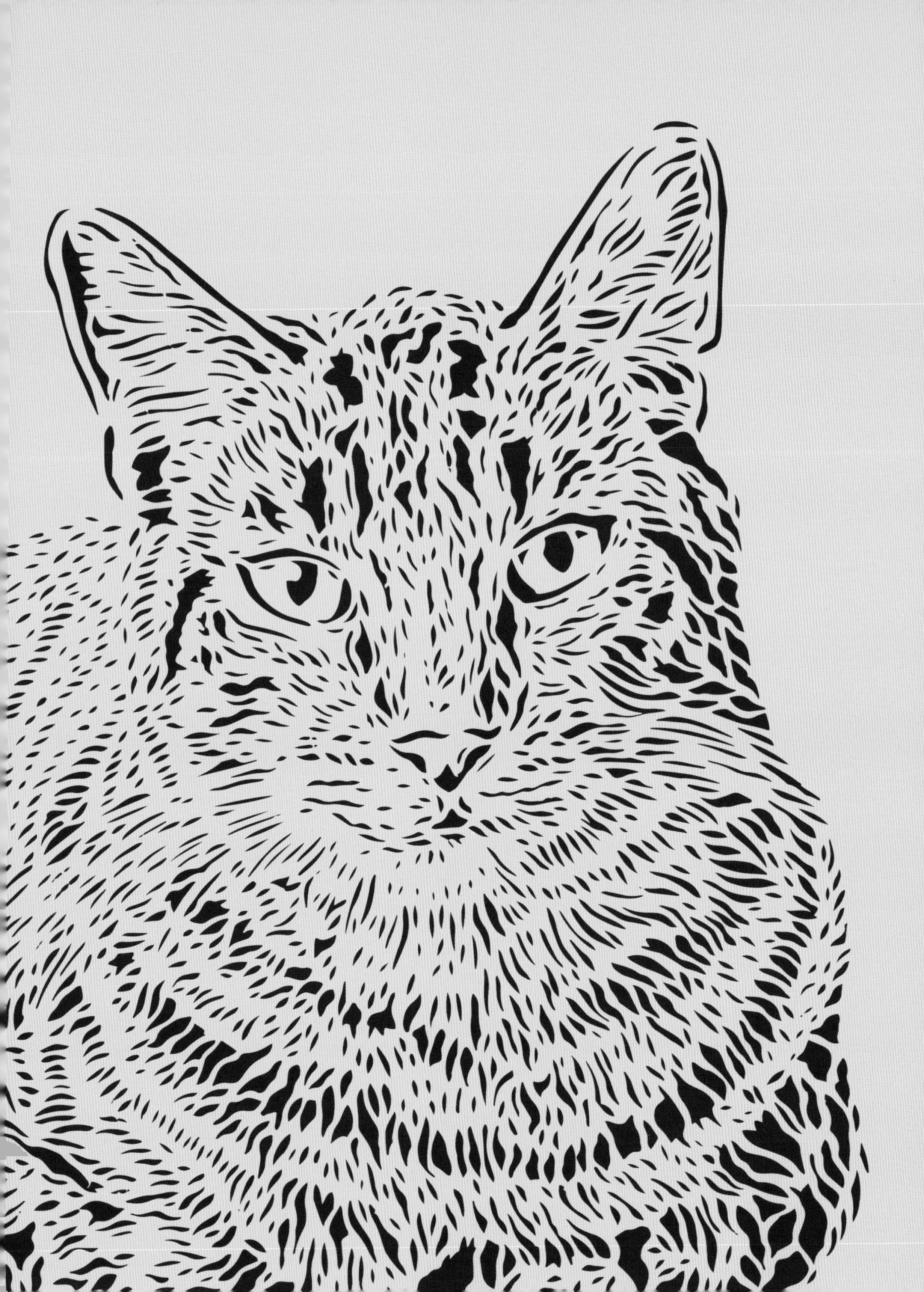

1. Stencil by Snik. We can see here how the knife is an appropriate tool for the finest cuts (see Snik's interview, p. 52).

2. Cutting table presented during my exhibition "Illustres," in the crypt of the Pantheon, 2018.

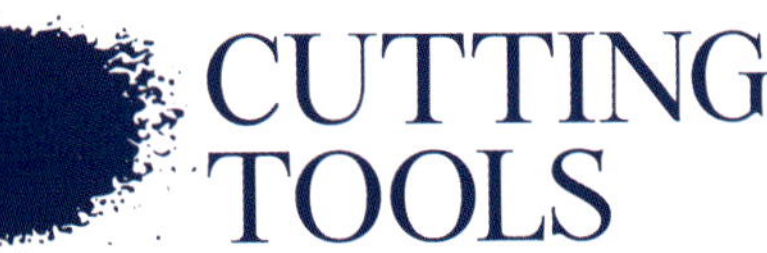

CUTTING TOOLS

The size of a stencil and its layout influence the choice of the cutting mode.

THE KNIFE

The utility knife is the emblematic tool usually associated with cutting out stencils. Several artists have made it their signature, such as Logan Hicks (see his interview, p. 124). There are different types; some have round handles, others angled. The roundness of the handle makes it easier to handle curves. There are knives with rotating blades, specially designed for curves, but they have less grip than conventional fixed blades.

A utility knife is suitable for cutting paper, cardboard and acetate but is not suitable for Plexiglas or harder or thicker materials.

Depending on the brand, there are different types of blades in terms of blade shape and thickness. The standard model is blade #11. Utility knife blades do not sharpen. If a blade is blunt or chipped, it should be replaced.

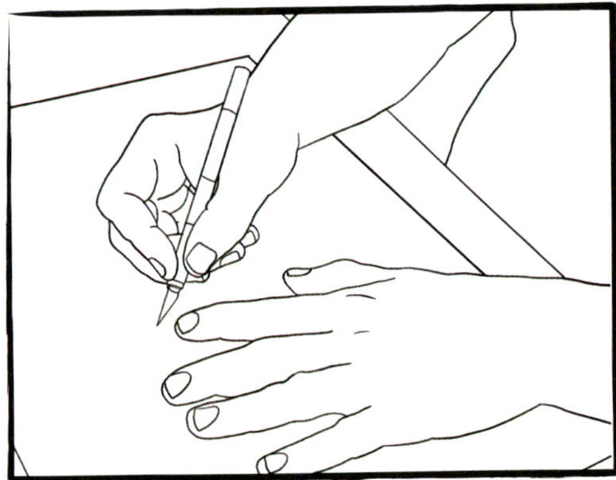

Be careful: to get a clean outline of paint, the cut must be cut at right angles. If it forms a bevel, the part stuck to the wall will be narrower and the line finer.

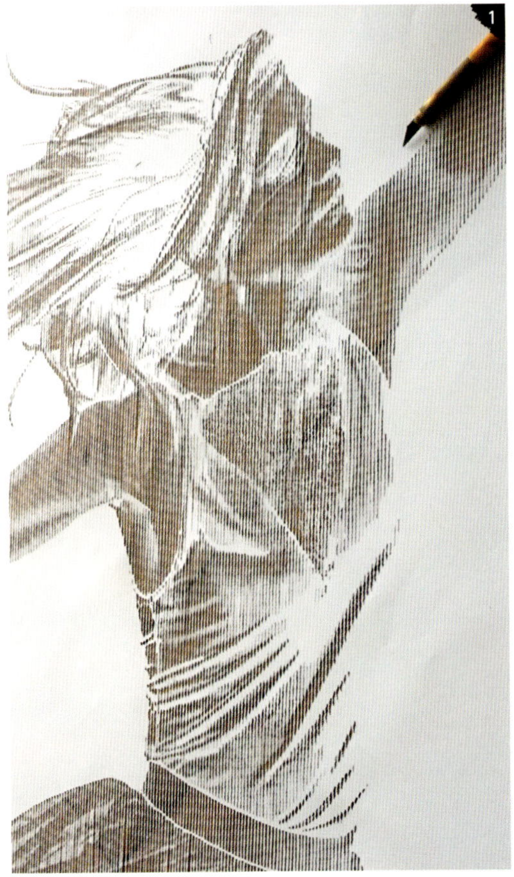

THE CUTTER

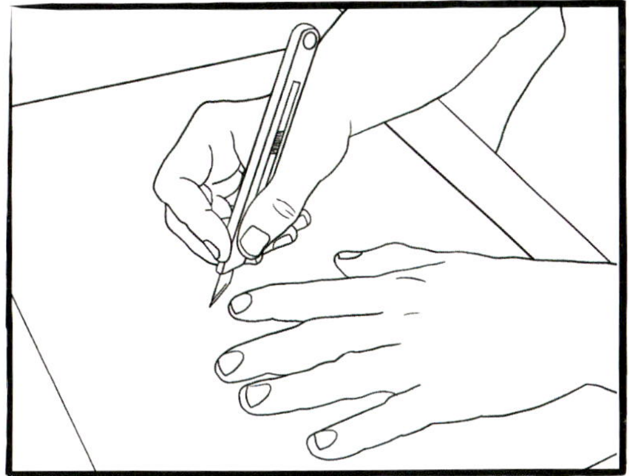

The cutter is a knife whose blade, composed of several breakable sections, is renewed as it wears out. Cutter blades are strong and thick and have a moderate bevel, which allows for strong pressure and deep cutting. However, their handle, generally flat with angles, is better for straight rather than curved cuts.

The cutter is ideal for cutting acetate.

THE LASER

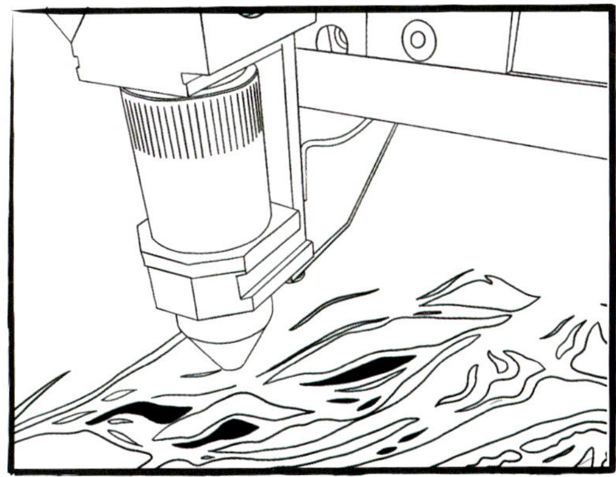

Stencils can be cut with laser cutters. These machines receive a numerical command defined from a previously created file. They do not create stencils; they only cut them. The supplied file must be vector-based, because the laser cuts on the trajectory of the vectors. The most commonly used vector drawing software is Illustrator (for details on its use, see p. 57).

The laser allows you to quickly and easily cut thick materials such as cardboard or Plexiglas with an exact, predefined production time and size. In addition, these cuts can be duplicated at will.

To cut metal, the principle is the same, but a water jet cutting machine may be used. If you want to make a wooden stencil, a jigsaw or a milling machine is another option.

THE CUTTING SURFACE

To cut your stencil with a cutter or a utility knife, another tool is essential: the cutting board. Some artists cut their stencils on wood or Plexiglas, but these materials are very hard and can break the blades. There are cutting boards available on the market that are self-healing, allowing you to save wear and tear on your blades, and to cut easily. They are sold in different sizes, so you can choose based on your desired stencil size.

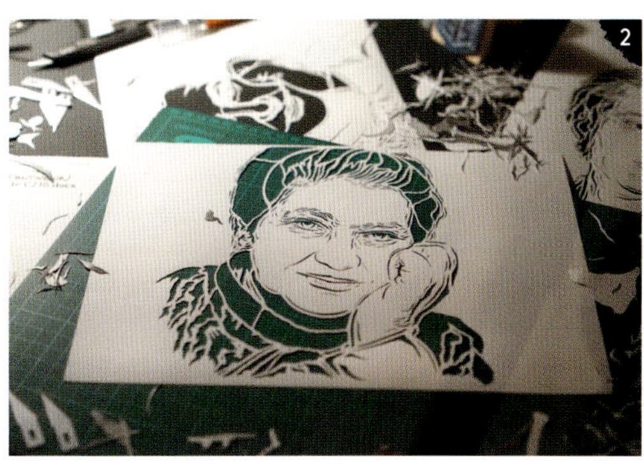
2

1. Note the fineness of the cuts that are possible in paper.

2. Monkey Bird applying part of his stencil on the M.U.R. of Oberkampf in Paris in 2017. To paint large surfaces, the stencil is usually done in segments.

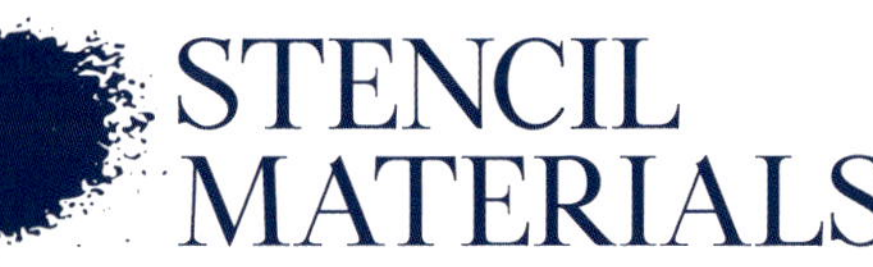

STENCIL MATERIALS

Depending on the use and purpose of a stencil, different types of material are used.

PAPER

Paper is the most accessible, the thinnest and the softest. Easy to cut, it allows you to create fine details. Paper is easily used up to a thickness of 180 gsm. Coated paper (its surface is treated so that it is less absorbent) allows a cleaner cut than uncoated paper, which is more textured. Paper also allows you to create curves in a stencil. Nevertheless, it has limits: it sometimes tears, and its porosity makes it curl when painted on. Finally, its thinness can be annoying: the paint tends to "leak" if the paper is not perfectly maintained against the support. To remedy this, it can be glued down with a spray can of repositionable glue, but the support surface receiving the stencil must then be perfectly flat.

Light and workable, paper lends itself well enough to single-use stencils that are glued on the support. This makes it possible to paint large areas where a thick stencil the size of a wall would be much too heavy and therefore unusable. For painting large walls, paper stencils are well suited if the subject is graphic and only one coat of paint is required (see "Stencil Sizes" on p. 26).

Regardless of a stencil artist's preference in terms of their final stencil material, paper is used to create stencil prototypes, which are then reproduced on another material.

A paper stencil can be shaped or folded to better conform to the shape of a nonflat surface, but in actual practice, stencils are rarely used that way.

Finely detailed designs in cut paper can be artwork in and of in itself, no painting needed—joining the tradition of paper cutting in the Swiss Alps in the eighteenth century, and also in China and Japan.

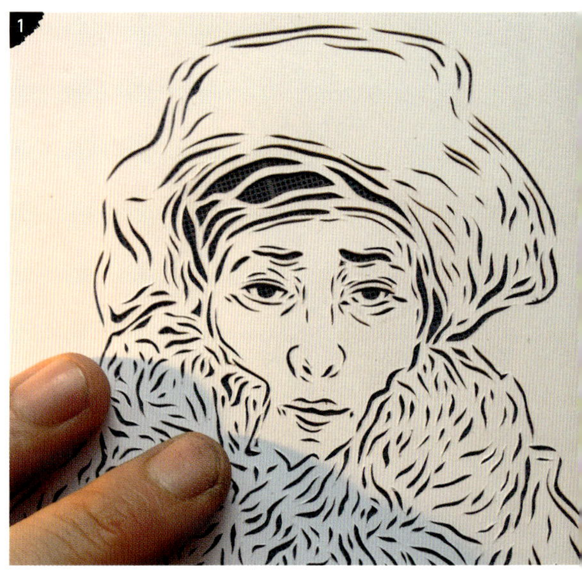

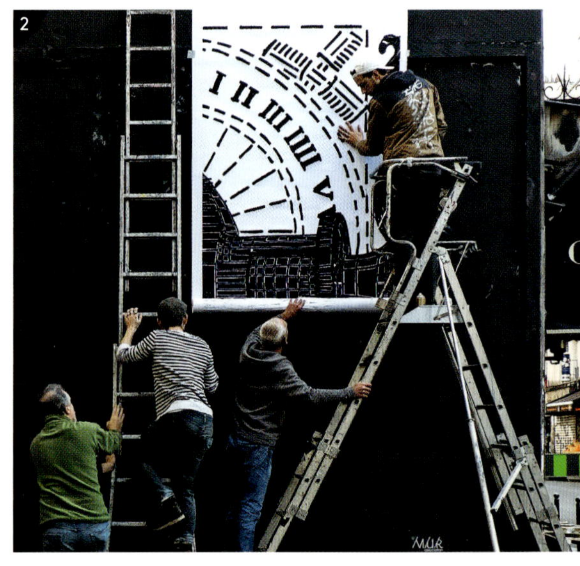

3. You can always ask for help in keeping your stencil against its support. In this photo I'm with my daughter Nina in Istanbul in 2014.

4. Using thick cardboard accentuates the cleanness of the painted work.

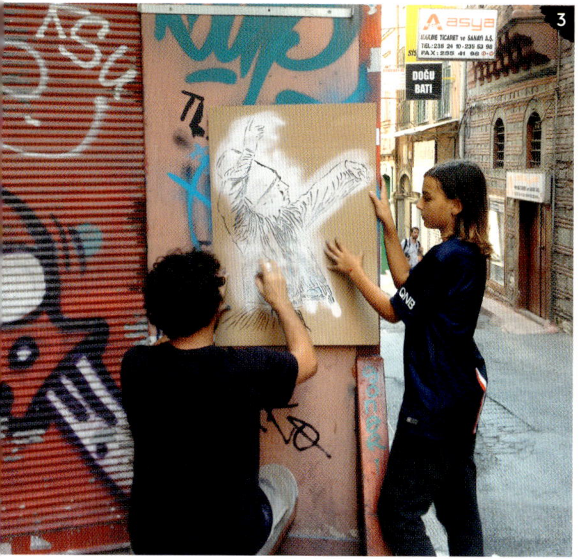

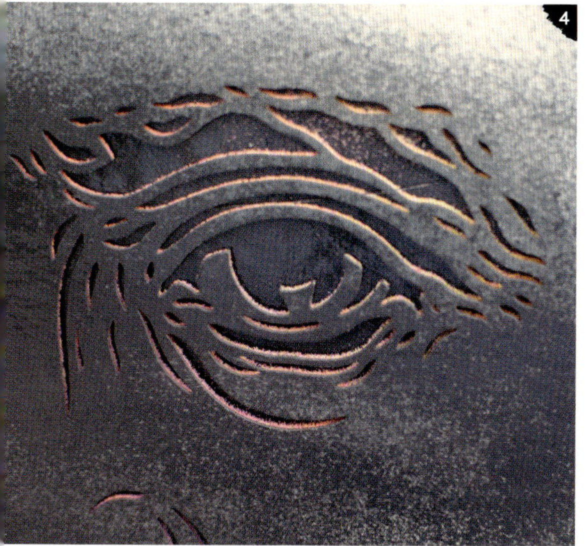

CARDSTOCK AND CARDBOARD

The thicker the material used to create a stencil, the less fragile and porous—that is, sensitive to moisture—it is, so the less it will curl. A thick material allows a very precise projection. Indeed, the thicker a stencil is, the more it will channel the projected paint in a right angle to the support.

We call it a map when the stencil material is a thick, compressed and compact sheet.

Kraft cardstock is a soft material, which makes it possible to be precise when cutting. It's sold in flat sheets of various sizes. It is also easily reusable.

Personally, I use a lot of kraft cardstock. I find that its fineness, strength and low porosity are a good combination.

It has two disadvantages: storage and transport. It's heavy, and it takes up a lot of space because it is non-foldable. It's difficult to handle, especially when your stencil collection gets extensive.

Packaging cardboard is not recommended, because the corrugation grooves don't let you make a clean cut.

ACETATE

Acetate is a fairly thin plastic, made from cellulose acetate, and is usually sold in rolls or sheets. I use the Rhodoid brand.

In a roll it's easy to transport, but it can be difficult to keep flat because it retains its curved form. Its main advantage is that it is completely waterproof, which makes it infinitely reusable. Its flexibility also makes it possible to remove the glycerol-thickened paint layers when they accumulate on the flexible plastic. These are generally the two reasons that stencil artists choose acetate.

Its main limitation? It's not soft to cut and therefore doesn't express curves well. With acetate it's easier to cut simple shapes and straight lines, such as geometric patterns, summary drawings or text that you want to repeat.

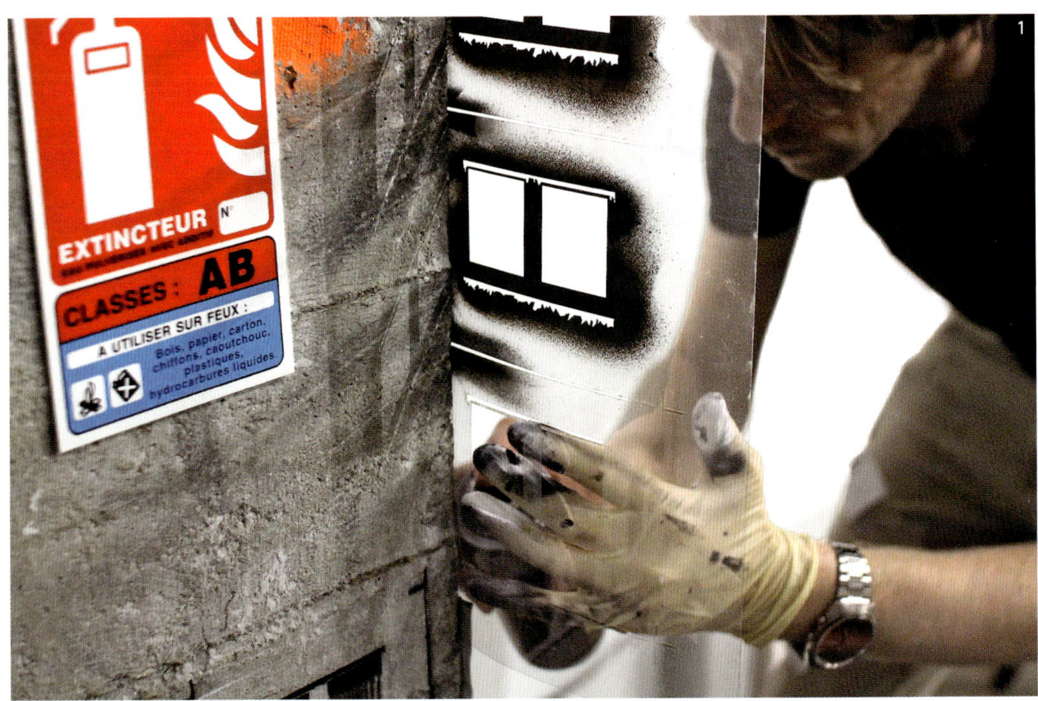

1

1. Evol at work (see his interview, p. 130). The transparency of acetate helps you see exactly where you are painting.

2. Monochrome portrait of C215 by Epsylon Point in 2014.

3. Here, the masking tape applied by Aleteïa in a linear pattern makes it easy to create white lines that appear when it's removed (see his interview, p. 102).

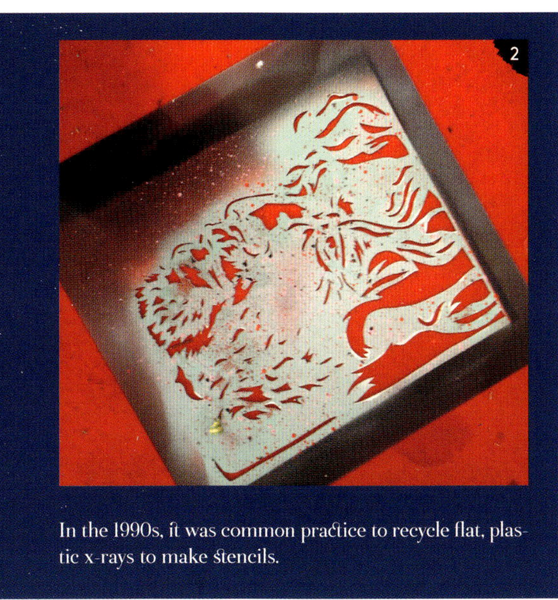

In the 1990s, it was common practice to recycle flat, plastic x-rays to make stencils.

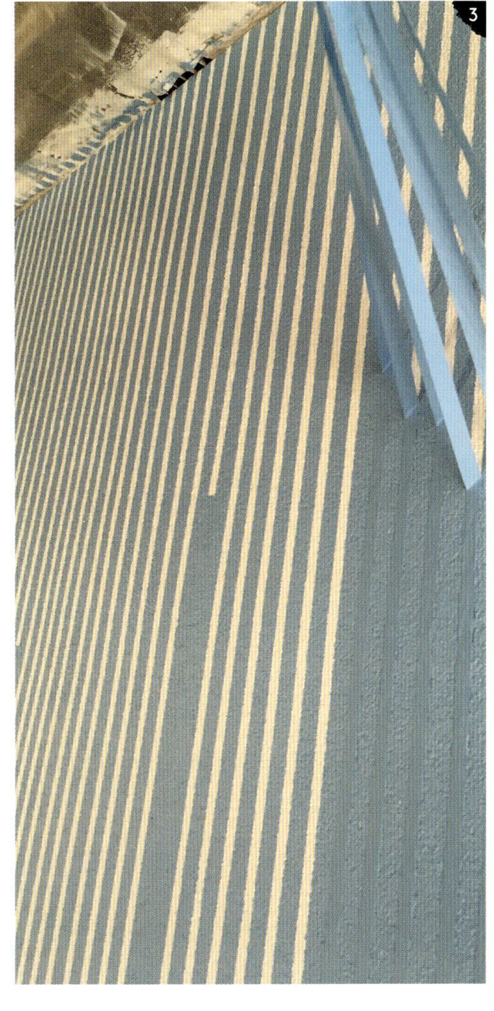

MASKING TAPE

Masking tape is undoubtedly one of the tools of the stencil art. Many artists, such as Felipe Pantone or L'Atlas, use it without considering themselves "stencil artists." However, the process of masking a support by drawing forms on it with adhesive, painting it and then removing the adhesive to reveal a motif is, of course, stenciling. Masking tape works well to create geometric forms or large letters, for example.

THE BASICS

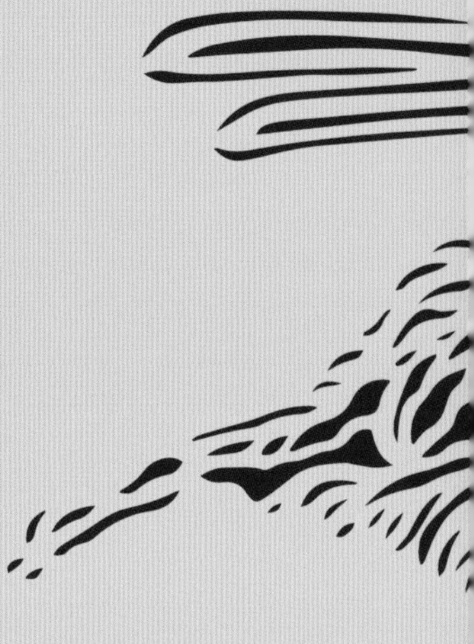

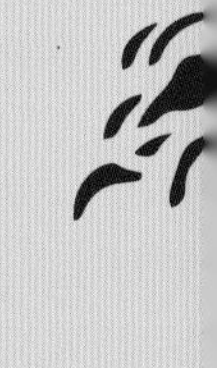

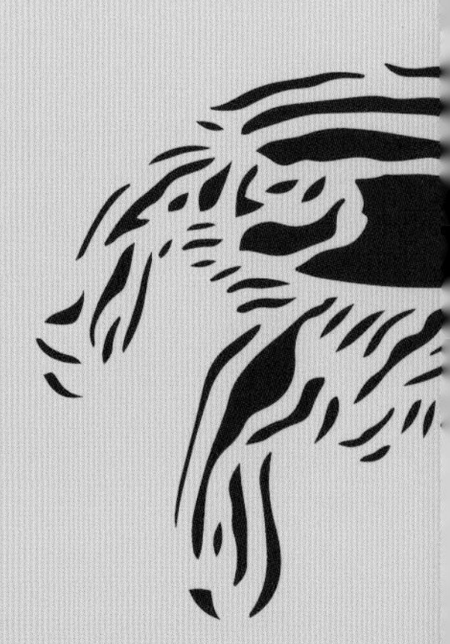

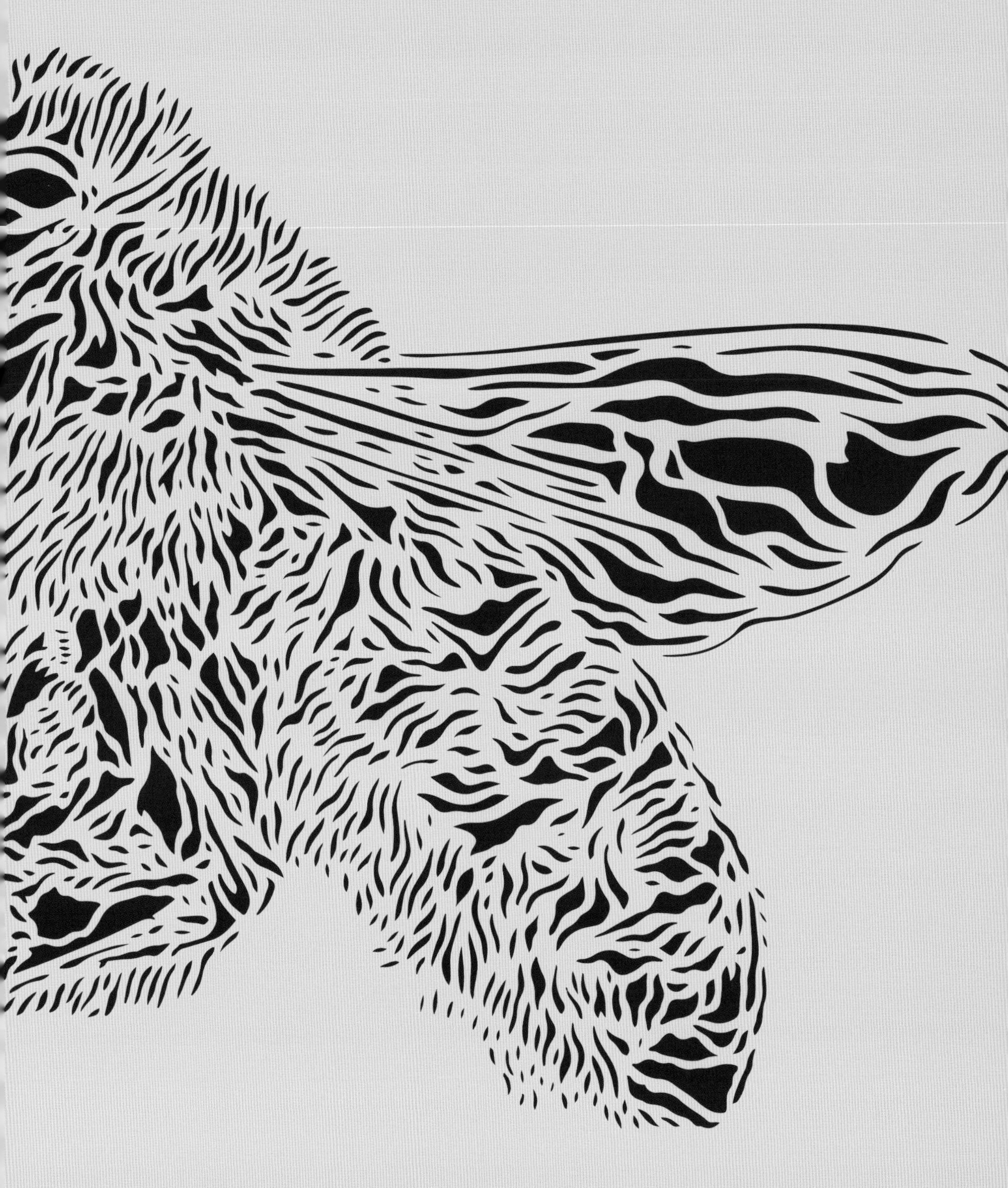

1. C215, Grenoble, 2008. Use of silhouette masking: Marie Curie.

2. Nemo, Paris, 2005. This iconic silhouette by Nemo is one of the many stencils that undoubtedly inspired Banksy.

3. Here, the dense network of bridges forms a bee's furry coat.

It's impossible to repeat it too often: a stencil is a masking tool that, after being painted and then removed, allows a negative pattern to appear.

The tool can be a central masking form, revealing a silhouette all around it—as is the case with those negative handprints in rock paintings—or it can contain a carved-out form, which will create a silhouette once paint is applied. Even today, some stencil artists still almost exclusively use the silhouette style. Banksy and many French artists, such as Blek le rat and Nemo, are masters of it.

In either case, each stencil is characterized by the presence or absence of bridges, and also by its frame and format.

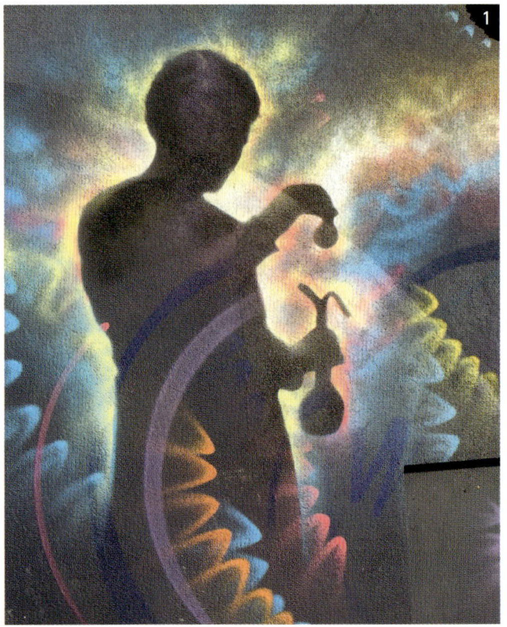

1

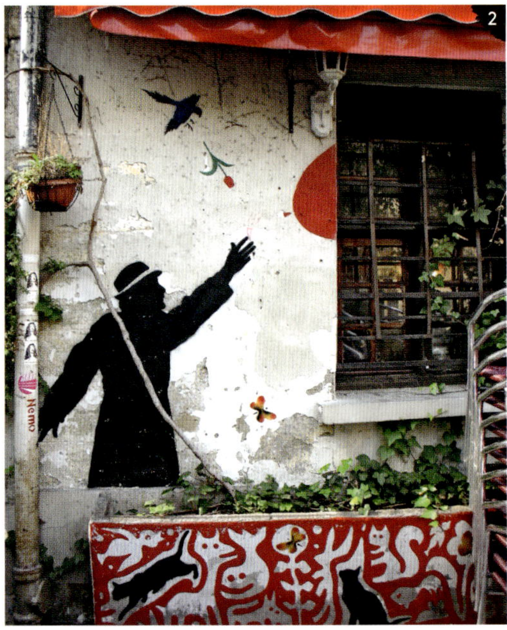

2

BRIDGES

Bridges come into play when the pattern corresponds to a cutout or a series of cutouts, "holes," carved out inside a frame. The carved-out parts form the design by creating the areas that will be painted.

To hold together a series of holes, whether large or small, many or just a few, complicated or simple, we need a contiguous network in the stencil. When the parts holding these holes together are thin, they are commonly called bridges. These bridges, like the solid areas, will appear in negative once the stencil is removed.

Traditionally, artists attempt to make the bridges as thin as possible so that they do not distract from the main design. There are several ways to make bridges invisible when the paint is applied, including covering them, either freehand or with another stencil, which will form a top layer (for more details, see "Bridging," p. 63). Sometimes it's artistically wiser to let the lower layers and their lines show through.

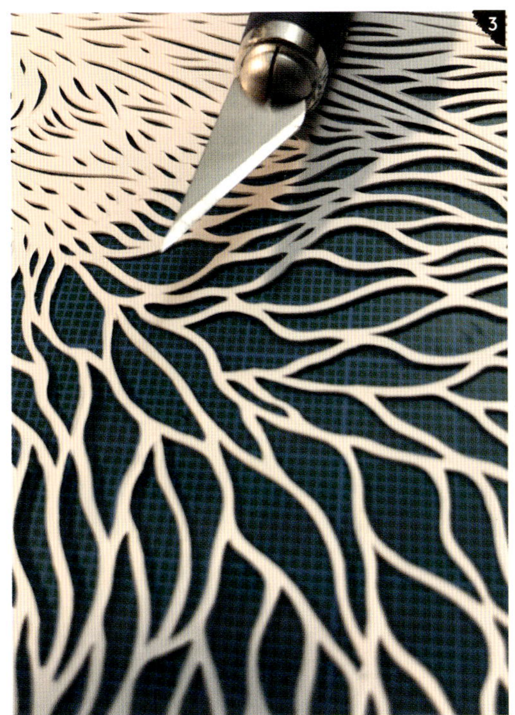

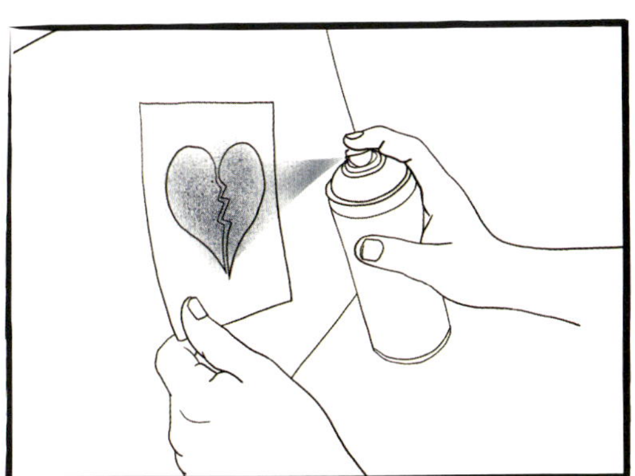

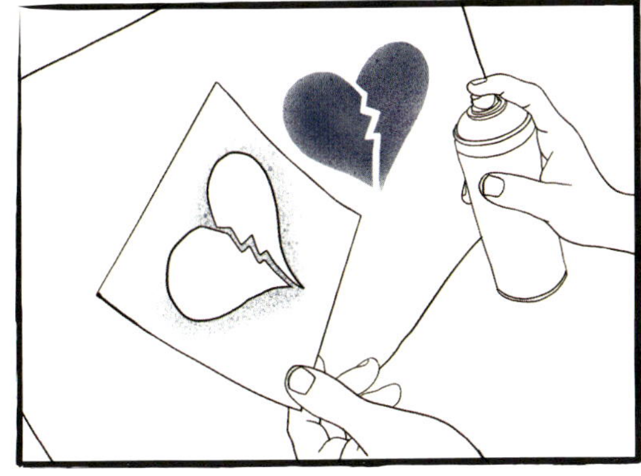

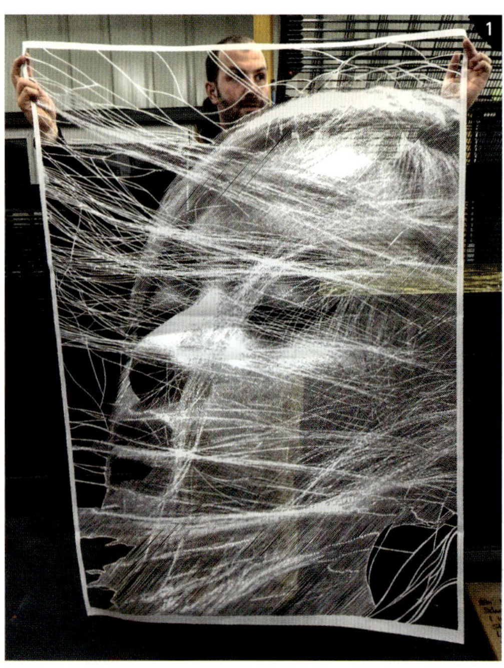

By maintaining a continuous connection between its different parts via bridges, the stencil keeps its shape and flatness. However, the stiffer the stencil material, the more rigid the stencil can be, and the more bridges can be dispensed with. Conversely, when using a flexible material, increasing the number of bridges helps keep the stencil flat.

The greater the number of bridges, the more the image is fractured. This can lead to different aesthetic results. Some follow the principles of optical mixing, explored by various movements in art history such as pointillism at the end of the nineteenth century. Other artists reference the granular or lamellar rendering developed by silkscreen printing and photography in the 1960s and 1970s.

I chose to make the marks of these bridges visible by including them in my designs, which determined my style. This is an artistic bias (see "Aesthetic Research," p. 64).

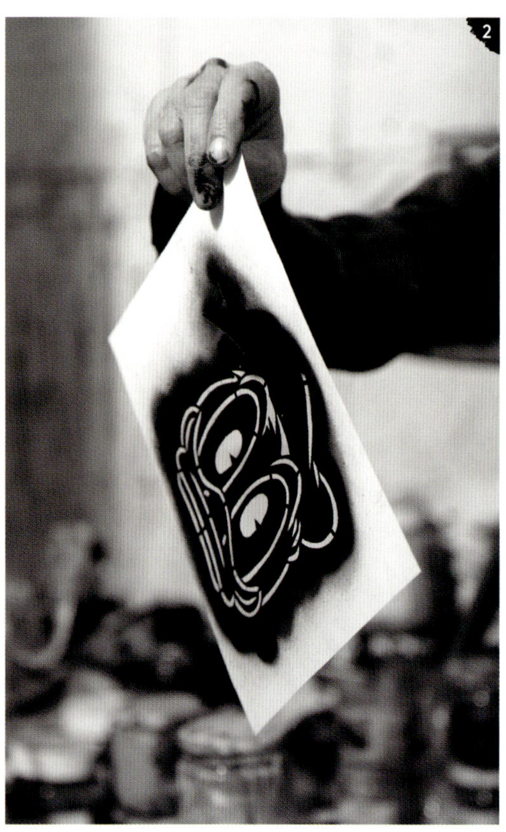

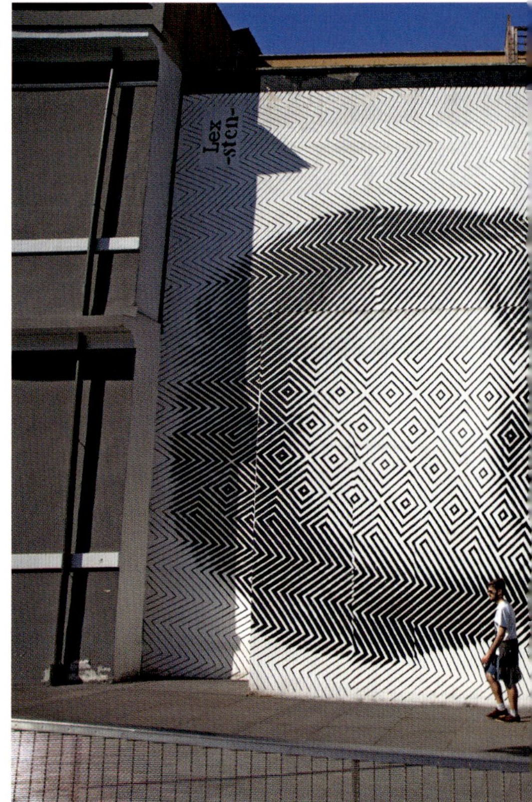

1. Snlk. The multiplication of bridges and their fineness can be pushed to infinity. The stencil itself then becomes a work of art.

2. Speedy Graphito. When the stencil represents a line, fine perpendicular cuts will create the least visible bridges (see interview with Speedy Graphito, p. 89).

3. Sten & Lex, on the terrace of the Macro Museum, Rome, 2012. Example of a halftone rendering (see their interview, p. 46).

FRAMES

Regardless of the aesthetic or structural decisions behind the stencil we have designed, a continuous border around the design will maintain its structure. This is the frame. The wider it is, the less risk we run of overflow.

This overflow, also called overspray, is sometimes intentional, like a stylistic trademark of street art. The artist is free to give the frame a nontraditional shape as he or she paints.

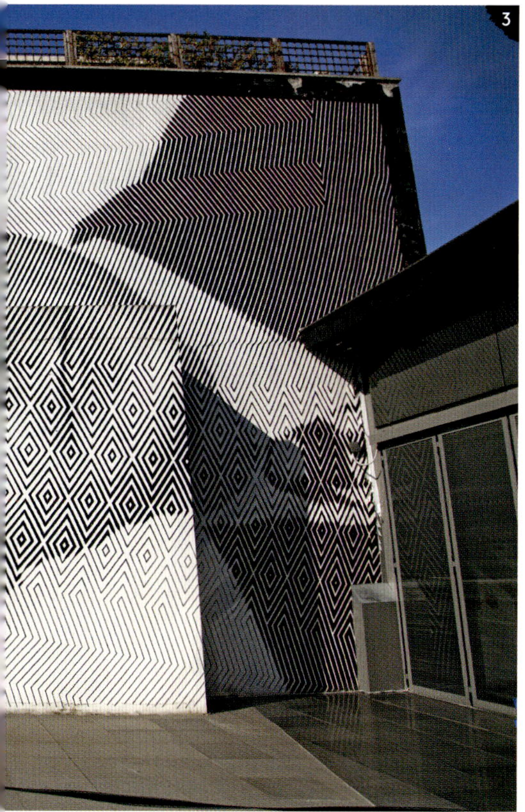

3

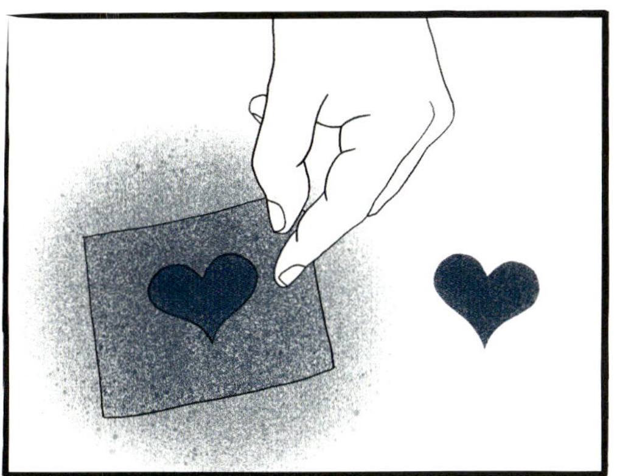

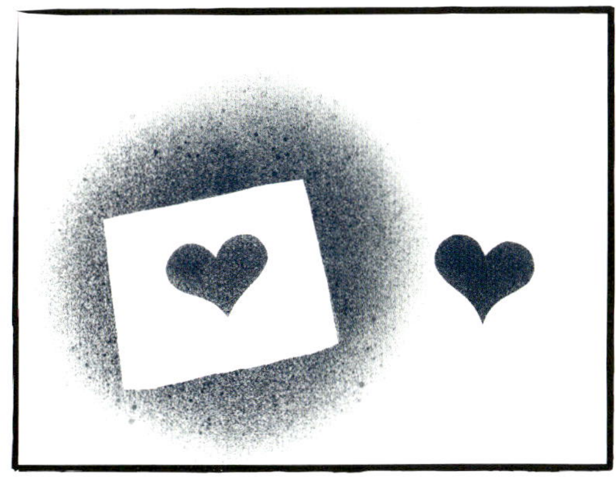

1. This monumental fresco by Shepard Fairey, alias Obey, *Liberté, Égalité, Fraternité,* visible in the thirteenth arrondissement of Paris, was stenciled using strips of paper.

2. Monkey Bird painting *Le Colosse aux pieds d'argile* in Nanterre (France), 2018. The huge size of the work required the use of a boom lift.

3. Speedy Graphito, Cornell Art Museum, Florida, 2018. From a very basic modular stencil, Speedy Graphito manages to create large sized artwork . . . all in pixels.

4. M-city created true architectural perspectives from stencils of three-dimensional buildings placed next to each other. Berlin, 2006.

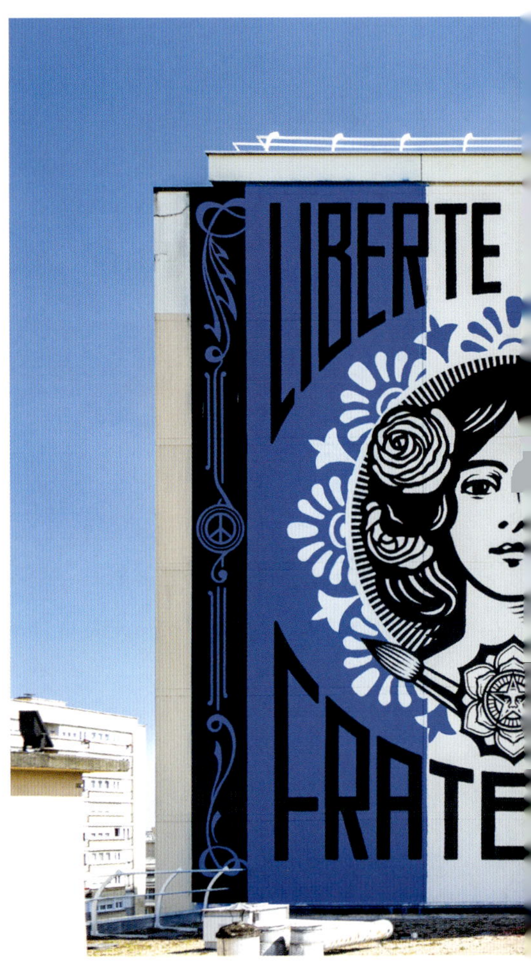

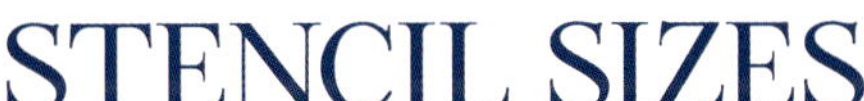

STENCIL SIZES

Usually a stencil is for small works. If the work is large enough to be painted by hand, the question arises as to whether a stencil is the most applicable tool. On a large scale, it can indeed be heavy, cumbersome and unwieldy.

Nevertheless, when there is no other choice or when very large, particularly graphic frescoes are created, some artists such as Logan Hicks, Jef Aerosol, Monkey Bird (see their respective interviews on pp. 124, 98 and 33) or Obey use an ingenious process. They create large paper stencils, fixed to the wall with repositionable glue, and tear the stencils off the wall after painting.

Others, such as M-city (see his interview below) or Speedy Graphito, have designed modular stencils, small monochrome stencils that can be combined, with which they produce very large-scale works.

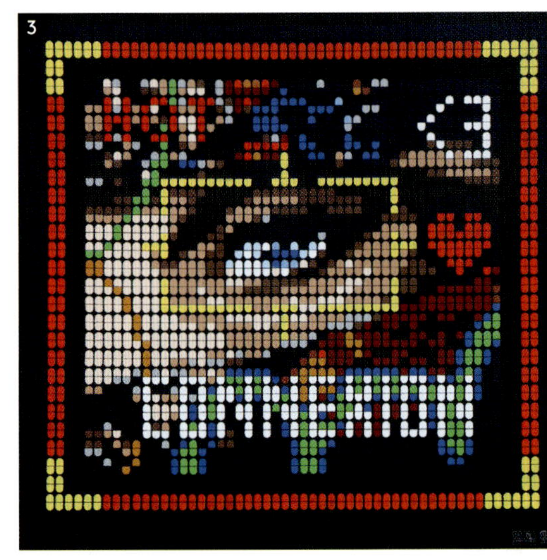

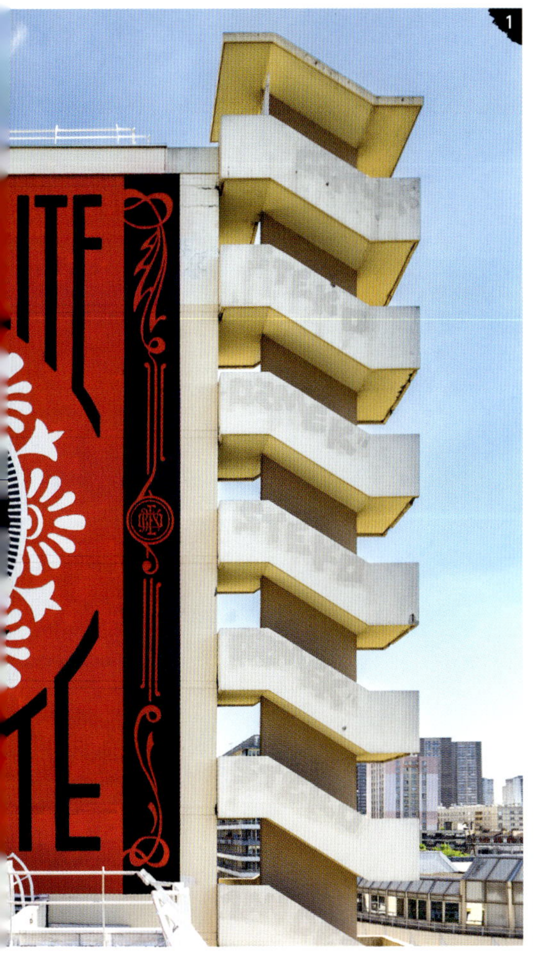
1

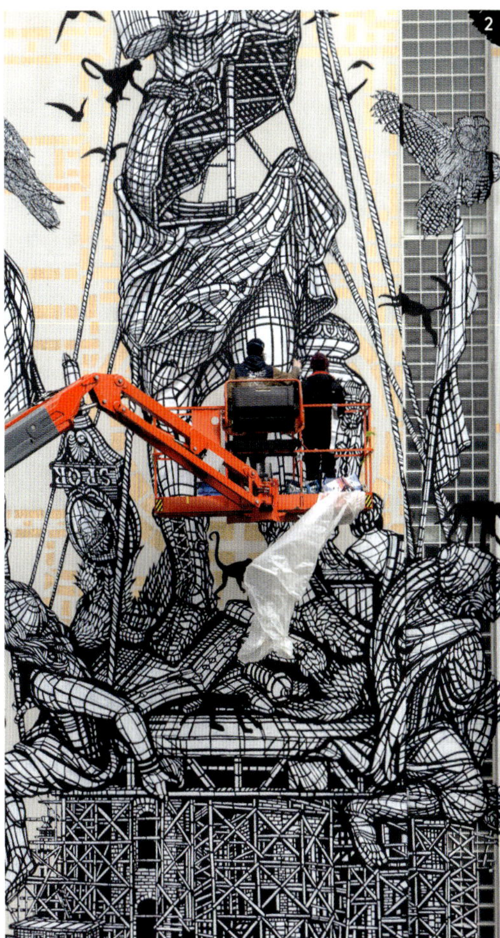
2

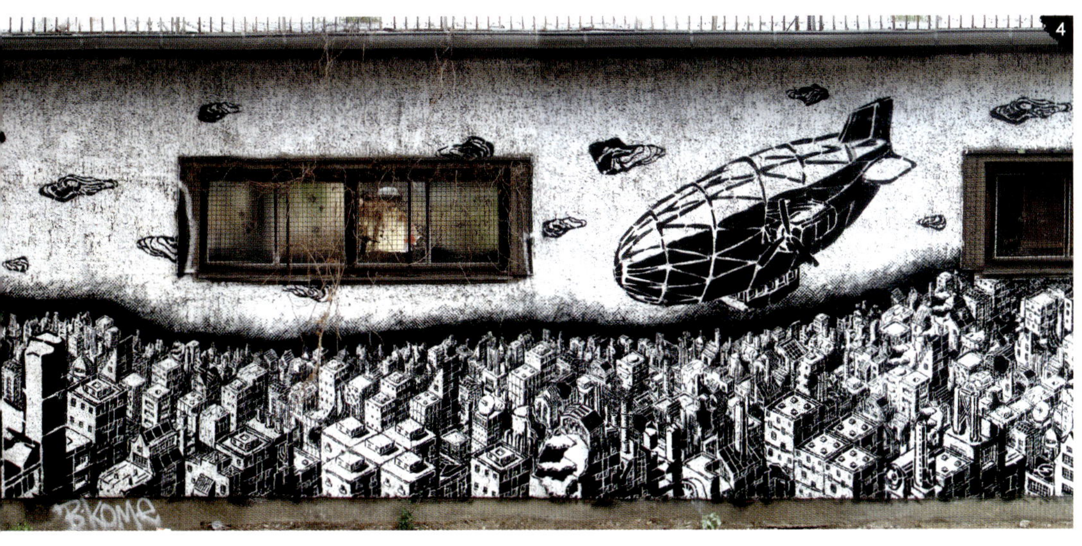
4

Some of the modular elements that make up M-city's frescoes.

INTERVIEW WITH M-CITY

M-city is a leading artist on the stencil scene, who first made his mark by painting large walls with modular black and white compositions as early as the 1990s. He travels around the world expressing his constructivist universe.
Website: m-city.org
Instagram: @stencilcity
Facebook: @stencilcity

Why did you choose stencils rather than another painting technique?
I like the techniques of graphic design more than those of painting. In general, I appreciate all techniques that allow for multiples, such as woodcutting, linocutting, etc. I've tried several times to combine stencil with classic acrylic paint, but I've never obtained satisfactory results. Stencil alone, without painting effects, seemed to me to be what worked best.

Another factor is the speed of the work: I don't like to spend weeks or months on a work; I prefer to get a fairly fast effect. And that's really the advantage of stencil. In fact, the creative process can be long, but then you can do experimental things quickly, repeat the theme and add new things. This is also true for creating big walls. Most of the time, I don't spend more than five days on scaffolding or a boom lift for the biggest sites. It takes a lot of time to prepare everything, but most of the work is done beforehand, in comfortable studio conditions.

How do you make your stencils?
My technique has obviously evolved over the years. The basis of my stencils is a sketch or a drawing. I'm a bit opposed to the idea of using a photo to create very realistic multilayer stencils. In the beginning, I would draw everything on paper or an x-ray and then cut it out. Then I used film photography to create stencils from the film, a bit like using a projector. A photo of the drawing was put on the enlarger, which is the projector that was used to produce photo prints in the darkroom. Later on, I drew on paper or on the computer, then scanned and printed. I glued a transparent sheet of paper on each side of the print. This allowed me to make stencils that were sturdy and reusable. Later, for larger formats, I used a projector.

What matters to me is multiplication. I consider it to be the essence of stencils. So I've created a kind of library in which I dig. Some elements are repeated and mixed with new ones. Of course, I went through different phases: flat stencils composed of several elements, complex stencils cut into one image, modular stencils cut individually and assembled freely. Some had a common perspective and scale, to be combined as blocks. That's why I called my project M-city. What distinguishes my works is that they're monochrome. Generally, I paint a black pattern on a light background.

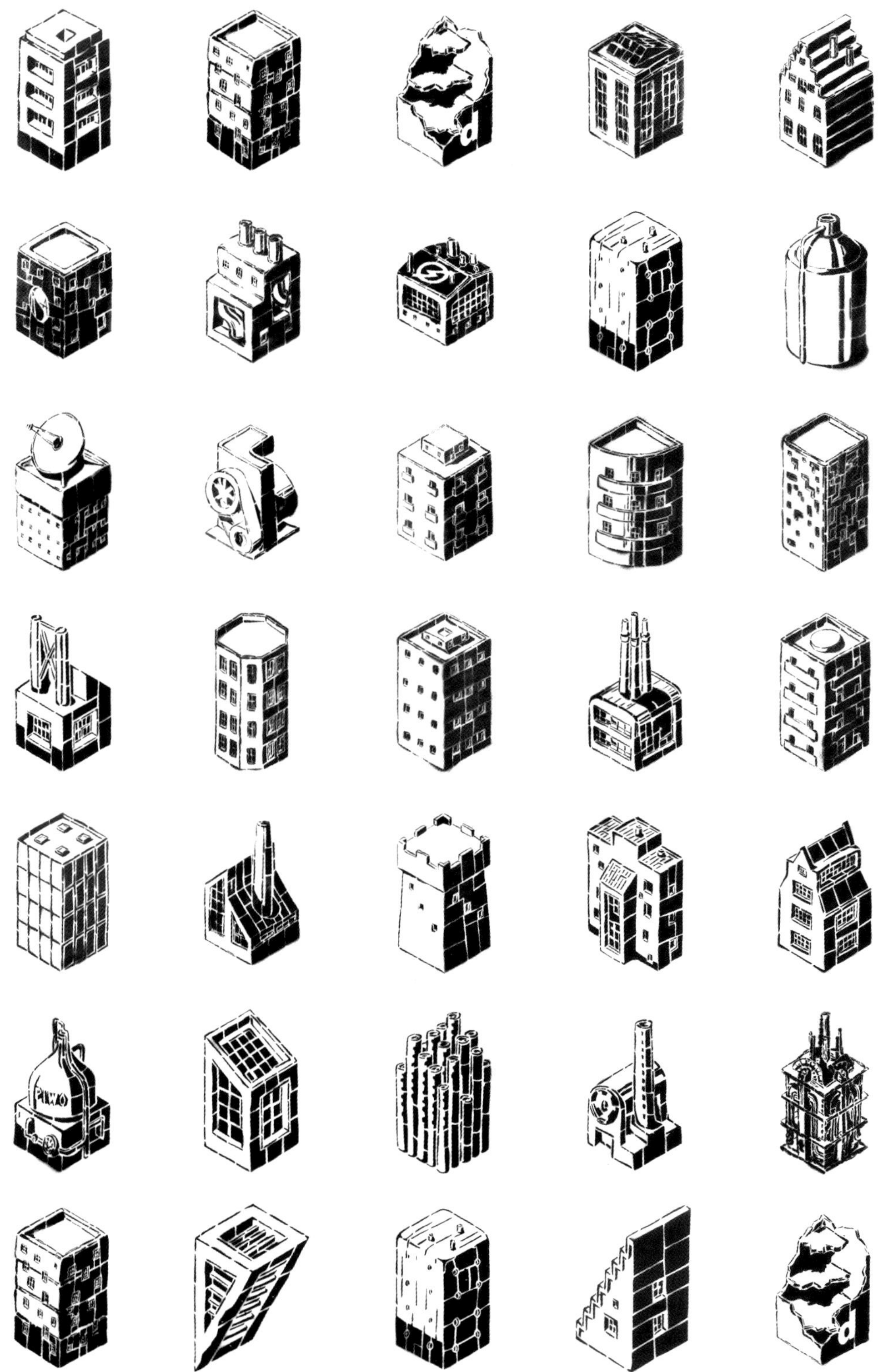
PIWO

1. Sao Paulo (Brazil), 2007.

2. Three steps in the creation of a stencil in the Leake Street tunnel for the London Cans Festival, 2008.

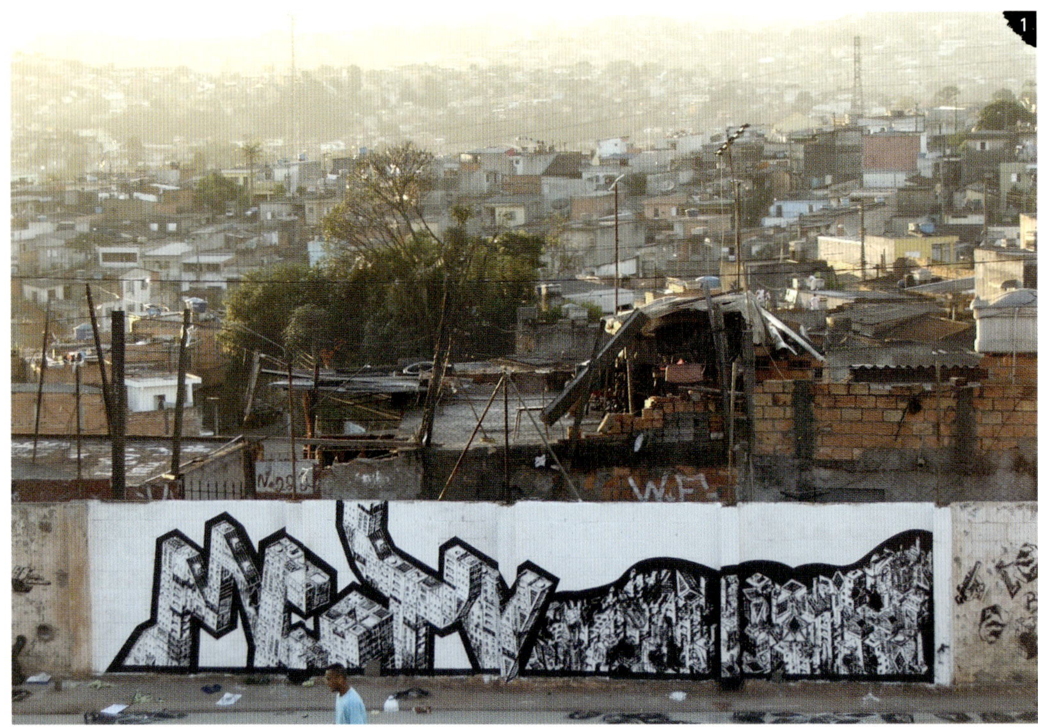

How do you see the evolution of the stencil technique since your beginnings?

In principle, the rules are still the same: a tool for cutting and a medium, such as the x-ray film that was used a lot at the time. Over time, x-rays were replaced by printed sheets and plastic materials. The appearance of projectors to paint large walls was a revolution. It clearly accelerated the process of creating very-large-format works. The diversification of manufactured paint colors also changed the situation, allowing the development of multilayer stencils with more color shades. And the latest novelty, not so new but more easily accessible today: the laser-cutting machine. But remember, it's just a helper, nothing more, like a brush or a roller for painting.

Which artists inspire you in your stencil work?

Mainly anonymous artists. I discovered stenciling on the walls of Polish cities in the early 1990s. At the time, they were messages to the population or criticisms of political authorities. Even the stencils that were considered artistic were against the system. A simple word, basic forms, an area of color . . . that's what caught my attention. The graffiti that we know today was less visible in the streets than those first stencils. In fact, in the beginning, stenciling was called graffiti. The distinction came later.

So I started with this stencil style, simple and fast. They were socially committed works, in a way.

What are the limits of a stencil as a tool?

I think I managed to defeat two of them. The first was the creation of a

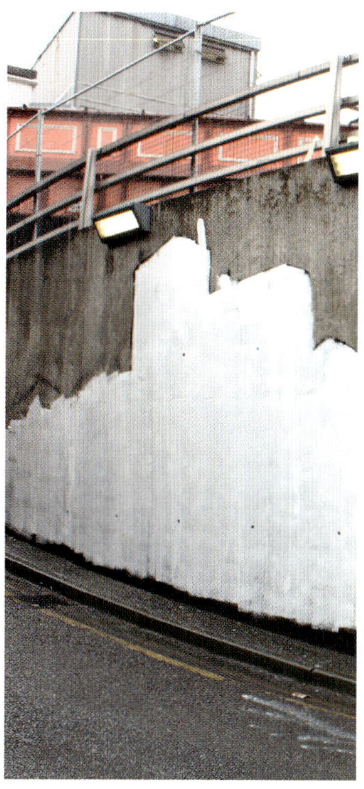

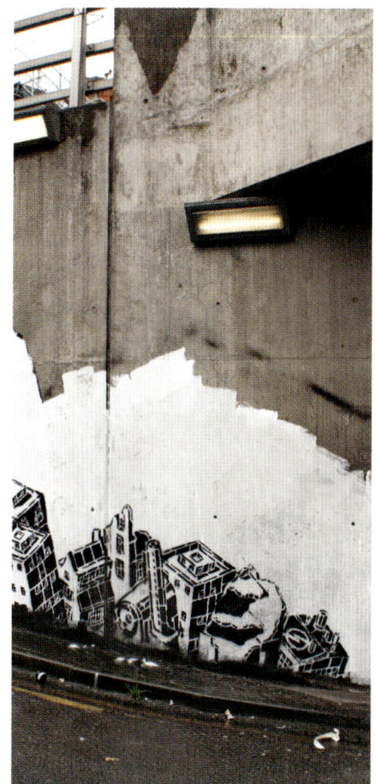

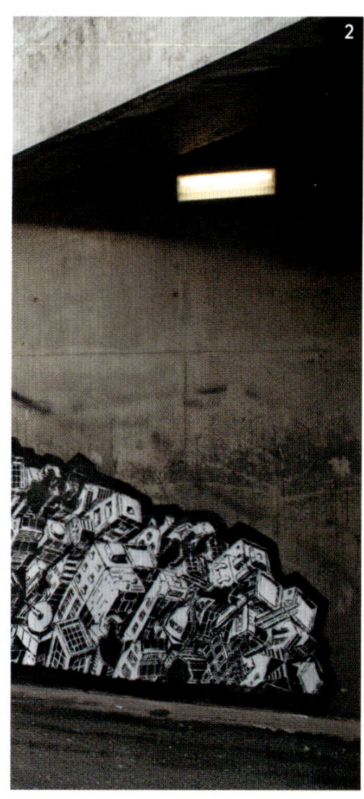

2

work composed of several large-size layers. A lot of people considered this problem as the main disadvantage of stencil, but that's not the case for me. I have always been able to enlarge an image using small stencils. The other difficulty was working on large walls. Through experimentation, I found a workable method by simply dividing the surface into large rectangles which, when combined, produce a single image.

For you, is a stencil a frame or a freedom?

The ease of creating a stencil, its universality, the speed of its execution and the simplicity of the message are more related to freedom. The use of an ordinary brush or roller is nevertheless simpler and more powerful when you just need to write a short message. The stencil template has be created in advance, so it's difficult to react immediately to a given situation.

Detail of a fresco done in Bogota (Colombia), 2010.

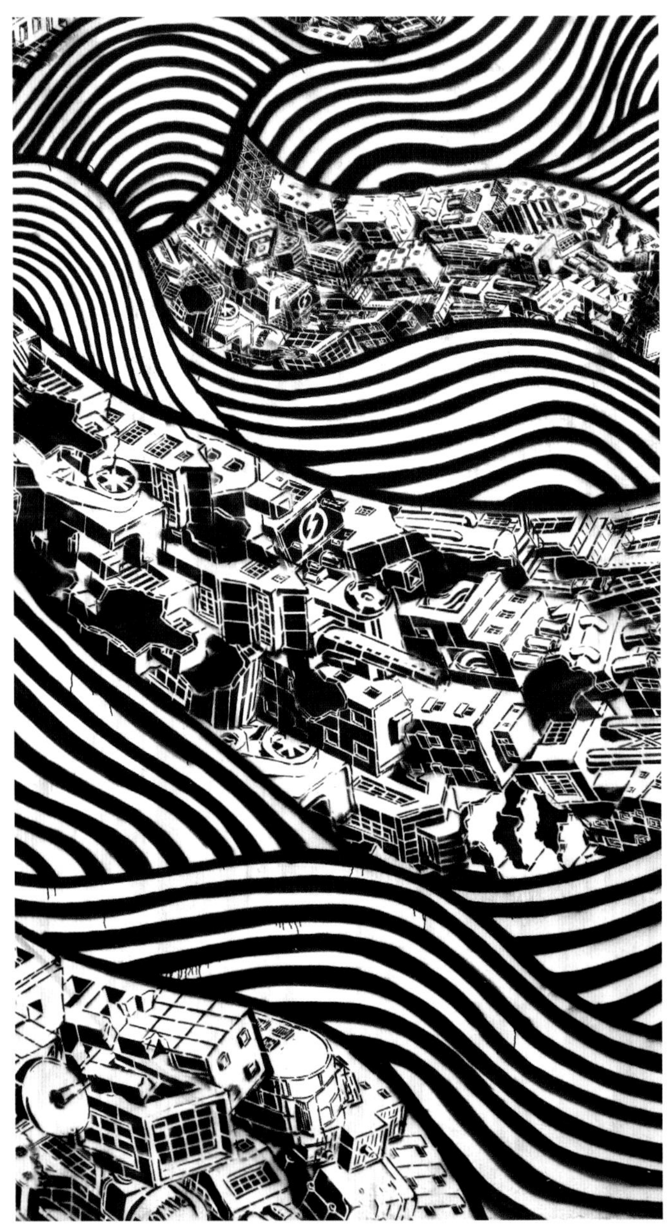

Can you describe your studio for us?

I've had several workshops over the past few years. All of them were located in incredible places, warehouses or factories, always close to the water, with an industrial landscape as a backdrop. At the moment I have a large studio in Gdansk, in a historical building that is more than a hundred years old. It is currently in ruins and is going to be restored. There are fourteen of us artists in it, and we had to repair everything: put in windows, insulate the walls and install electricity. We don't have running water yet.

The building is located 4 meters from the sea, in the heart of a former shipyard with a view of the cranes and production shafts of other shipyards. It is truly an incredible place and one of the last places in my city that welcomes independent art. My private space is more than 200 square feet (60 square meters). I have all my things there, objects that tell the story of fifteen years of work. I also have some more technological equipment, such as a 3-D printer, drones, a laser-cutting machine, and a beautiful view from the window. Part of my studio serves as a gallery. I organize small events where I invite an artist to exhibit his work. My studio is open to the public; my art has nothing to hide.

INTERVIEW WITH MONKEY BIRD

This young duo from Bordeaux with their neosymbolist creations is contributing to renewing the aesthetics of stencil art today. Their oversized frescoes, entirely painted using stencils, are technical feats that make these two artists major figures of this scene.

Instagram: @monkeybirdcrew
Facebook: @MonkeyBirdCrew

Why did you choose stencils rather than another painting technique for large walls?

We developed our stencil technique during our studies in visual communication and product design. We quickly decided to cooperate under the same name, out of friendship, but also because this duo dynamic made us stronger. We pooled our research, developed an identity, tools and a language. At first, we were looking for proliferation with small stencils, but we were soon frustrated by the limits of the format: given our universe, we were looking for monumentality. So we evolved our work to gain scale, first by working with several stencils and principles of symmetry. Then we took a new step by making giant stencils in rolls, which are put in place using a boom lift.

How do you make your stencils for large walls?

We compose our line drawings precisely, to get a result at the right caliber, then we scan the image and prepare a mockup with software. This allows us to anticipate an action and a result in situ. Then we print the image to the scale of the wall. We cut the stencils by hand in our studio. Then we pack all the stencils and leave with them, by train, by plane, to go and paint our wall.

As for the painting, we mainly use a palette of black, white and gold. We first make a marking of the silhouette and gold ornaments. Then we paint the silhouette in black with acrylic mural paint. Finally, we paint the stencil in white on black, which reveals all the details and volume.

Which artists have inspired you in your stencil work?

We were in our twenties when street art exploded among young artists and then among the general public. It all happened very quickly. Edouard was already initiated to spray paint and wall painting because he belonged to a small group of graffiti artists. Banksy unveiled new possibilities to interact with the street, with a relevant message and exceptional ability. His speed of execution immediately convinced us of the potential of this medium. When we started painting in the street, at a time when it was not yet saturated, it was absolutely exciting, and we were interested in everything that was being done in the field. Roa and Phlegm fascinated us with their monumental works. C215 completely opened the field of possibilities with very detailed stencil work and particularly the negative line. Beyond its practical usefulness, this approach testified very early on to the pictorial potential of stenciling.

La Courbe, Grenoble (France), 2017.
Fresco made for the Street Art Fest.

We are very attached to monochrome and line drawing, and the non-use of color is the fruit of a passion we have for the linear complexity of the copper engravings of Piranesi and Gustav Doré, the balanced volume of statues, the structures of architectural plans and the semantic codes of symbolism.

What are the limits of a stencil as a tool? What about large walls?
For us, it's a great tool, a discipline in the lineage of printmaking. We create a matrix and can make a limited number of prints, sometimes a monotype. Its real advantage is that it allows us to use inks on any support as long as it is relatively flat. A good stencil maker has his own know-how, his own style . . . he needs to know how to manage a double identity of artist-craftsman. Its real limit is for us the same as if we worked freehand: we paint on a "closed" support. The performance aspect of a monumental painting aside, we are nonetheless painting on a support, "a container." Public painting, beyond its pictorial effect, must know how to anchor itself in a preestablished context. We are therefore very dependent on the qualities of the wall and the environment.

For you, is a stencil a frame or a freedom?
For us it is a framework, let's say a foundation, conducive to building a structure. Freedom seems elusive to us; it is exercised by itself in the poetic part of our approach, which we do not master.

Can you describe your studio for us?
It is a 1950s industrial premises converted into workshops, located in a suburb near Paris. We built a framework and installed a transparent roof that insulates us, while preserving a maximum of light. There are very large hexagonal windows and mirrors on the walls to capture direct light. Outside, there is a large building with all the mirrored windows reflecting the sunset, which we would not normally be able to see. Plants are suspended from the ceiling, and we can water them with a pulley system. We have two spaces of 82 square feet (25 square meters) each, one for working, the other for storing and handling large formats. There are many antiques and old woods, tools, pouches and rolls of stencils. There are a total of five worktops. The space is fully modular according to the type of project to be carried out. It's a modest place, but very much reflects our tastes and influences.

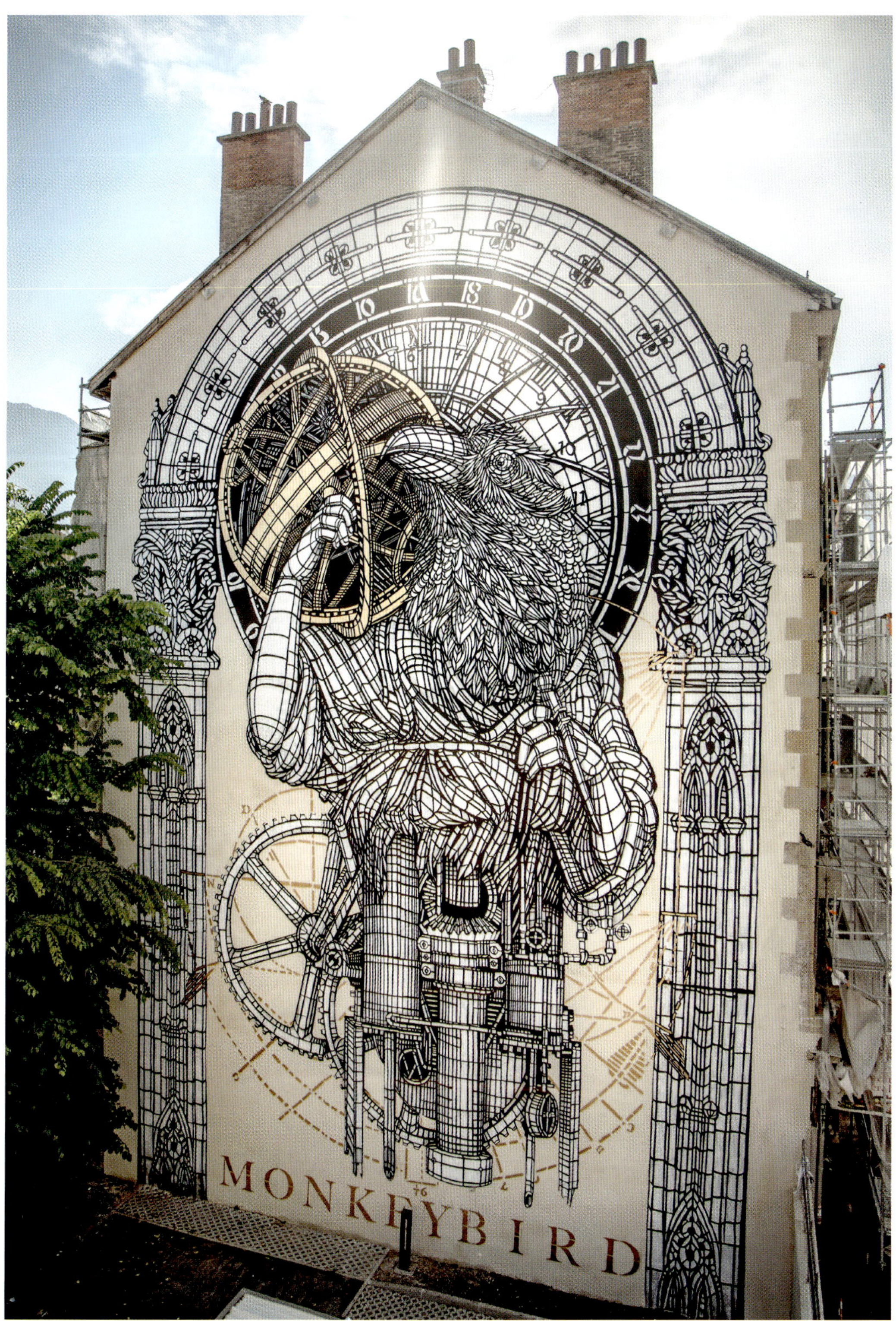
MONKEYBIRD

1. Fresco in progress, Loures (Portugal), 2016. As part of the festival Loures Arte Publica.

2. *Les Paons*, Grenoble (France), 2016. Fresco created for the Street Art Fest.

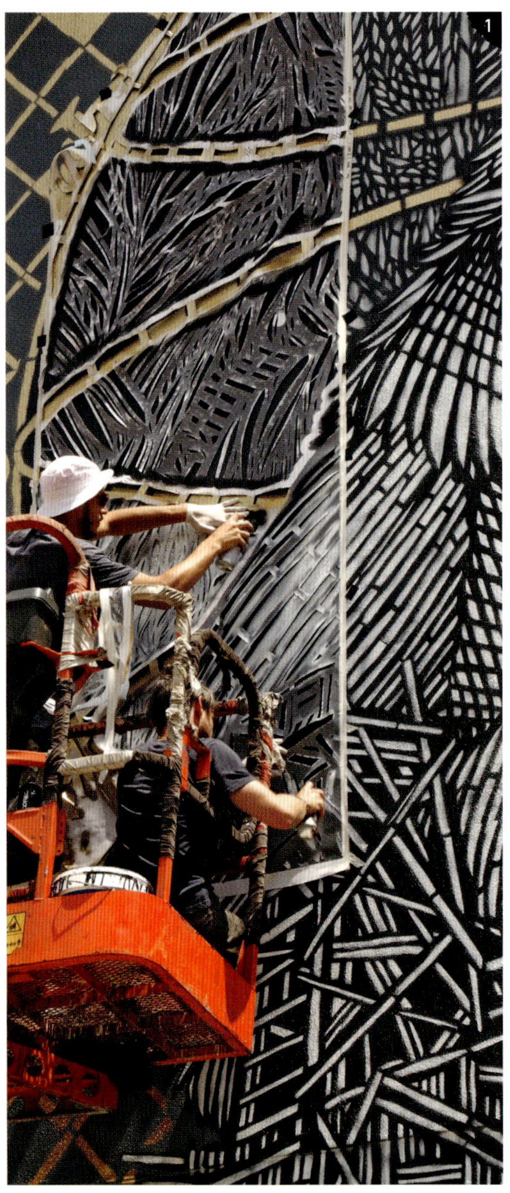

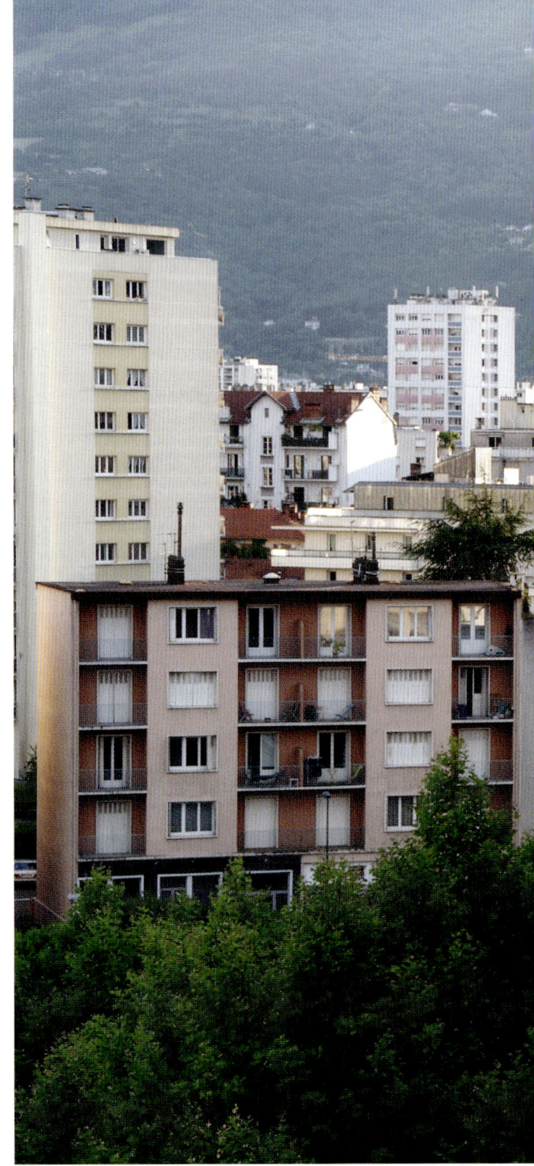

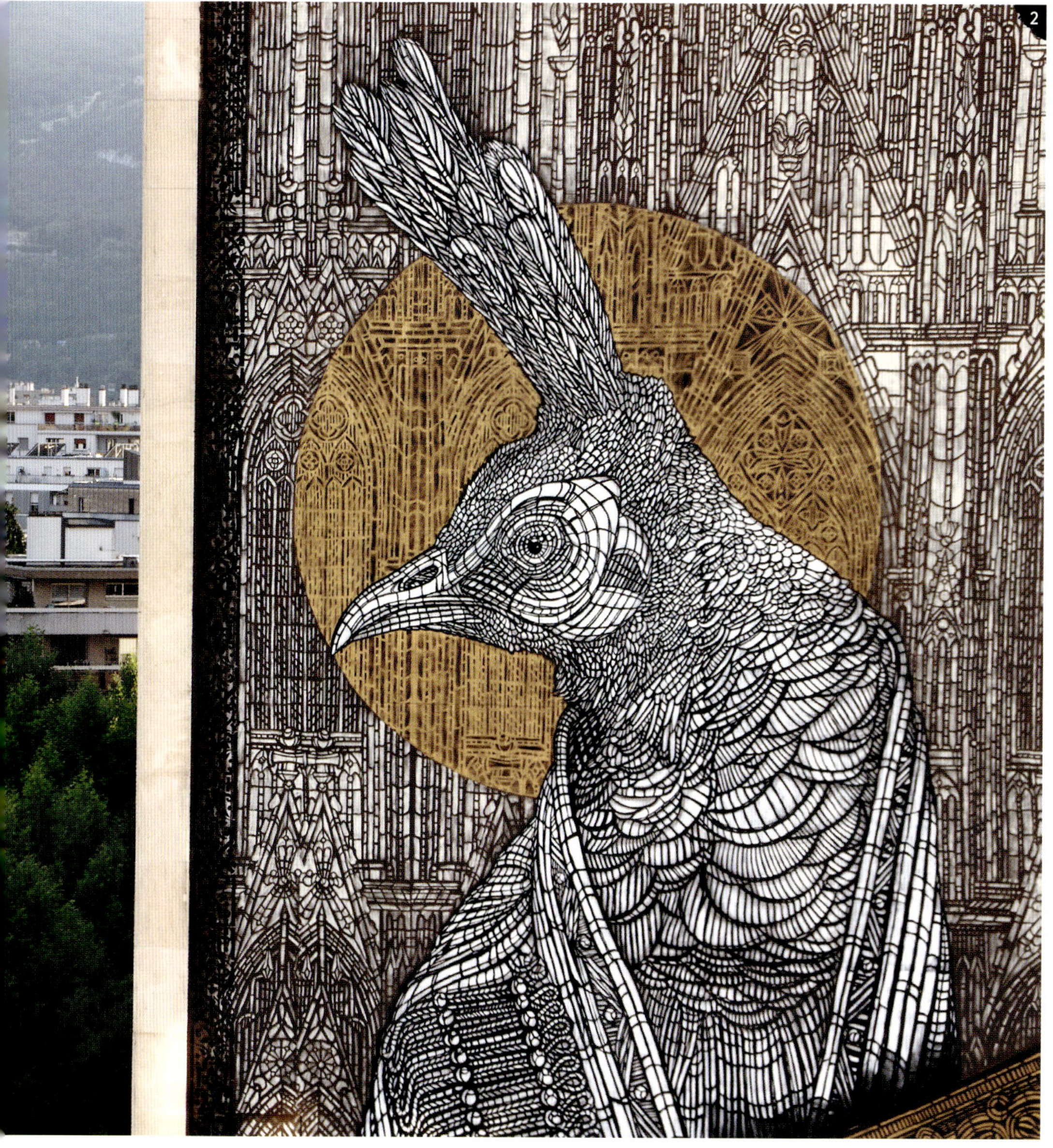

CREATING A STENCIL

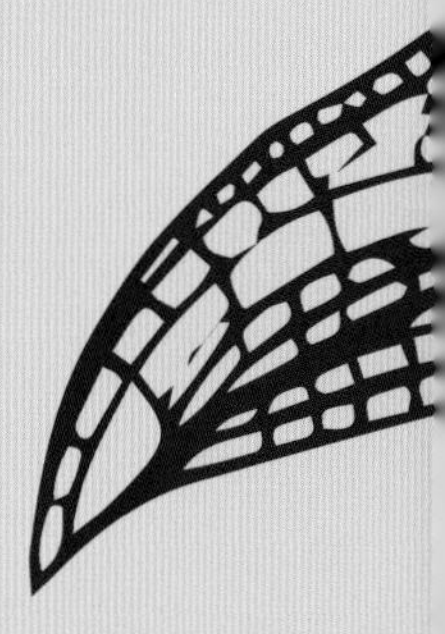

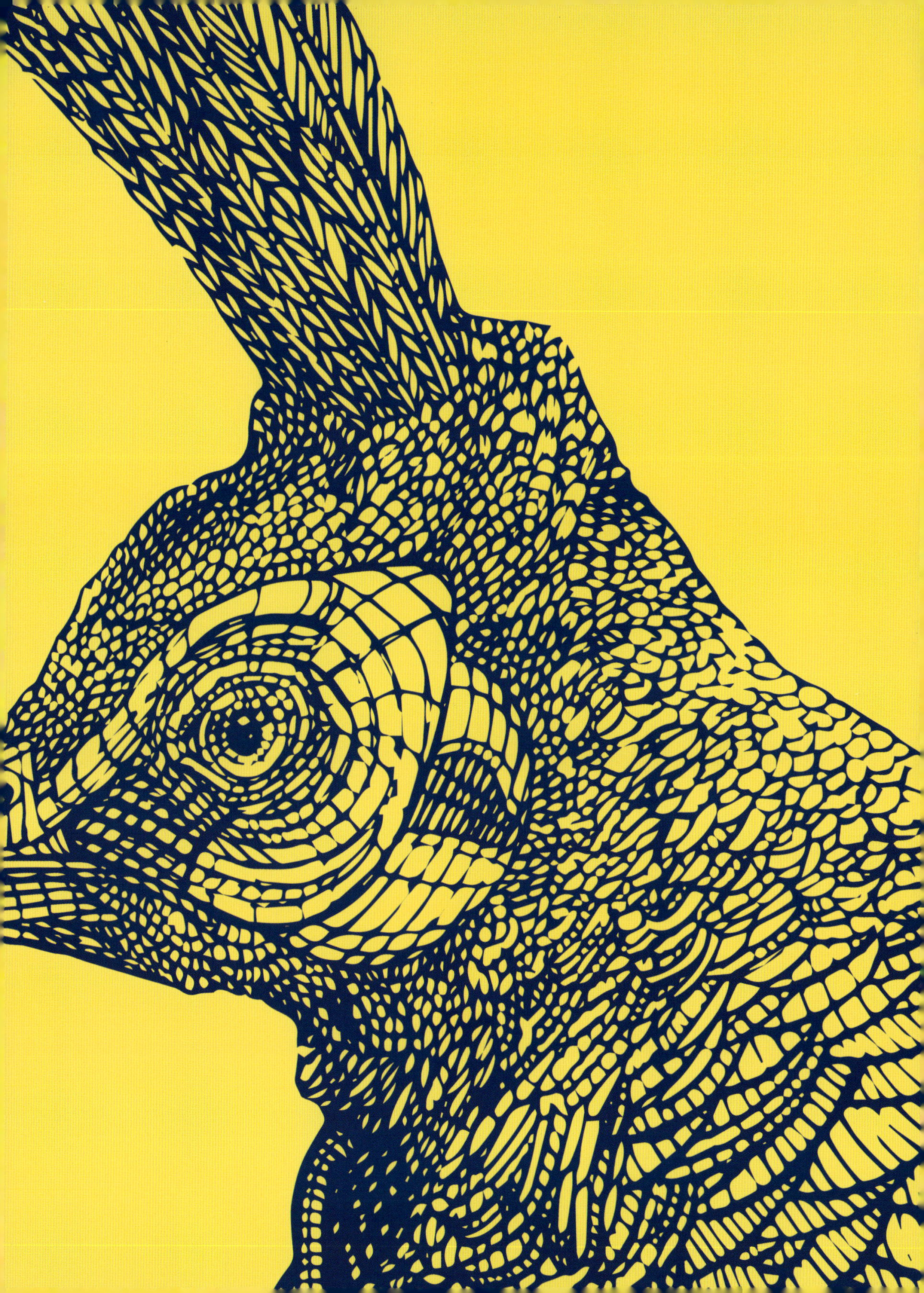

1 & 2. C215. Portrait of Eugene Delacroix, 2019.

3. C215. The superimposition of the same stencil painted in several colors and offset, creating an abstract work while preserving a certain readability.

4. Stinkfish. Study of superimposition of small colored stencils on a portrait.

THE LAYOUT

A stenciled work of art consists of lines separating the voids and the solids. Impossible to escape this principle of drawing. The stencil tool is thus made up of a group of holes held together by a frame and bridges, each hole being delimited by a line that returns to its starting point.

The lines that make up these different areas can be drawn prior to cutting, either manually on the material to be cut or digitally using software such as Photoshop or Illustrator, which will form the templates for future cutting. Others are cut directly in the support, without prior drawing.

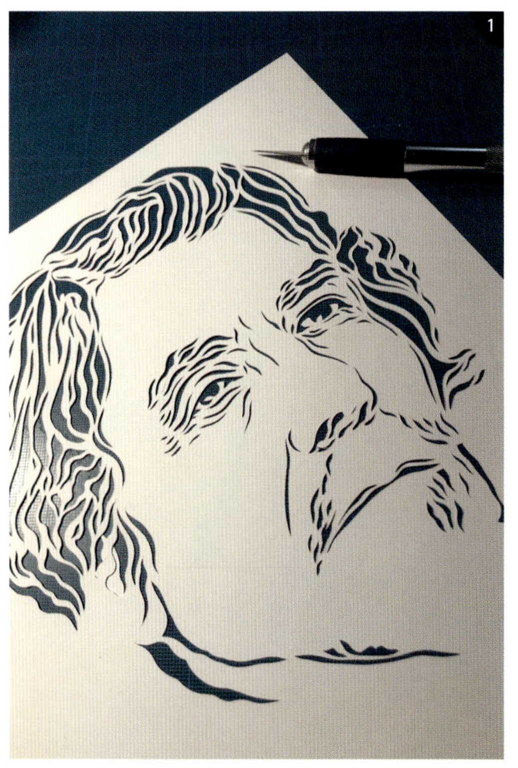

1

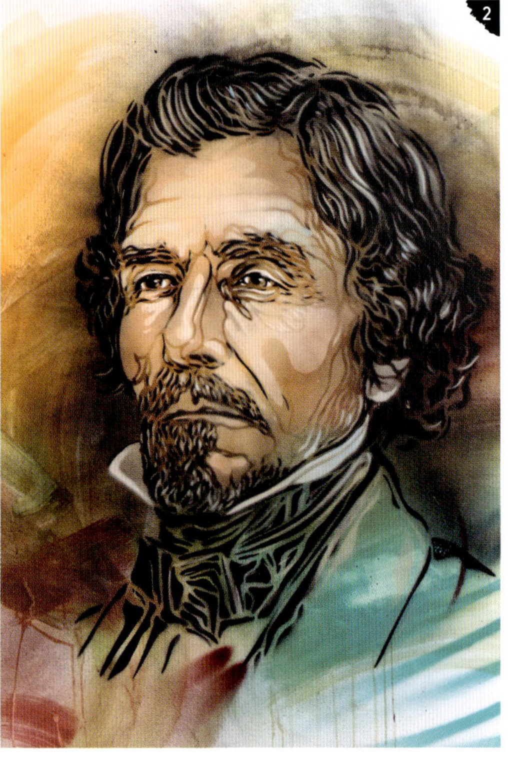

2

A MODEL?

Creating a stencil does not necessarily involve transferring a preexisting image. No transfer is absolutely mimetic: a stencil can come close to an existing image, never reproduce it exactly. There are many ways to render a given image, and each approach constitutes a style. Each "reproduced" image, therefore, is unique.

The final work can also be the product of applying, together or by superimposition, a repeated stencil or different stencils. or by superimposition, either of the same or of different stencils.

ENLARGEMENT

To make a large stencil from a smaller drawing, you can use an overhead projector on which an acetate drawing or even a stencil can be placed. The projection will allow you to redraw your image's outline at the desired size. It is also possible to laminate an enlarged print of the design you wish to create on cardstock or acetate.

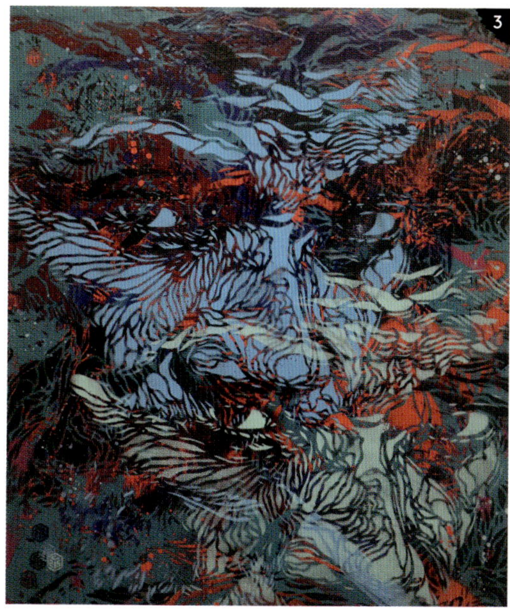
3

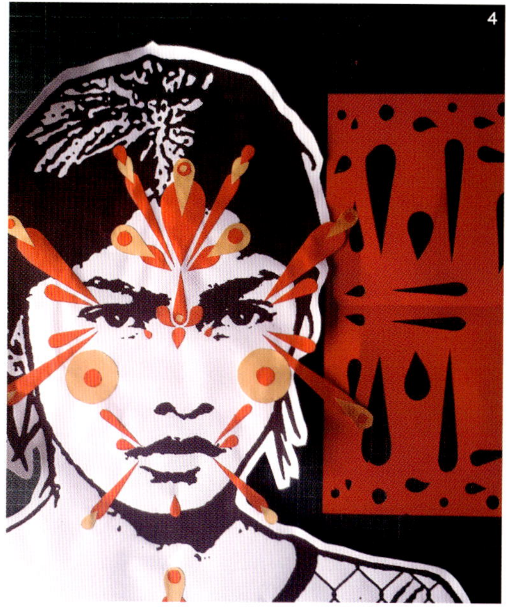
4

PHOTOSHOP AND ITS FILTERS

Photoshop is a well-known image-processing software. It, among others, can be used by those who are just starting out and also by those who have difficulty drawing. Some of its functionalities, such as filters, make it easy to transform visuals into an image that is suitable for stencil cutting.

FILTERS

Several filters serve to divide the initial image into as many areas that can be converted into holes, which will form the final stencil design. Among the optical filters offered, some (such as the Pixelization > Halftone color filter) echo the aesthetics of offset printing screens developed in the 1960s and 1970s. The result is a breakdown into small dots of various sizes that with distance will assemble visually to form the image.

SELECTING LAYERS

For those who have difficulty distinguishing and tracing the different levels of light or color in their work themselves, the software also allows you to mechanically select layers, isolating the levels of light and the various colors to create separate files. Each one of these files can be transformed into a stencil, and the assembled stencils will faithfully reconstitute the desired image. The tutorial opposite shows you how to put this into practice.

TUTORIAL: MAKE A STENCIL USING PHOTOSHOP

Here's a simple way to create a single or multilayer stencil with Photoshop. The software often offers several alternatives to perform the same action. With time and practice, you will be able to refine your method.

Step 1
Select the image you want to turn into a stencil. It can be figurative or abstract, simple or complex. Anything goes! Once you've chosen your image, open it in Photoshop.

Step 2
Switch the image to black and white (Image > Mode > Grayscale).

Step 3
Contrast the image to reduce the number of gray levels (Image > Settings > Levels). Use the black and white sliders to adjust the black and white values to the desired effect. For standard contrast, place the sliders at the beginning and end of the histogram peak. You may need to repeat this several times to achieve satisfactory contrast.

Step 4
Select the number of layers that will make up the image layers (Filter > Filter Gallery > Trim > Levels). For a monolayer stencil, select 2 levels: you get a black and white file. For a multilayer stencil, you can select three, four, or five or more levels, depending on the number of layers you want. I advise you to limit yourself to three or four levels, because with that you will reach a sufficient level of complexity so that the eye will reconstruct the nuances of the image by itself. The additional layers will not add much. For this example, three levels have been created (black, white and gray). Also play with the Simplicity and Fidelity values visible under the level settings, to simplify the contours of the future shapes to be cut.

Step 5
Using the Brush tool, create several black registration marks that will be used to properly align all layers of the stencil when applying paint.

Step 1

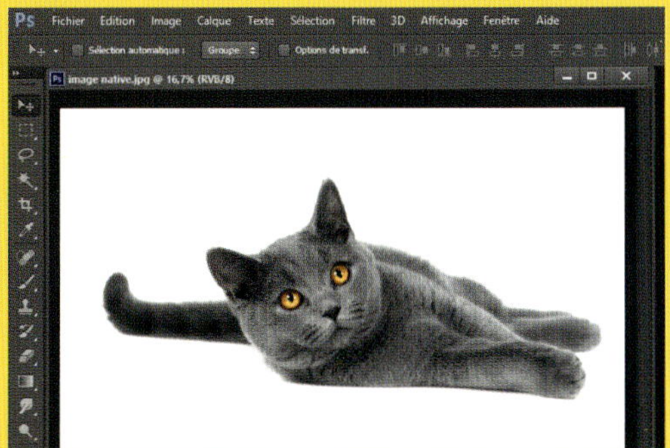

Step 2

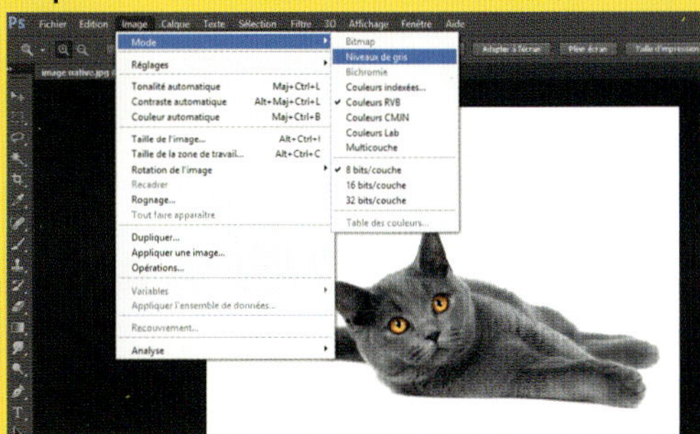

Step 3

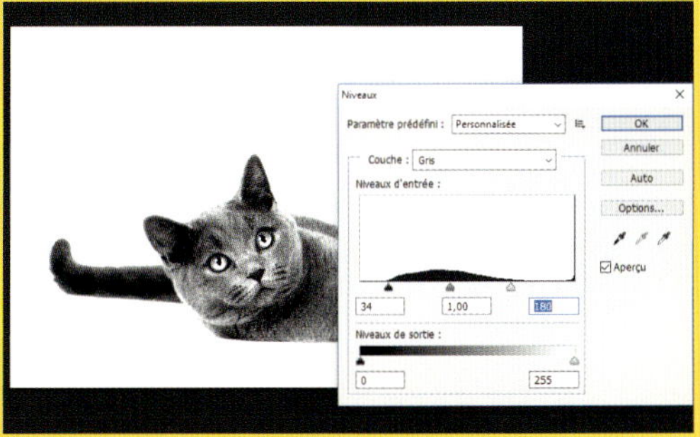

Step 4a

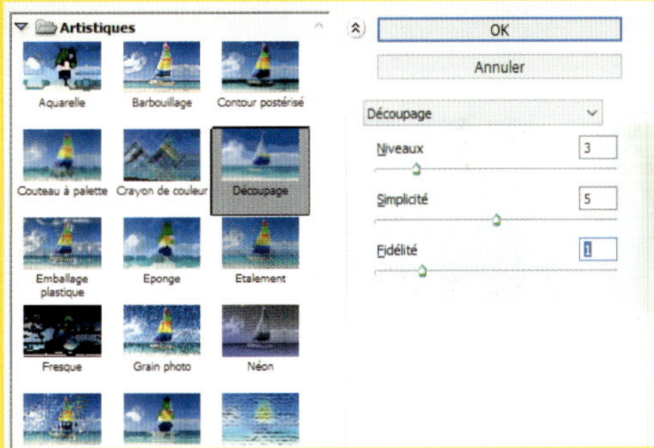

Step 4b

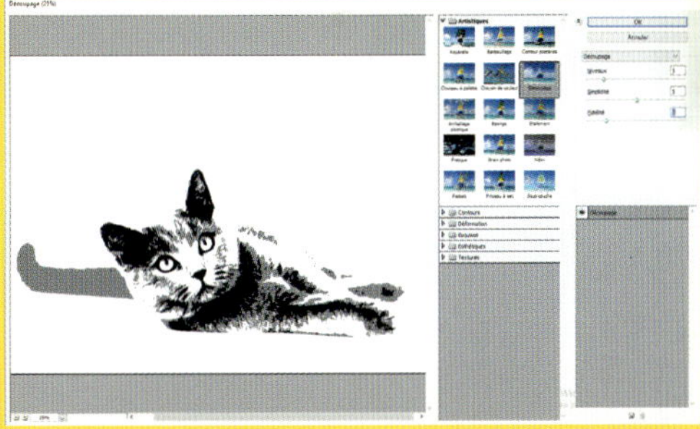

Step 5

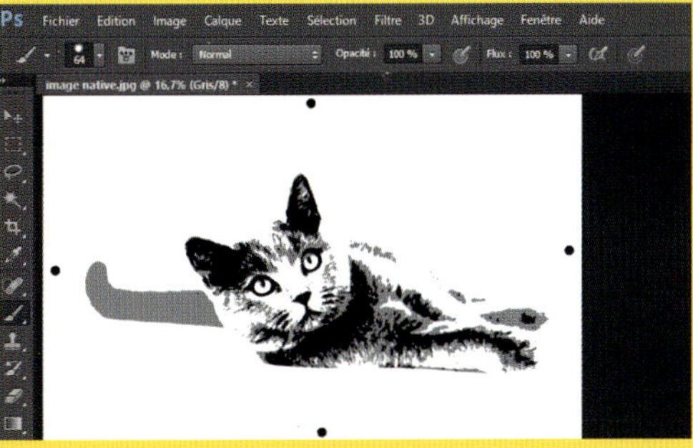

Step 6
Duplicate your file so that you have a separate file for each layer of the stencil (Image > Duplicate). Here, the file obtained in step 5 is duplicated once, so that you have two files. Remember to name each file clearly (layer1, layer2, layer3, etc.).

Step 7
You will now generate a black-and-white file for each layer of the stencil (the black represents the areas that will be cut). On one of your files, select the Magic Wand tool and uncheck the Contiguous Pixels box in the taskbar. This will allow you to select the entire range of the same color with a single click. Set the tool to a tolerance of 5 and click on a black area. All black areas of the image are selected.

Invert the selection (Selection > Invert). Switch the selection to white (Edit > Fill > With White).

You get the black-and-white file of one of the stencil layers.

In your second file, select the gray color with the Magic Wand tool. So that the black registration marks don't disappear, once again check the Contiguous pixels box and select each mark by holding down the Shift key. Then swap the selection and change it to white. Your file now contains the second layer of the stencil, which you simply change to black (Edit > Fill > With Black).

Step 8
With the Brush tool, create bridges and simplify the drawing of your images when necessary. Keep in mind that wide bridges will be visible but will make the stencil strong; conversely, thin bridges will not be visible but may weaken the stencil. The images for steps 8a and 8b show the creation of bridges and simplified tracings at the level of ears and eyes.

You can also create your bridges after the stencil is printed, by placing a grid over your images and leaving consistent bridge areas along these squares to maintain the pattern.

Step 9
Print your files on plain paper that you can laminate onto card or print them directly onto cardstock. Cut out the black areas, making sure to also cut out the registration marks that will allow you to align the different layers. When you paint your stencil, first place a piece of masking tape on the support under each of the marks. This way, they will not appear once the stencil is painted.

You can also vector-base your files in Photoshop or Illustrator (provided they already contain the bridges) and have them laser-cut by a specialized printer.

Step 7a

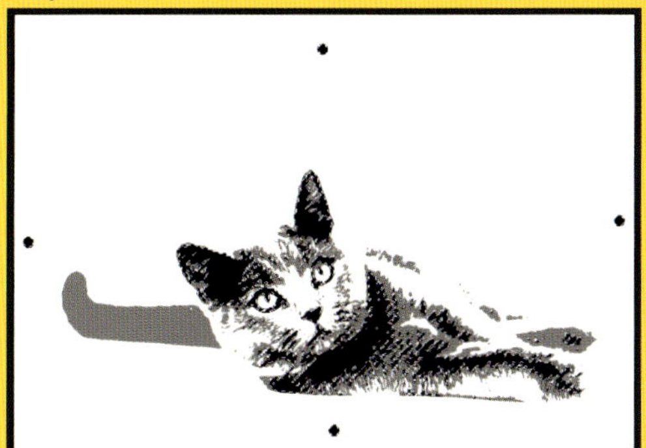

Step 7b

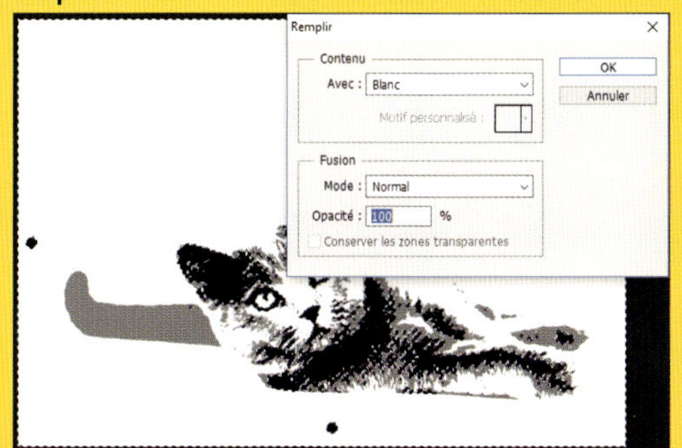

Step 7c

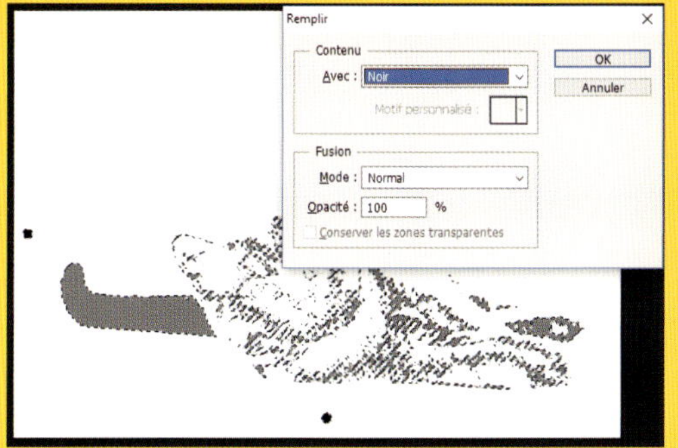

Step 7d

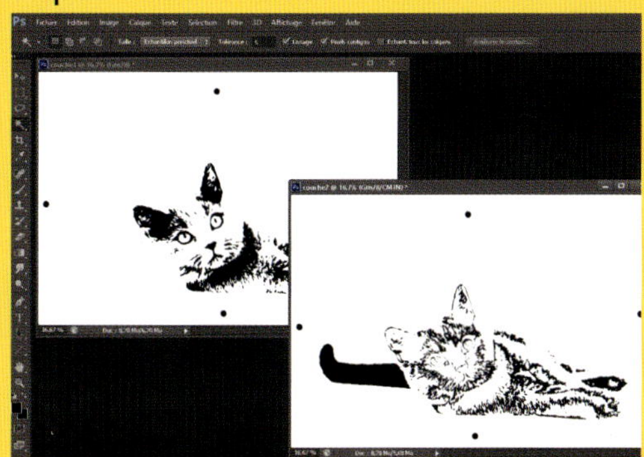

Step 8a

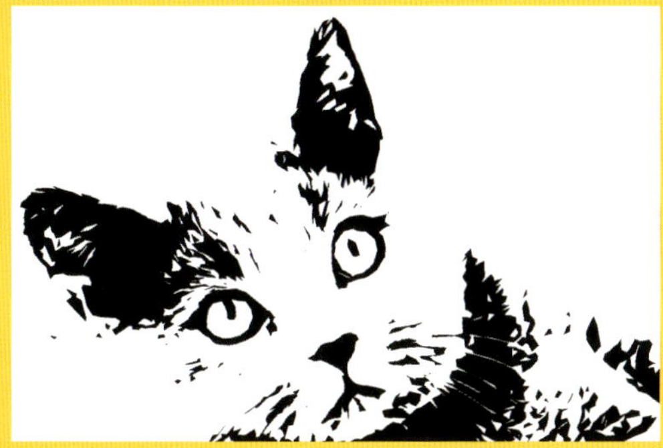

Step 8b

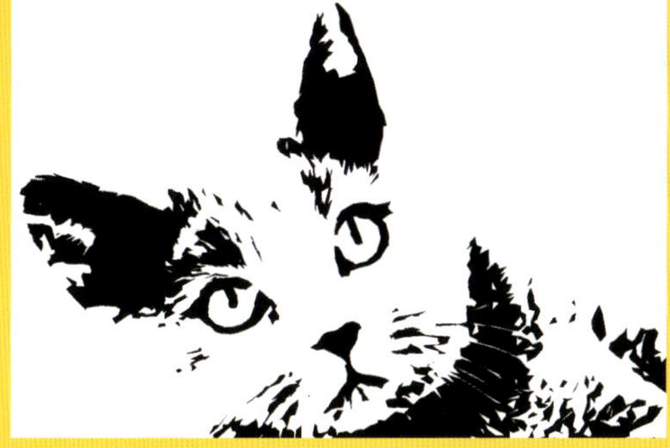

Anonymous portrait, stencil poster, 2010. In Sten & Lex's studio.

INTERVIEW WITH STEN & LEX

This duo of Roman artists, active since the early 2000s, became known for their radical aesthetic. Adepts of monochrome painting, their sense of optical mixing inspired by serigraphs of the 1970s has allowed them to develop a style that today borders on abstraction.
Website: stenlex.com
Instagram: @stenlex

Why did you choose stencils rather than another painting technique?
We have always been attracted by everything that is printed: grainy photographs from old newspapers, stamps, prints, engravings, banknotes, silkscreens . . . and especially black-and-white prints.

As a printing technique, stencils offer the possibility of simplifying a photo, of returning to its essence and purifying its contrasts. This is particularly the case with monolayer stencils (single layer). With the advent of digital graphics, the transformation of photos into one or more layers has become quick and easy.

From the beginning, we wanted to make portraits, mainly of anonymous, middle-class people, students and professors from the 1960s and 1970s. This strongly guided the choice of our technique. However, not all photos are suitable for stenciling; the play of light and shadow is a determining factor in getting a good starting point. All this was mostly done in a very spontaneous way, because in the beginning we did not want to be artists at all but doctors!

How do you make your stencils?
In 2010, we started producing what we call a poster stencil. The process brings together two of the main mediums used on the street: stencil and poster. We stick a stencil cut out of paper on the wall, then paint on it and destroy the matrix. This technique makes each creation unique, because the matrix remains on the wall and deteriorates little by little. The form can no longer be reproduced, which is contrary to the very nature of the stencil. Our obsession with this technique has finally led us to renounce its reproducible nature, creating in a way a paradox of the stencil.

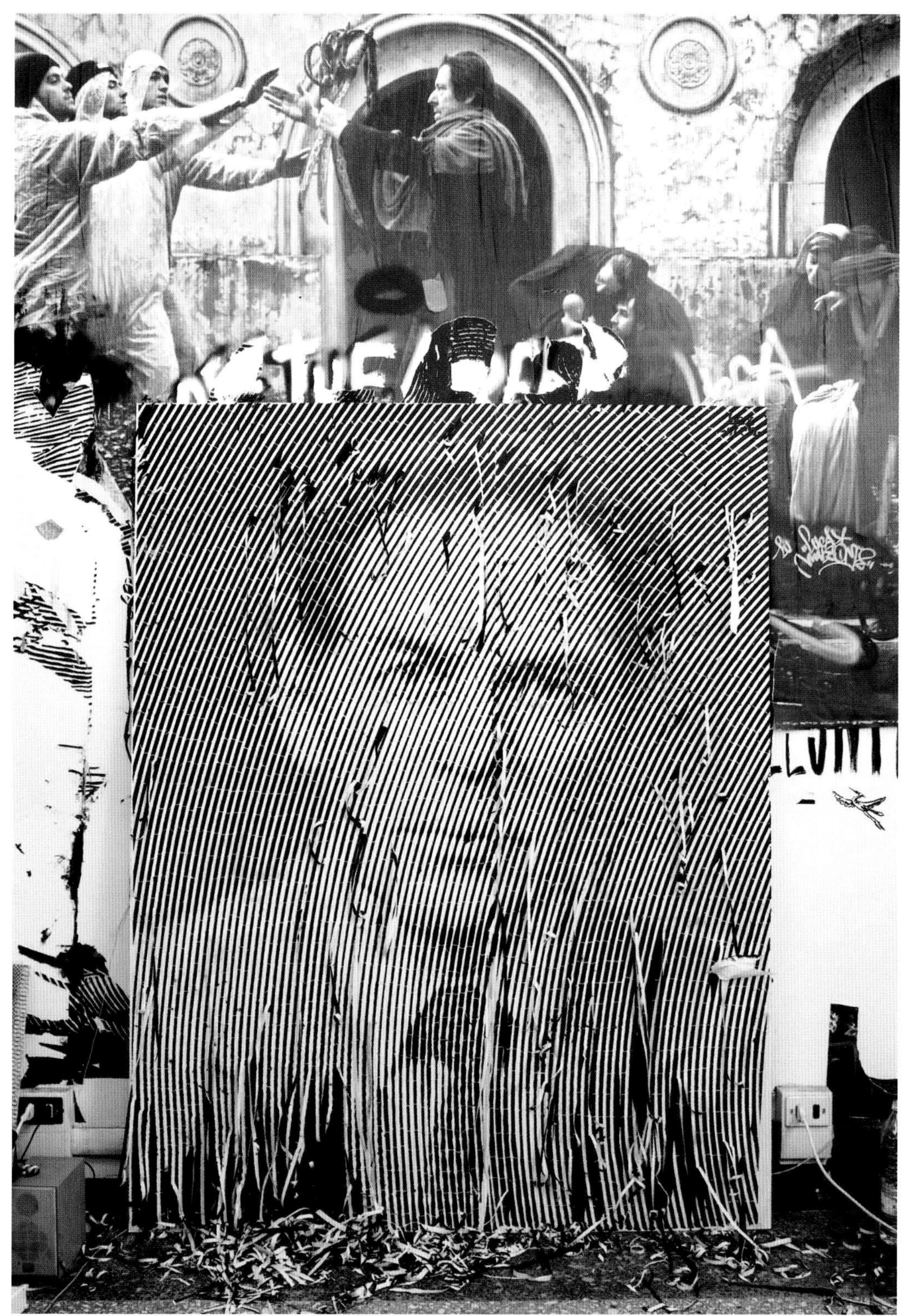

Anonymous portrait, stencil poster, Campobasso (Italy), 2011. Created as part of the Draw the Line Festival.

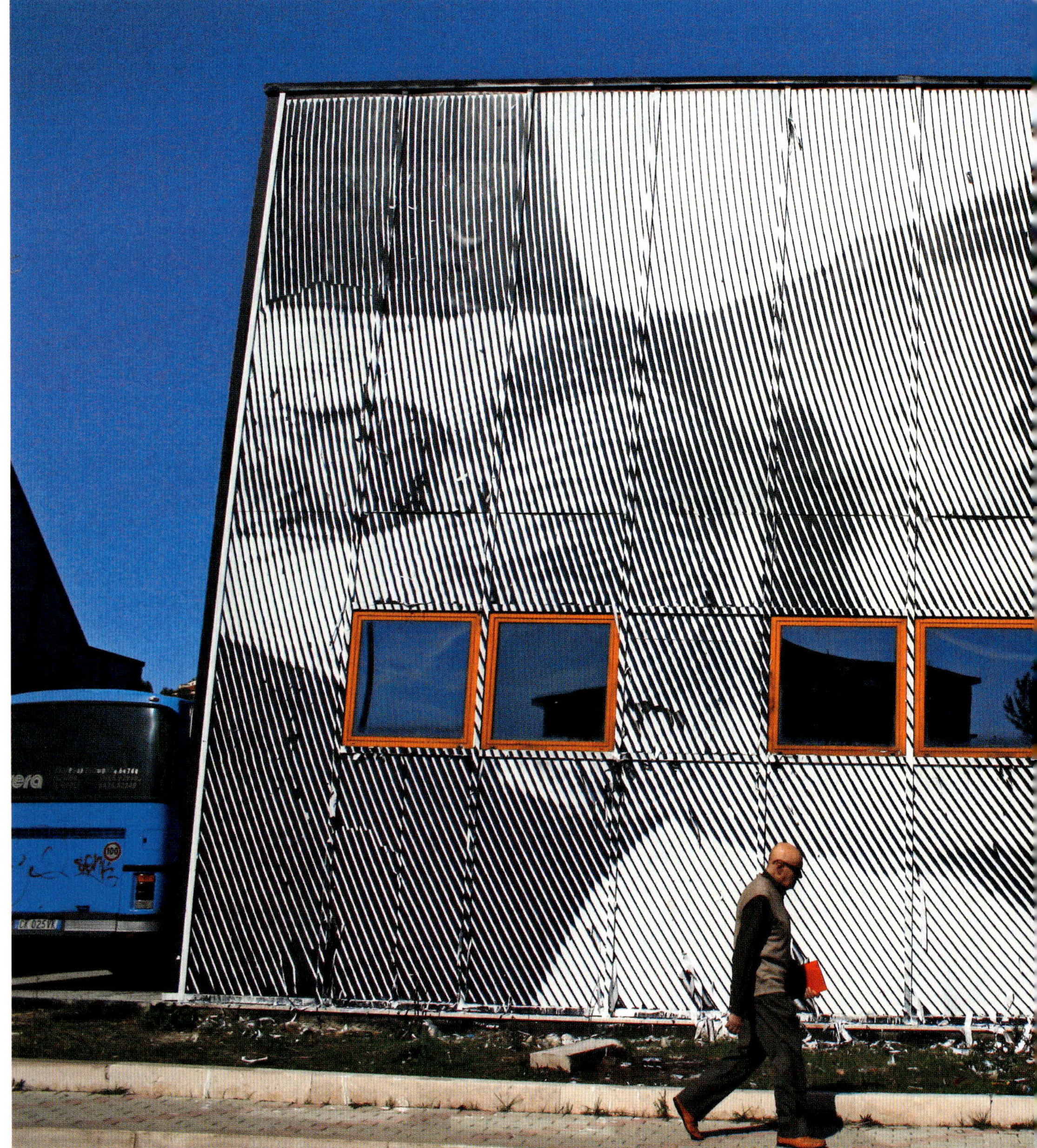

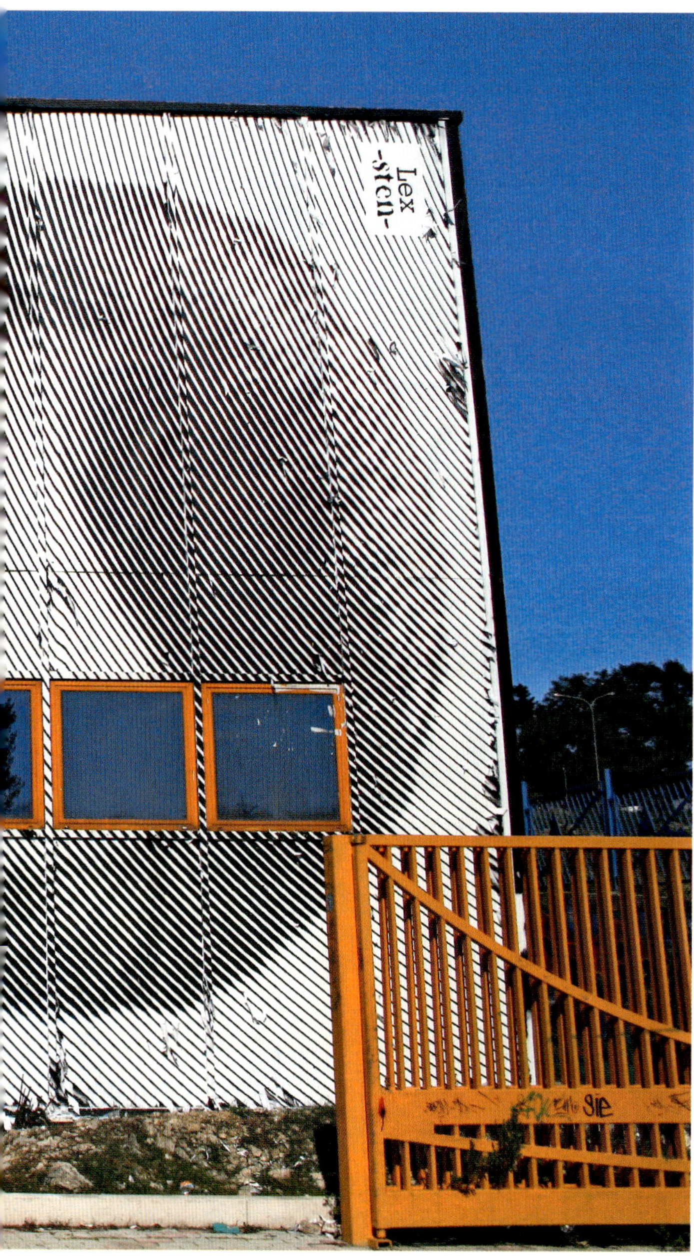

How do you see the evolution of stencil techniques since you started out?

Stencil graffiti of the last twenty years has gone in different directions: hyperrealism, multilayer, black and white optical play, illustration, freehand drawings, lettering . . . Each movement has had its representative artists. When we started in 2001, there were no references on the Internet about stencil or street art. We felt we were doing something new. That was the best period for us. A few years later, thanks to websites like Wooster Collective, Stencil Revolution, Fotolog or Flickr, and books like *Stencil Graffiti* by Tristan Manco, we discovered a whole universe that was developing in the big Western cities, like an invasion.

One of the first stencil festivals in which we participated was called Difusor; it was in Barcelona in 2007. Artists like Dolk, Vhils and M-city were there. Then, in 2008, the Cans Festival created by Banksy in London set out an international vision of stencil art. It was real recognition for the stencil artists of our generation. Ten years later, stenciling as a process is no longer as valued as it was then. Perhaps because, on its own, this technique could not support an artistic "movement."

In any case, most of those who participated in the festival are now great artists.

Stencils have been used less in recent years because most muralists work on very large buildings. Stencils are more suitable for small surfaces. A thirty meter wall can be painted in two days, whereas it takes up to twenty days or even a month to cut out a stencil of that size. This book is important because it shows the link between the artists and the technique they use.

Portrait imitating the screen-printing of the 1970s, made with spray cans of non-opaque colors, 2008.

Who are the artists who inspire you in your stencil work?
The Stencil Revolution website inspired us a lot. It was the largest database of stencils and stencil makers. Most of the artists were represented there, and we greatly admired the work of some of them such as Evol, Logan Hicks and Swoon. One of the masters who inspired us is Gustave Doré, even though he is not a stencil artist. Since the beginning, we have been trying to express ourselves through a monolayer stencil. To create our three-dimensional portraits, we start with lines that make us think of those in the engravings that Doré made to illustrate the *Divine Comedy*.

When we started with poster stencils, the master was JR. His way of working on different types of architecture was really unique. In 2013, we started creating abstract stencils, in the tradition of our peers Momo, 108, Moneyless and our elders, including Frank Stella, Sol LeWitt, Alberto Burri, Piero Dorazio and Mimmo Rotella.

What are the limits of stencils as a tool?
Stencils have many technical limitations, but we manage to overcome them. Bridges make its matrix fragile, whereas to paint in the street, the support must be solid. Yet, the bridge is a trademark, and in many cases the balance of the bridges makes the beauty of a stencil. We don't have this problem because we glue our stencils directly onto the wall. Overspray is also a risk, but with a little experience, you can avoid it. If you make multilayer work, it can be difficult to mix the colors. But in the end, the stencil is only a tool. The important thing is the final artwork, not the way you do it.

For you, is a stencil a frame or a freedom?
Stencils are a constant struggle between frame and freedom. The process we use, the poster stencil, was created after many years of work, for functional reasons. We wanted to paint a stencil without bridges. The only way was to glue it onto the support.

Can you describe your studio for us?
We moved to a new apartment a few months ago, and we now have a dedicated room, but in general we like to paint on site. So most of our production is done outside Rome. When you have your studio in your apartment, you never stop working, and at the same time there are too many distractions.

Can you explain your technique used in the years 2008–2009, which superimposed transparent colors in order to create dark surfaces?
It was one of our very first experiences with color. We decided to use primary colors in the manner of the colored pixels in photographs found in newspapers in the 1960s and 1970s. Instead of pixels, we used lines and gave color to the portraits by superimposing four transparent layers. The transparency between two colors gives a third color, and that's a very interesting aspect. It brings to mind the quadrichrome of printing, the famous CMYK (cyan, magenta, yellow, black). Working with colors is still difficult for us—our works are mostly painted in black and white—but when we made this series of portraits, we felt we had taken a big step forward.

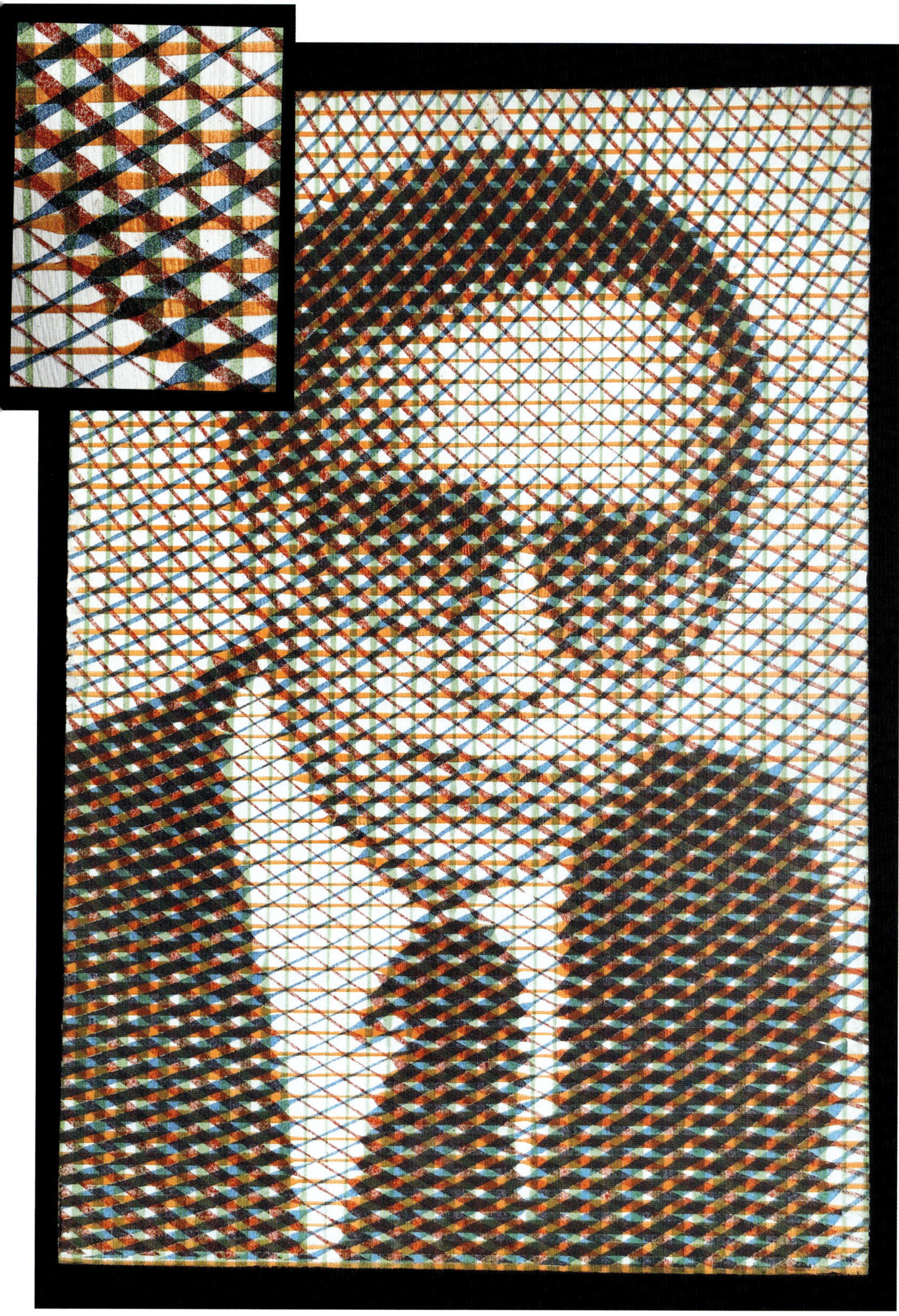

The artists at work, 2018.

INTERVIEW WITH SNIK

This duo of Bristol-based artists is one of the most radical explorers of complex stencil design today. Multiplying the levels of cuts and breaking up their drawings to the extreme, they make work that tends toward hyperrealism. Their fragile and delicate cuts alone can reach the level of works of art.

Website: www.snikarts.com
Instagram: @snikarts
Facebook: @snikarts

Why did you choose stencils rather than another painting technique?

We love many aspects of stenciling, from design to cutting to large-scale mural painting. Sitting for hours and hours cutting out every little element is very relaxing; it's good for the mind. We always cut our work by hand, which takes several days or even weeks for a single piece. This adds a meditative dimension to the process. Cutting stencils can't be done hastily or without care; otherwise the final result will suffer. Stencils also allow a great freedom of choice of colors and materials. The work can constantly evolve and offers great diversity: the studio stencil, for example, is very different from the street stencil, both in strength and design.

How do you make your stencils?

Our stencils are a mix of digital and freehand work, but our cuts are always hand-done. We design our source material ourselves, either by hiring photographers or taking the photos ourselves. Once the lights and tones of the image are reworked, we scan it via Photoshop and print it in large format. Then comes the time for cutting, which can take hours, weeks, and sometimes, for very large projects, months at a time.

How do you see the evolution of stencil techniques since you started out?

When we started out, the stencil scene was very different. Internet coverage was low, there were no communities. Social networks changed not only the stencil world, but the whole street art world. Stencil artists now have access to a very high level of exposure, and their work is becoming more and more technical at the same time. I remember a monumental piece that M-city did for the See No Evil event in Bristol, which was supposed to be ten stories high and completely astounded me. That work had penetrated my spirit.

With Instagram, Twitter, etc., access to the work of artists from all over the world is now immediate and commonplace. The public is used to seeing new offerings. To continue to be visible, one must constantly push the level higher. But the evolutions have not only been concentrated in the streets. Logan Hicks, for example, has totally changed the multilayer game with extremely detailed stencils. You can feel that the stencil art scene is stronger than ever.

Who are the artists who inspire you in your stencil work?

When we started, we were attracted to the multilayer style that Logan Hicks mastered. The monolayer black-and-white style was already known, but the multilayer offered more depth and detail, which was more suited to us. The Everfresh Crew was also a great source of inspiration. Their large-scale collages and stencils using the environment or context to tell a story are breathtaking.

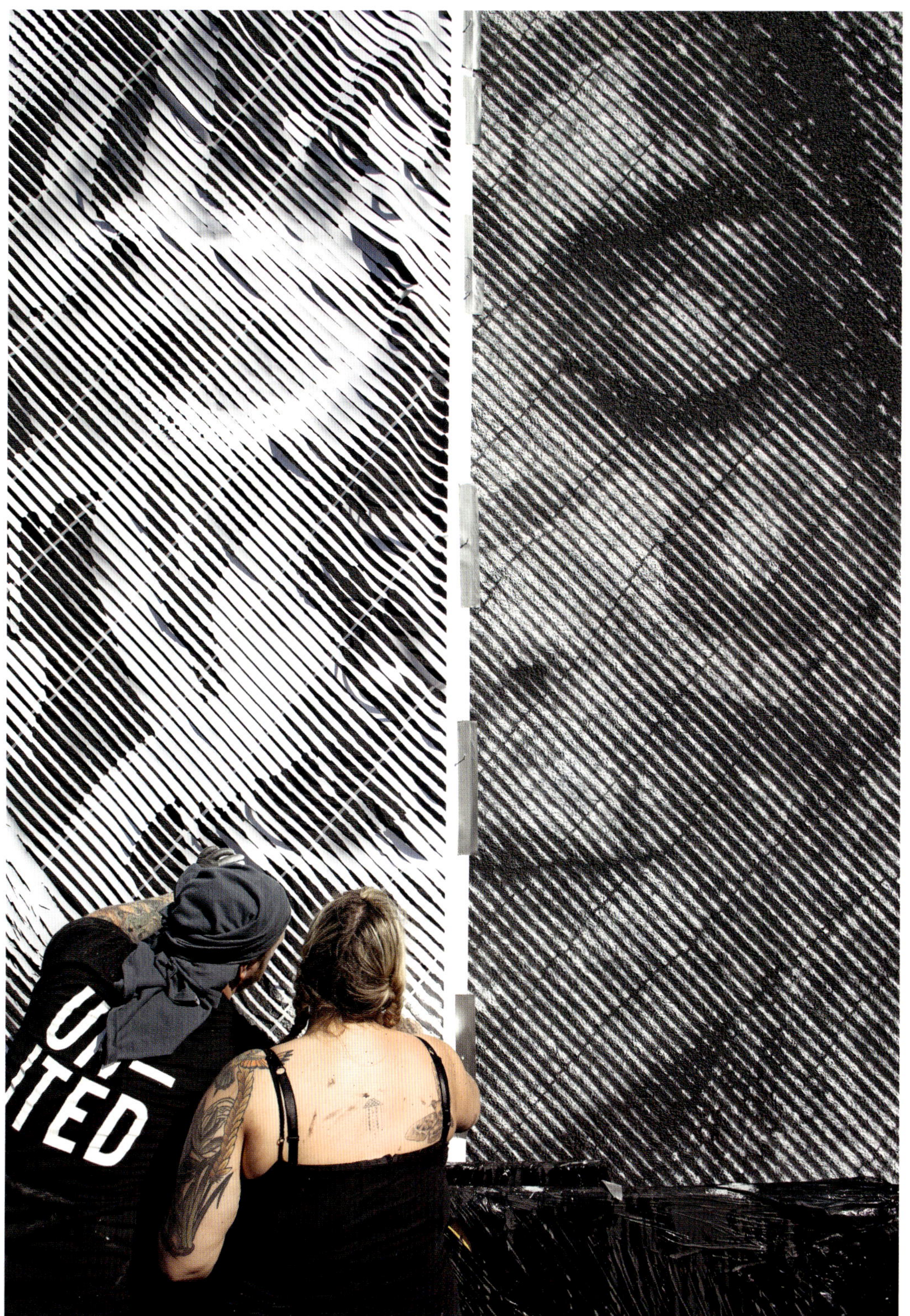

What are the limits of stencils as a tool? For you, is a stencil a frame or a freedom?

The slowest part in making a stencil is the cutting, no doubt about it. Even if you use a machine, it has to cut the layers, whereas a graffiti artist only has to paint according to his inspiration, without any delay. Apart from that, I don't see any disadvantage to stencils. They can be used several times and always create different effects. The scaling potential is also helpful; an image can be used as a basis for a mural as well as a work on canvas. There is also a form of freedom in deeply knowing the image we are going to paint, as a result of our time spent cutting it. We don't have to question, as we paint, the dimensions needed for the surface. This is a considerable advantage because it allows us to devote ourselves fully to painting. It's a personal choice, and I understand that many people think stenciling is restrictive, but every medium has its disadvantages. The important thing is to use the one that suits you best. For us, it is clearly stencils.

Can you describe your studio for us?

We work in a small studio in our house. But it's spacious enough for us to cut large-format stencils for the street and also to paint a canvas. There are a lot of different paint colors for our multilayer stencils, and there's nonstop music playing. We live in the country. It's a pleasure for us to stop work for a while, to take a walk with the dog, to listen to music and to let new ideas emerge. One day we would like to have a huge studio, but at the moment it's not the space that counts, but what we produce and develop inside it.

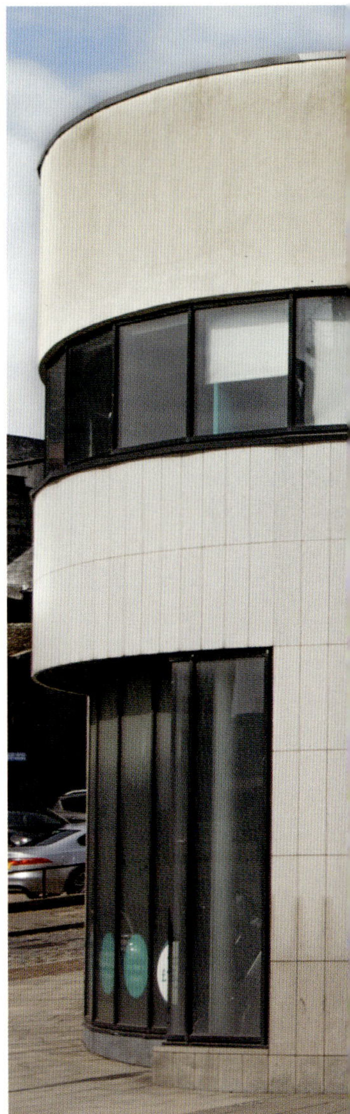

Hold Fast Hope, Aberdeen, Scotland, 2018. Eight-layer stencil made for the Nuart Aberdeen festival.

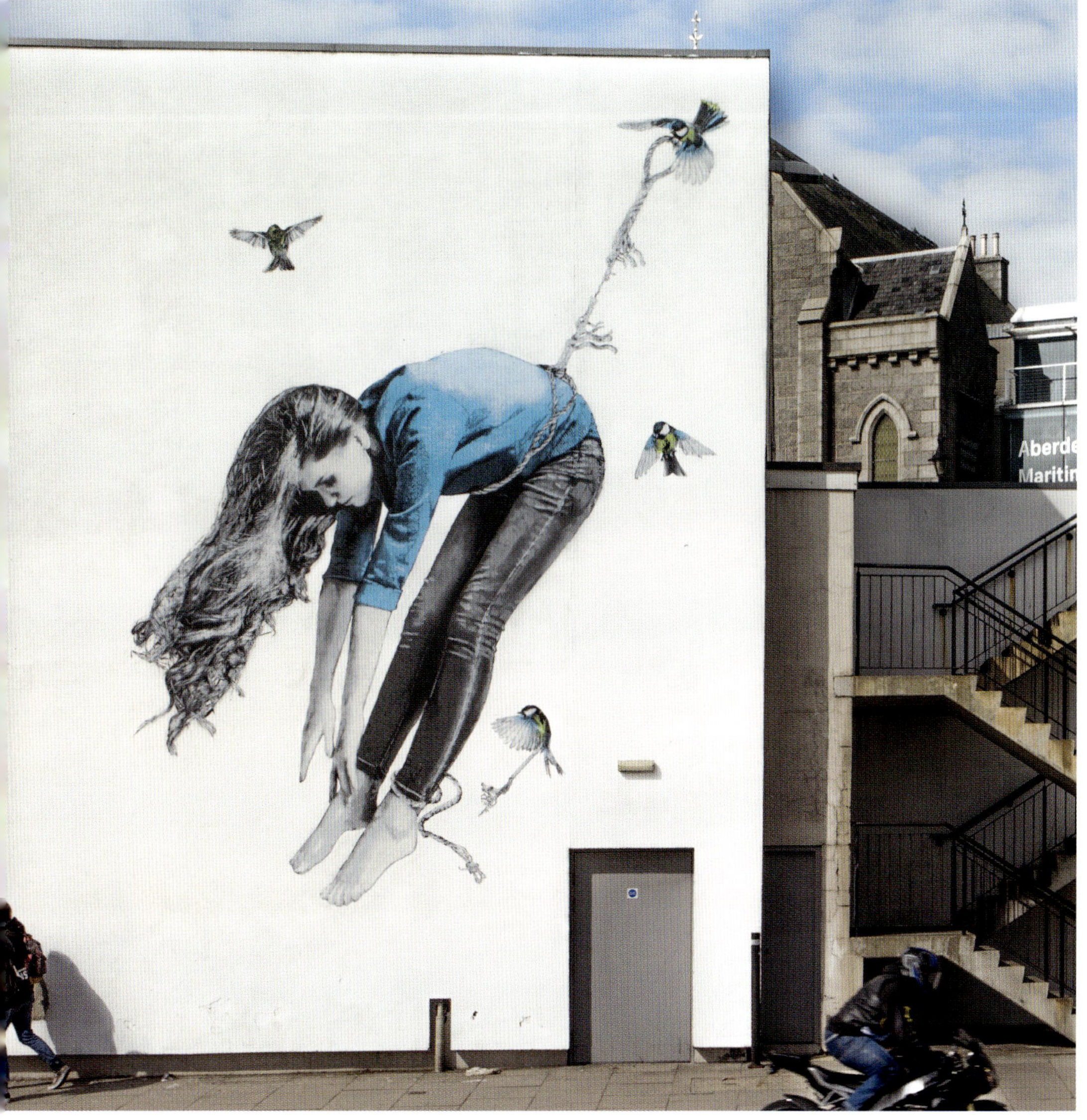

Everything Connected (in collaboration with Nuno Viegas), Berlin, 2018.

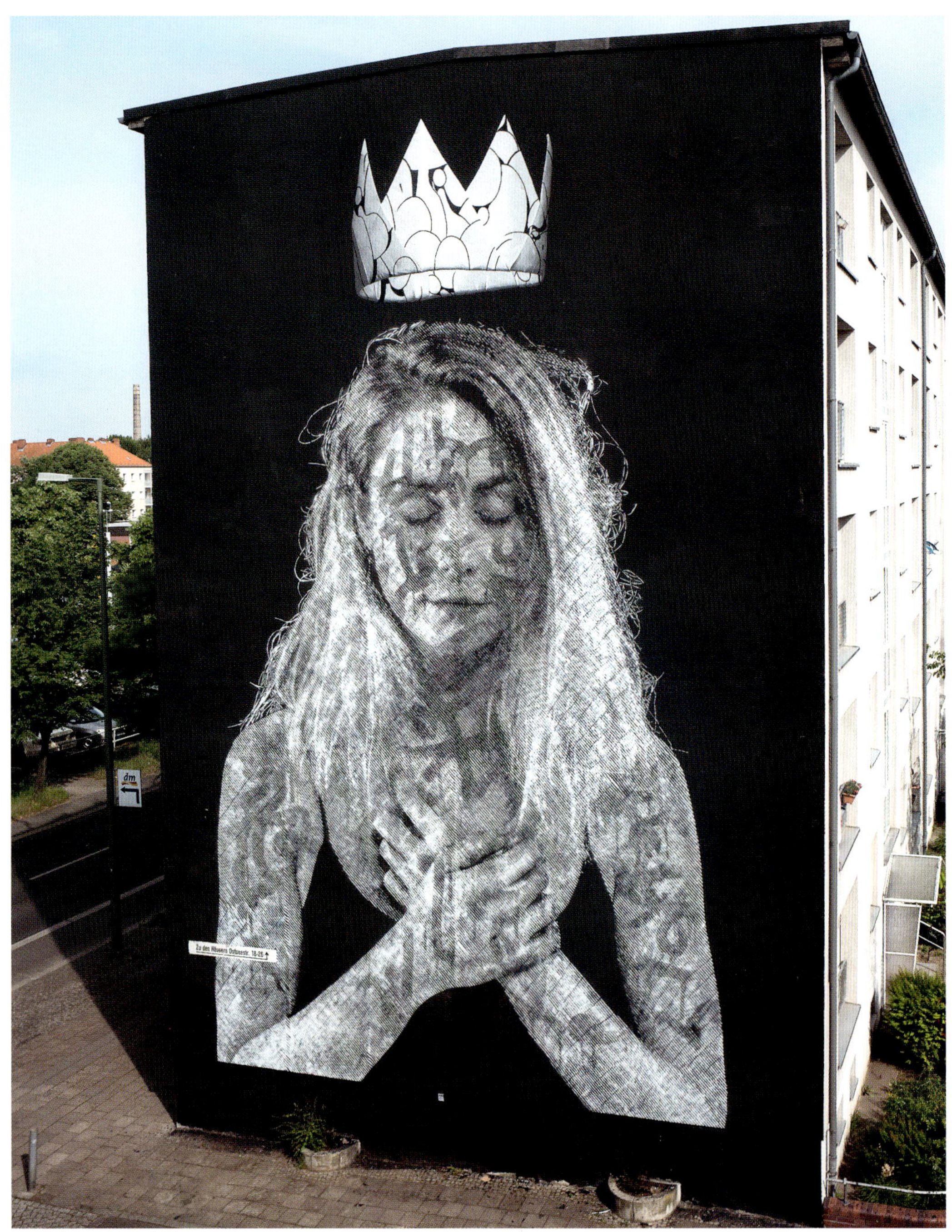

ILLUSTRATOR

The other very useful software for creating stencils is Illustrator. It allows you to define zones from harmonious curves. Moreover, the product of these vectors is ideal for artists who wish to to have their stencils cut out by plotters or laser-beam-cutting machines. Photoshop also allows vector-based designs, but the forms obtained will never have the quality and the simplicity of those purposely designed on Illustrator. The artist Stew (see his interview below) has concocted for you two tutorials to familiarize you with this software.

Stew's Tutorials

The Pen Tool

Illustrator is a vector graphics software; i.e., it works with coordinates and not pixels. My favorite tool is the Pen tool, used to create complex vector graphic forms. (The Curvature tool works as well.) Here's a small tip: before clicking on this tool, select the Selection tool directly (white arrow), so that you can easily switch from one to the other thanks to keyboard shortcuts: the Command key (on Mac) or Ctrl key (on PC). The white arrow will allow you to isolate a point.

Please note that to draw with Illustrator, you need to have both hands on the table: one hand holds the mouse (or the stylus), and the other one is near the keyboard, ready to use those famous keyboard shortcuts!

On a new document, click with the Pen tool: a point appears. Move the cursor and click again: a second point appears and a straight line connecting them appears. Continue the operation until you return to the first point and thus close your form. It's very important to close your forms—this will save you a lot of trouble down the road.

If you want to constrain your angles to 45° or 90°, press on the Shift key at the same time that you create a new dot.

If you want to draw a curve, when you create a new point, keep the left mouse button pressed down and drag the mouse: a Bézier curve will appear with handles on both sides of the point that you will be able to pull on in order to modify the appearance of your curve.

Don't forget to select the anchor point you want to modify with the white arrow. To do so, hold down the Command (or Ctrl) key. With the Pen tool, but this time combined with the Alt key, you will be able to modify your curve at will by manipulating the handles of the anchor points independently of each other. Press and hold the Alt key throughout the operation. You now know all the subtleties of this tool to create and modify vector shapes.

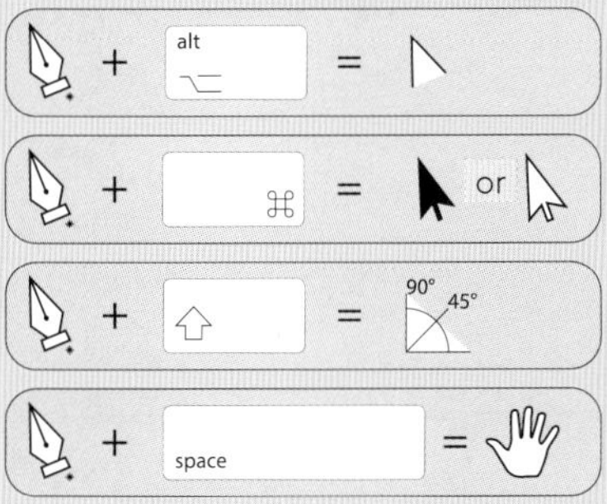

+ alt ⌥ =

+ ⌘ = or

+ ⇧ = 90° 45°

+ space =

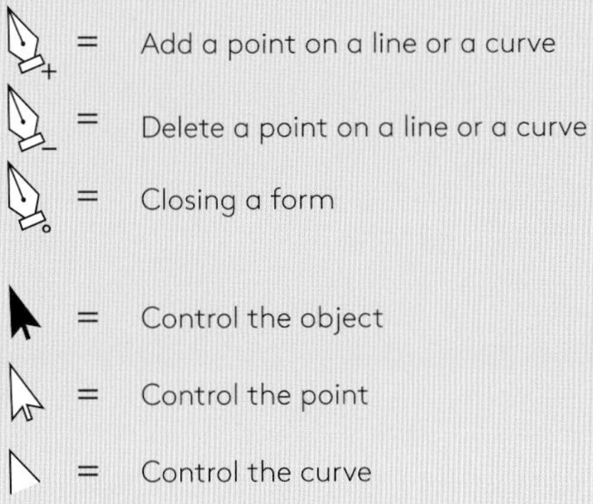

= Add a point on a line or a curve

= Delete a point on a line or a curve

= Closing a form

= Control the object

= Control the point

= Control the curve

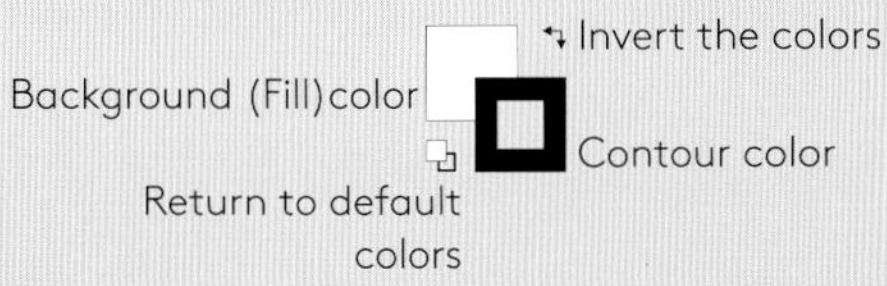

Invert the colors

Background (Fill) color

Contour color

Return to default colors

A stencil of my logo

We are now going to make a stencil, using the creation of my logo as an example. The idea is that you will then be able to transpose this process to your own designs.

Step 1

I have previously drawn a sketch that I import into my page. Since I want a geometrically perfect result, I will use the predefined shapes drawing tool. With a sustained click, I can access all the tool's options: Rectangle, Ellipse, Polygon, etc.

Step 2

I create two circles of different diameters. To create perfect circles, I hold the Shift key down, and if I want to create the form according to its center, I hold down the Alt key. I then select the two circles and align them with the help of the Alignment panel (panels are accessible via the Window menu). I can hollow them out using Pathfinder. Pathfinder has several options; you can familiarize yourself with them by superimposing two objects and selecting them with the Selection tool (black arrow). Try all the options. I work with the Divide, Exclude and Merge commands. Once my two circles are aligned and hollowed out, I repeat the operation with two other smaller circles, then I create a square the thickness of my circles that I duplicate to create rectangles that I will use to form the horizontal and vertical lines of my logo.

Step 3

Once all the shapes are in place, with the black arrow I select the elements one by one and divide them using the Divide command in the Pathfinder panel. Thus, each superimposition of shapes becomes a shape in itself, with its anchoring points. Then, thanks to the white arrow and the Delete key, I eliminate the shapes I'm not interested in. I repeat the operation for each element of the stencil.

Step 4

Once the dividing work is done, I remove the unneeded points with the Pen tool (by simply placing it on them), and I join all the shapes together using the Merge command in the Pathfinder panel. All I have to do now is print my logo on a sheet of paper and cut it with a cutter or use a laser-cutting machine.

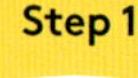

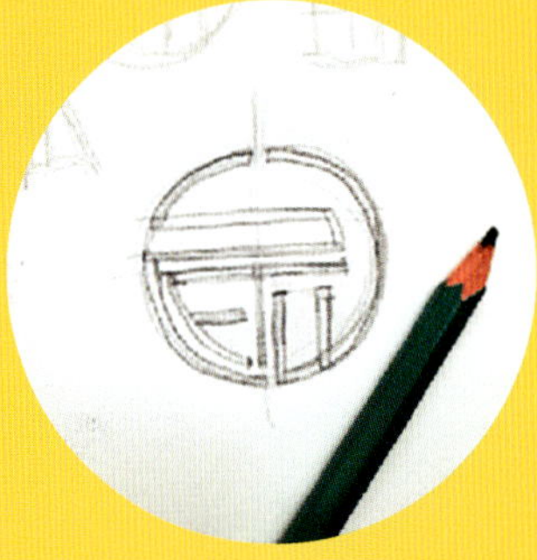

Step 2

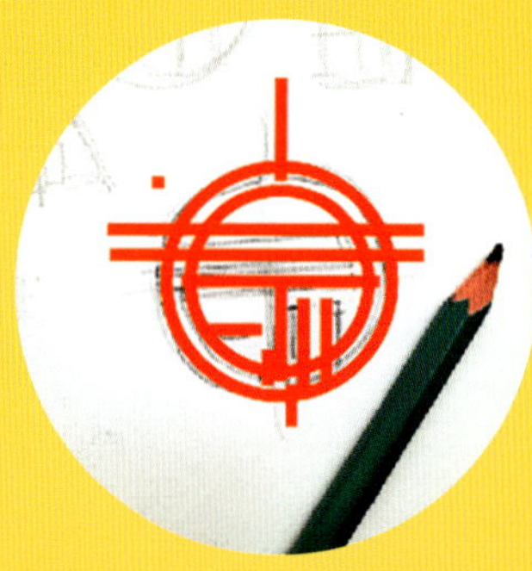

Step 3

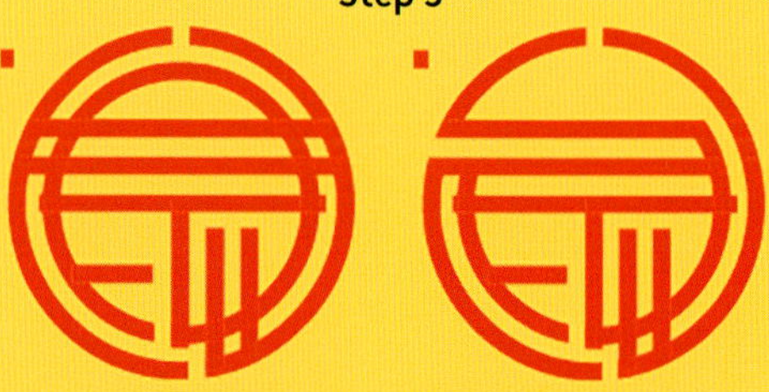

Step 4

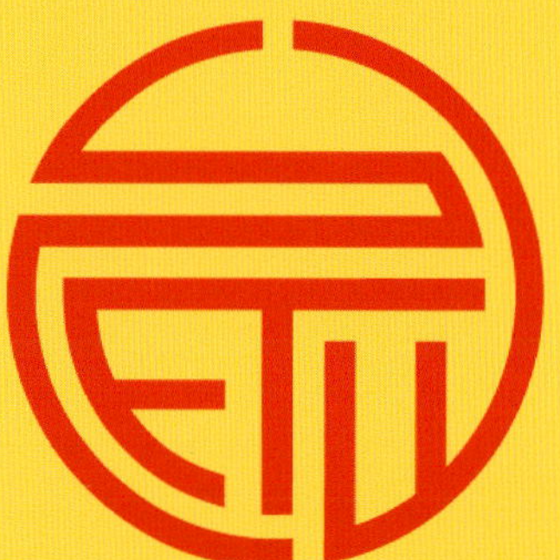

INTERVIEW WITH STEW

Traveling companions since 2006, Stew and I started stenciling together. His fascination for Japanese graphic arts led him to go all the way with his iconography: Japanese scenes, birds, samurai . . . everything in his work refers to Japan, including his approach to stamping. When his stencils are saturated with paint, he turns them over to print them on the walls.
Site: stewearth.com
Instagram: @stewearth
Facebook: @stewearth

Why did you choose stencils rather than another painting technique?
I would say that it was the other way around: stencil art chose me. My first stencils were logos that I used to mark our musical gear when we organized techno parties. I was just a suburban graffiti artist at the time, and I rather disparaged this technique. Over the years, during which I spent hours drawing silkscreen illustrations on my graphic tablet, I realized that my work was becoming more and more detailed and accomplished. From silkscreen to stencil, it was only a short step. Very quickly, I learned to think stencil, to see stencil—the empty and the full, the positive and the negative, the yin and the yang. This philosophy completely corresponds to me, and it obviously allows me to reproduce and accumulate my designs, but it also means I can put finished work on the streets—the fruit of my work in the studio.

How do you make your stencils?
Generally, I start with iconographic research. I then draw the images that inspire me on paper or directly on the computer as vector graphics, which means that I can print out my sketches in any size I want to use. Then comes a real moment of meditation—cutting out slowly and sinuously. I always start in the center and cut the small parts with a scalpel, and like a surgeon I stay focused until I've finished; no mistakes allowed. The initial sketch is usually rough; it's while doing the cutting that I refine the points and redesign the curves.

How do you see the evolution of stencil techniques since you started out?
A stencil is a tool an artist makes with a precise goal in mind: expressing an idea, illustrating a subject. I don't believe that stencil techniques can really evolve: we're taking about making holes in paper—it's an ancient technique!

It's true that the choice of paper is very important and determines the finesse of your drawing; it can be almost as delicate as a piece of lacework. But although this technique has become more and more precise and complex in its creation—I'm talking here about execution finesse, but also of the number of layers or matrices—the technique is the same for everyone: to hide a color or to make it appear.

Who are the artists who inspire you in your stencil work?
More than one specific artist, it's the whole Japanese textile craftsmanship of the seventeenth century that has inspired me. In fact, the patterns of kimonos were printed using stencils called katagami. This technique was very important for me because it allowed me to make the bridge between silkscreen printing and stencil art.

Stencil and stamping on canvas (detail), 2017.

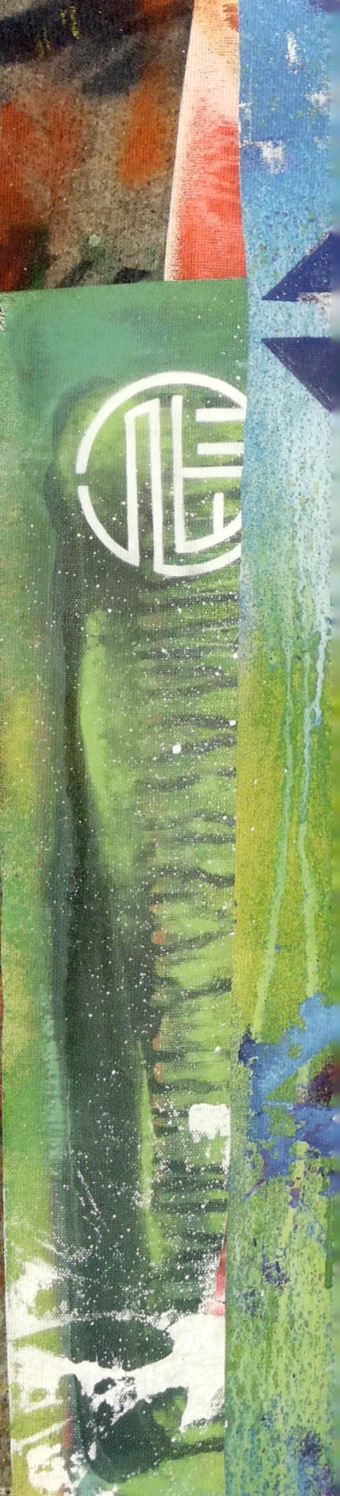

What are the limits of stencils as a tool?

First of all, I would say its fragility: the matrix must be handled gently, a stencil must be dry before being stored flat . . . but no complexity or dimension is inaccessible with this technique. It simply requires preparation time, tools and therefore a quiet place to work.

For you, is a stencil a frame or a freedom?

A stencil is rather constraining by its static format, its plastic rigidity, its fragility. On the other hand, it allows me to repeat, duplicate, break up a pattern and spread a message quickly. Like the matrix, it is everything and its opposite. You have to succeed in finding spontaneity with this technique; that's why I like it so much. I found this freedom by using the matrix as a stamp, the excess paint drawing the negative of my pattern. Using the tool in this way allows me to reconnect a little with my former graffiti art.

Can you describe your studio for us?

I am lucky to have a "stewdio" that suits me! A hundred square meters in an industrial wasteland within an association of about thirty artists and craftsmen. There are all kinds of books, a photo of my wife and daughter, a guitar, a lemon-and-olive-oil, music, a desk with my computer and my tablet, a glass table on which I cut my stencils and of course an open and colorful space in which to paint!

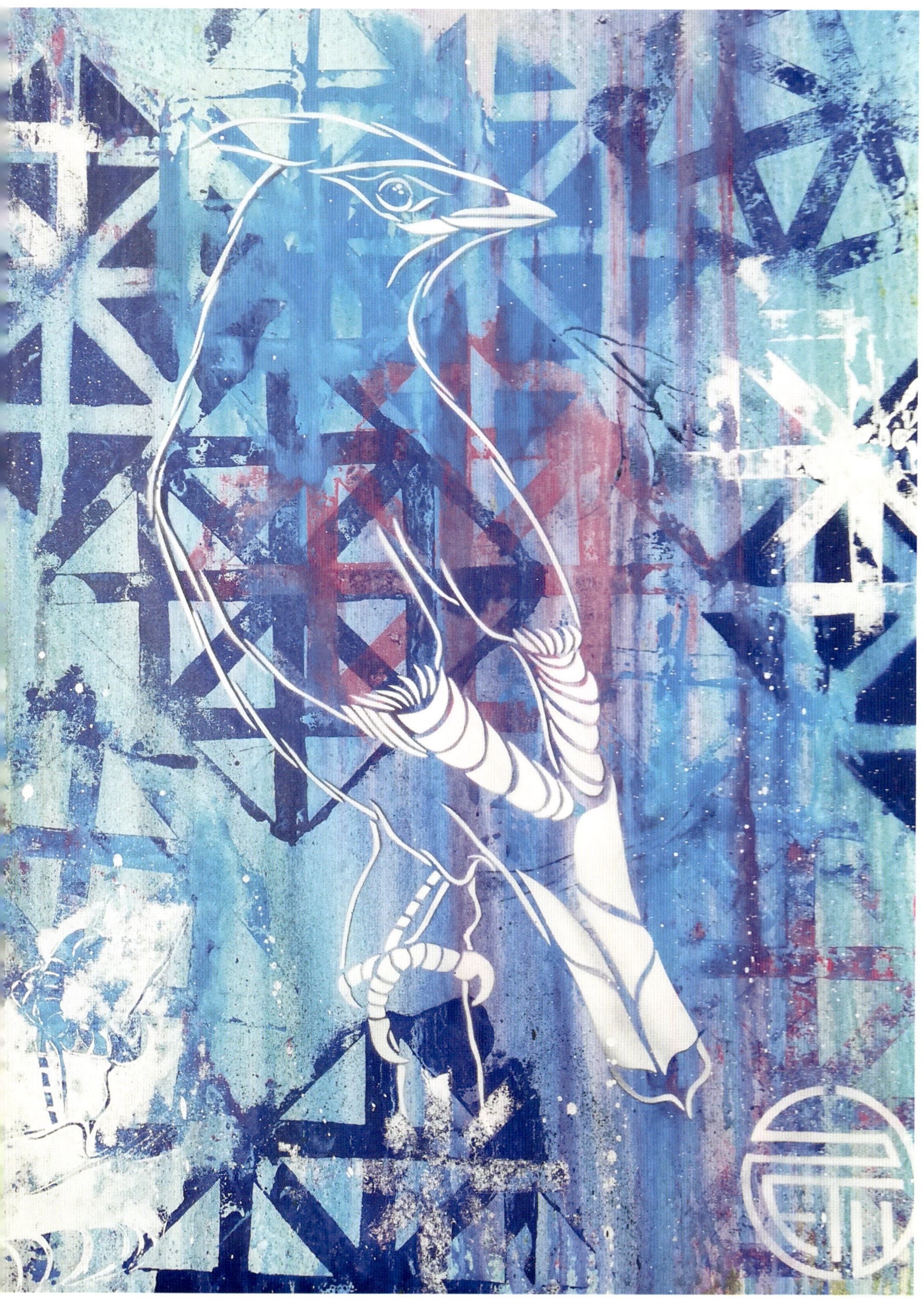

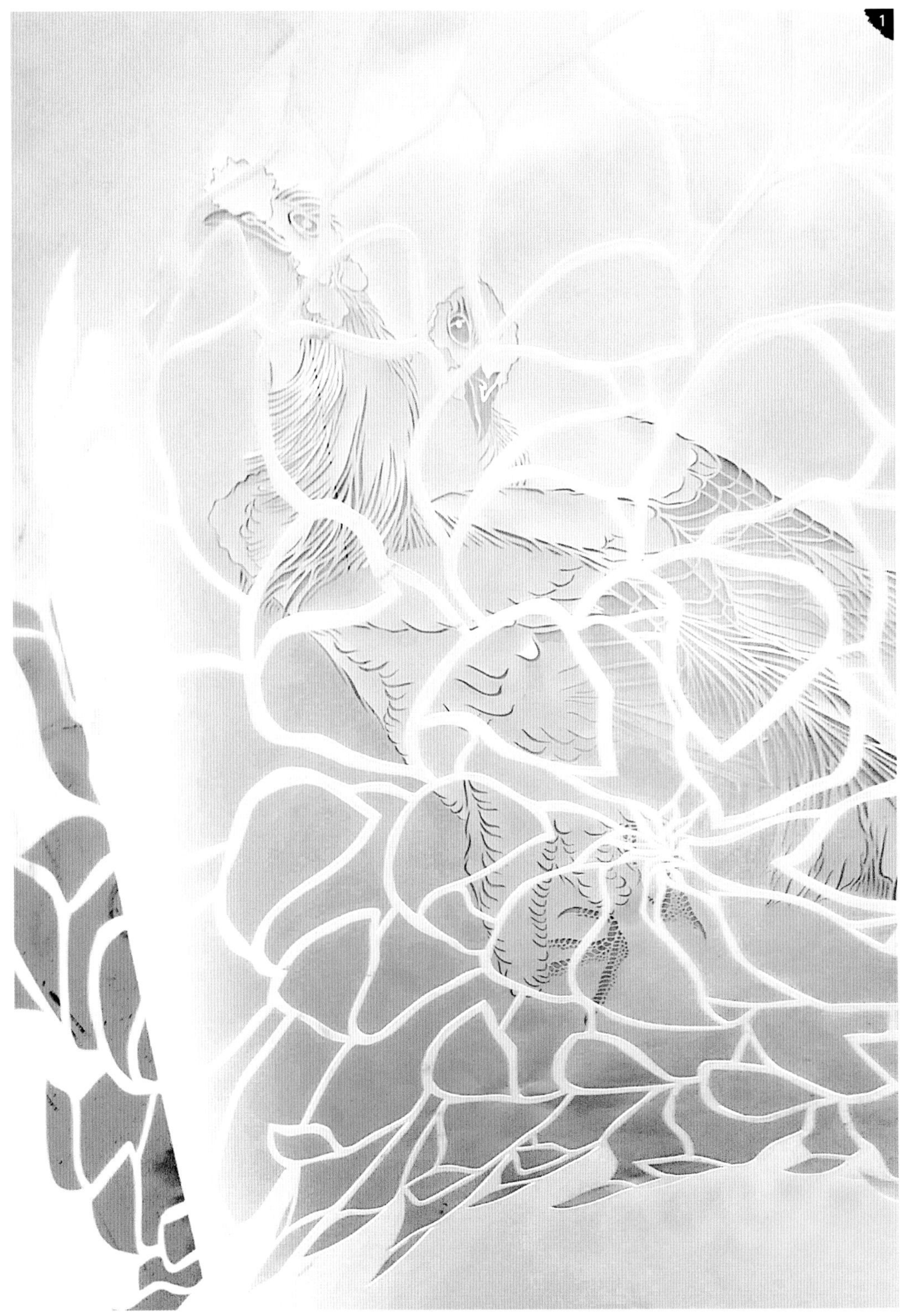

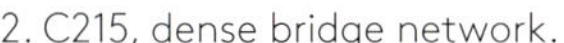

1. Stew, cutout paper, 2016.

2. C215, dense bridge network.

3. Stinkfish, Istanbul, 2018. A stencil can be used to apply only the outlines, which will be hidden afterward.

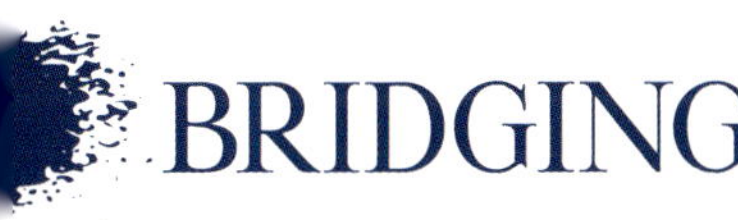

BRIDGING

Bridging is a structuring and aesthetic notion specific to stencil art. It consists of maintaining the masking parts together by a network of thin reserve zones, more or less wide but continuous, which maintains the overall structure of the stencil. Once painted, these bridges will appear in negative in the painting. The stencil artist is free to hide them or, on the contrary, to play with them.

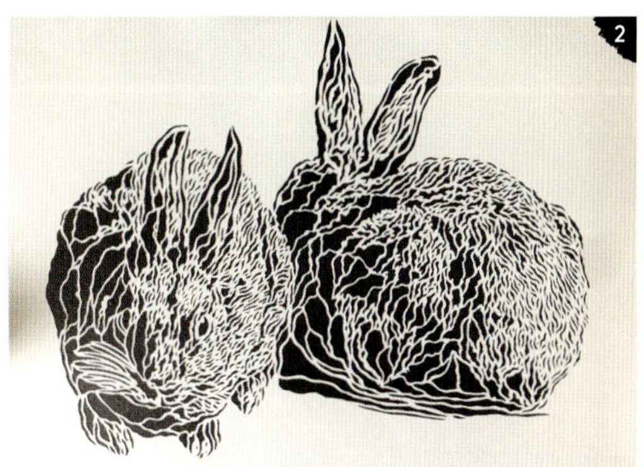

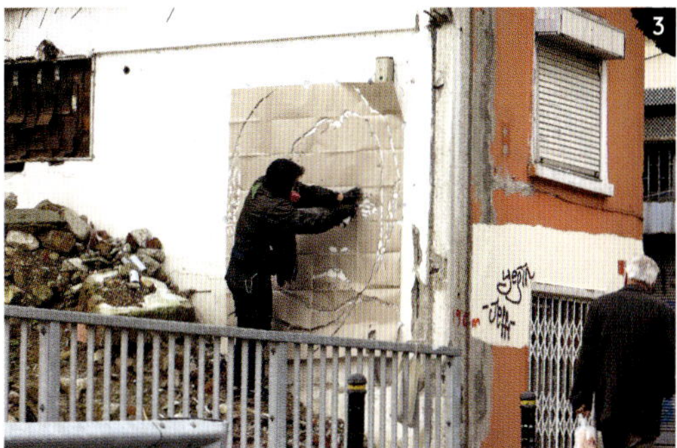

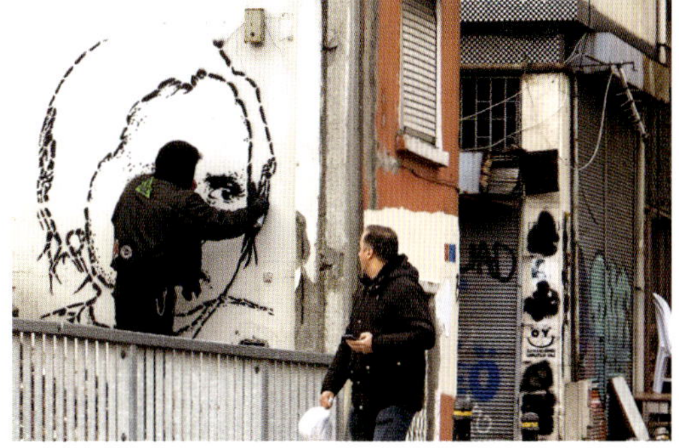

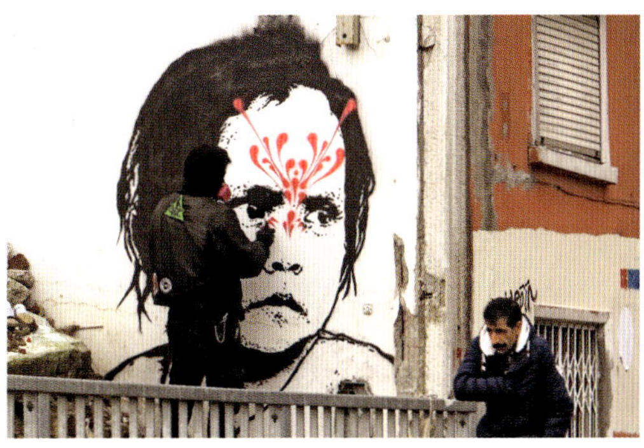

DISSIMULATION

For a long time, by superimposing layers or creating ultrathin bridges, stencil artists tried to conceal these bridges. In fact, they were considered unsightly and reminded the viewer that the work was made with stencil, a technique considered absolutely minor until the 1980s. Several techniques prevailed in order to avoid the aesthetic disgrace of a bridge: a full, flat silhouette like Blek le rat or Nemo or Miss Tic do(see his interview, p. 120). Stencils of basic drawing like Banksy does, sometimes supplemented by freehand erasing work. Stencils with multiple levels—each new layer hides the bridges of the previous layer, like Logan Hicks' or Snik's work; or stencils that strive to create bridges so thin that they will be invisible to the eye or covered thanks to the phenomenon of paint diffusion under the said bridge. I even met a duo of artists in Brazil, named Alto Contraste, who glues a fishing net on the upper surface of their stencils, which hides the bridges.

1. Monkey Bird. In certain aspects, the stencil reflects the aesthetics of stained glass.

2. C215, 2008. Stencil on cardboard.

3. C215, Birmingham (UK), 2008.

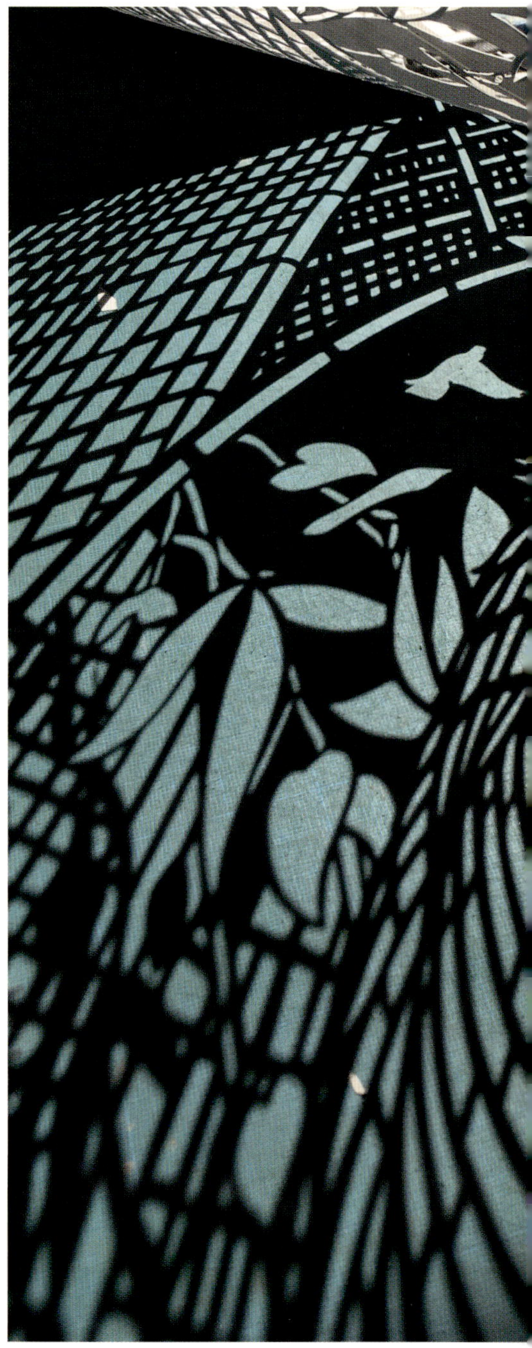

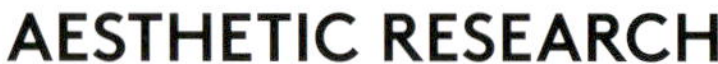

AESTHETIC RESEARCH

The design of a bridge, whether it is determined by manual cutting or via software, always consists of separating areas of paint. In my work, the determination of these lines constitutes, so to speak, my drawing.

I discovered, around 2009, that other artists had previously explored this approach: the American Buzz Blur had been doing paper cutout portraits since the 1990s, and a Parisian street painter whom I greatly admired, who died at the end of the 1990s, known as Le Bateleur. The portrait of Miles Davis, painted in white in the Châtelet-les-Halles neighborhood, which survived until 2005, left a deep impression on me.

Following him, other artists also researched the aesthetics of bridges. The young French duo Monkey Bird is currently the most original and creative example.

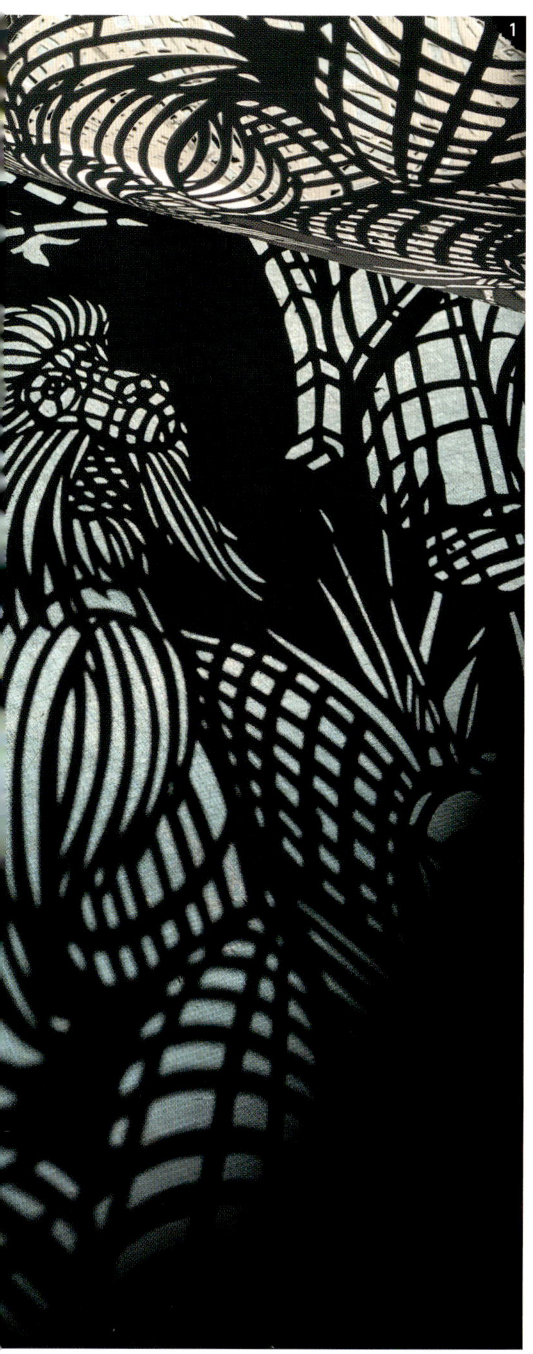

1

For my part—and this is, I think, what makes my work and my style specific—rather than trying to hide the bridges, I decided from the beginning to integrate them into my drawing, like half-tone reserve lines, which allowed me to make my lines more complex. So I multiplied the bridges, and thus the areas, especially in the lines of the face, for wrinkles, shadows, gradations. This multiplication of bridges also had an important material advantage: my stencils have become very solid and rigid, which facilitates their storage in my drawing boxes. Don't forget that around 2005, when I started stenciling, it was absolutely forbidden to paint in the streets of Paris, as in most European cities. It was therefore a good idea to be able to put away your material very quickly after painting your work.

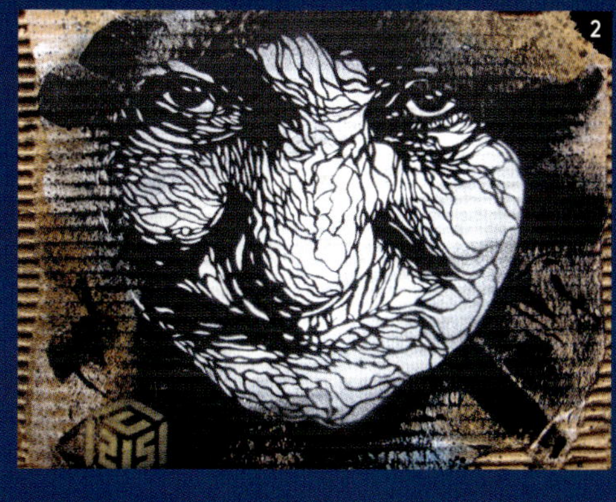

2

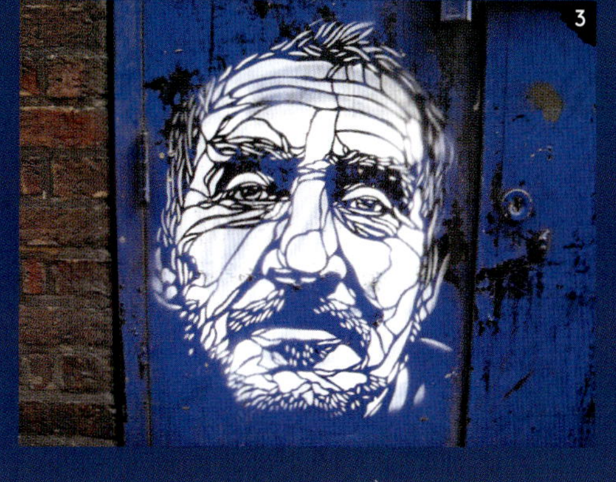

3

1. Portrait of Gustave Courbet, cut out of paper, 2018.

2. Nina, Ivry (France), 2001.

INTERVIEW WITH C215

C215 made his debut on the stencil scene in the 2000s. Since then, his urban paintings, mostly portraits, decorate the walls of cities all over the world: children, anonymous people, the homeless or personalities who have marked History . . .
Website: www.c215.fr
Instagram: @christianguemy

Why did you choose stencils rather than another painting technique?
When I started stenciling around 2005–2006, it was impossible to paint without authorization in Paris. At the time, a repressive policy under Tiberi's mandate systematically condemned any identified inscription, and the works were erased in less than two days. It was possible to paint in only two streets: rue Ordener and rue Dénoyez, run by rather virulent graffiti collectives. So much so that most of the street artists of the time (36, Duster132, et al.) only intervened through ephemeral posters here and there.

For my part, I wanted to be one with the supports, and my portraits had a "tribal" aesthetic. Stencils allowed me to stick to this aesthetic while intervening quickly on small surfaces. I first stuck up a few stencils painted on posters, like everyone else, then I started to work directly on street furniture (electrical boxes, post office boxes). I also wanted to paint portraits of my daughter Nina in the street, not far from the places she used to go to.

How do you make your stencils?
I cut the paper directly with a scalpel. I work from unretouched photographic prints. These serve as templates to keep the same proportions from one stencil to another. I create stencils from one to several layers. I scan them and archive them, because these original cuts are fragile and small. Then I enlarge them and print them out on Kraft card.

How do you see the evolution of stencil techniques since you started out?
When I started out, the most influential artist in the field was Banksy, and everyone was looking to create situation stencils with unusual or sarcastic subjects. There were few portraitists except for Sten & Lex, Btoy and Jef Aerosol. My generation was very much concerned with emotions, anonymity and the humanization of the city. Today, there are innumerable portrait painters. Fortunately, I have since seen the emergence of artists with very original ideas. Alongside M-city, Roadsworth, Logan Hicks, Evol, Ben Eine, Faile, each of whom had a very singular concept, are Add Fuel, Yellow, Stew, who, among other artists, have endeavored to make their work stand out.
I have also seen a new generation of stencil artists who have tackled the issue of gigantism, like Monkey Bird. These young artists, or even a "veteran" like Speedy Graphito, have largely taken up the challenge with original aesthetics.

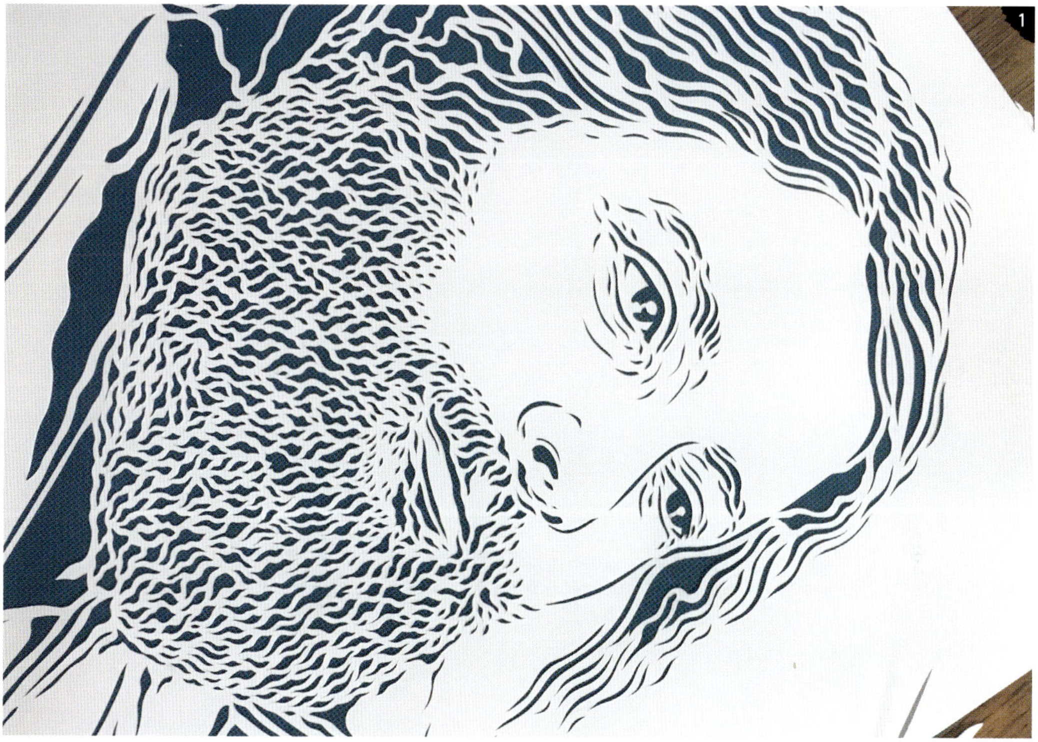

1

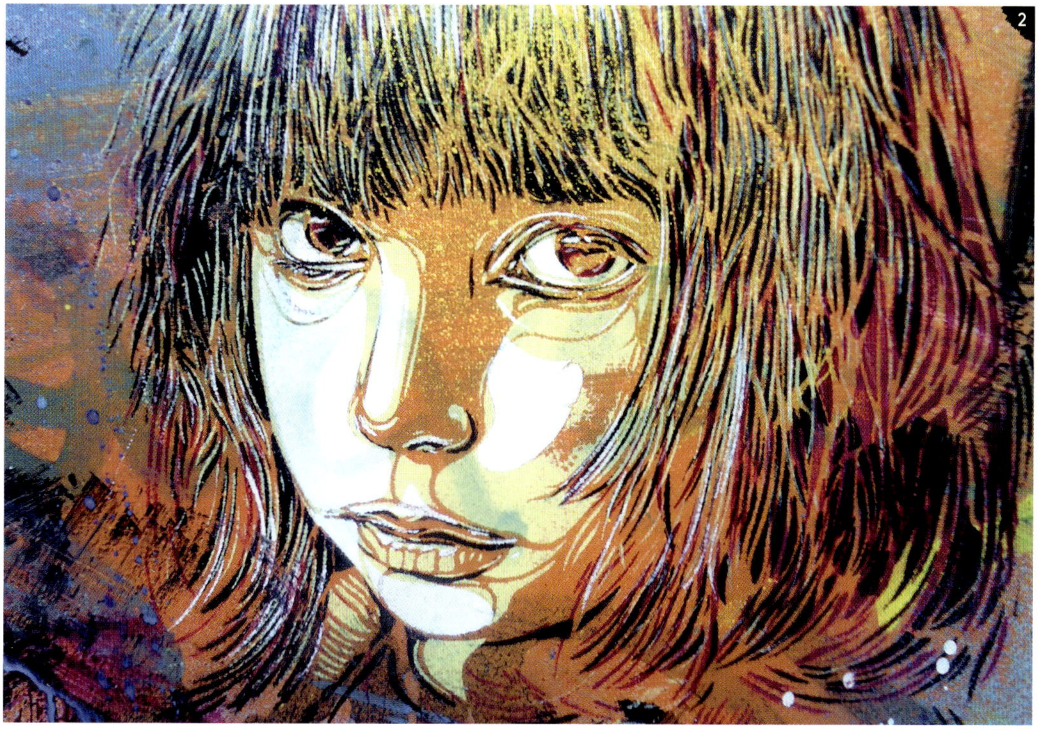

2

View of my studio, 2014.

Who are the artists who inspire you in your stencil work?

Surprisingly, the artists who have inspired me the most and who inspire me still are not necessarily stencil artists. Swoon, for example, is a portraitist from the world of lithographers, just like Ernest Pignon-Ernest. Ben Vautier, the genius of interaction and vanity, just writes words. Finally, Caravaggio, the master of chiaroscuro, is a classical painter . . .

What are the limits of stencils as a tool?

Personally, I don't see any, except that creating stencils leads to a certain habit, which makes each artist imitate himself a lot. Having said that, the urban context has changed so much that it is now possible to paint in most Western metropolises, so I am not sure that it is still very useful for a street artist to use stencils to paint in the street. If I was starting out today, I think that I would do like most artists of the younger generation: very big walls.

For you, is a stencil a frame or a freedom?

For me, a stencil is primarily a freedom, because the manual creation of each one of them is a place I can escape to. Every hour, every day spent cutting, makes me forget about society. Cutting stencils is my passion, and I will cut stencils for sure until the end of my life, whether it's still my profession or not.

Can you describe your studio for us?

My studio certainly has the structure of my works. A very orderly, very aesthetic first part allows me to cut my stencils in a pleasant environment. It is the framework of my private life; I never show it, any more than I show myself cutting my stencils. I feel protected, free. A second part, in which I welcome people more willingly, houses all my stencils, the spray cans and the supports on which I will paint my works. Rather messy, even chaotic, and very dusty; I spend little time in there painting, and I leave very quickly to escape the toxic fumes from the aerosol cans.

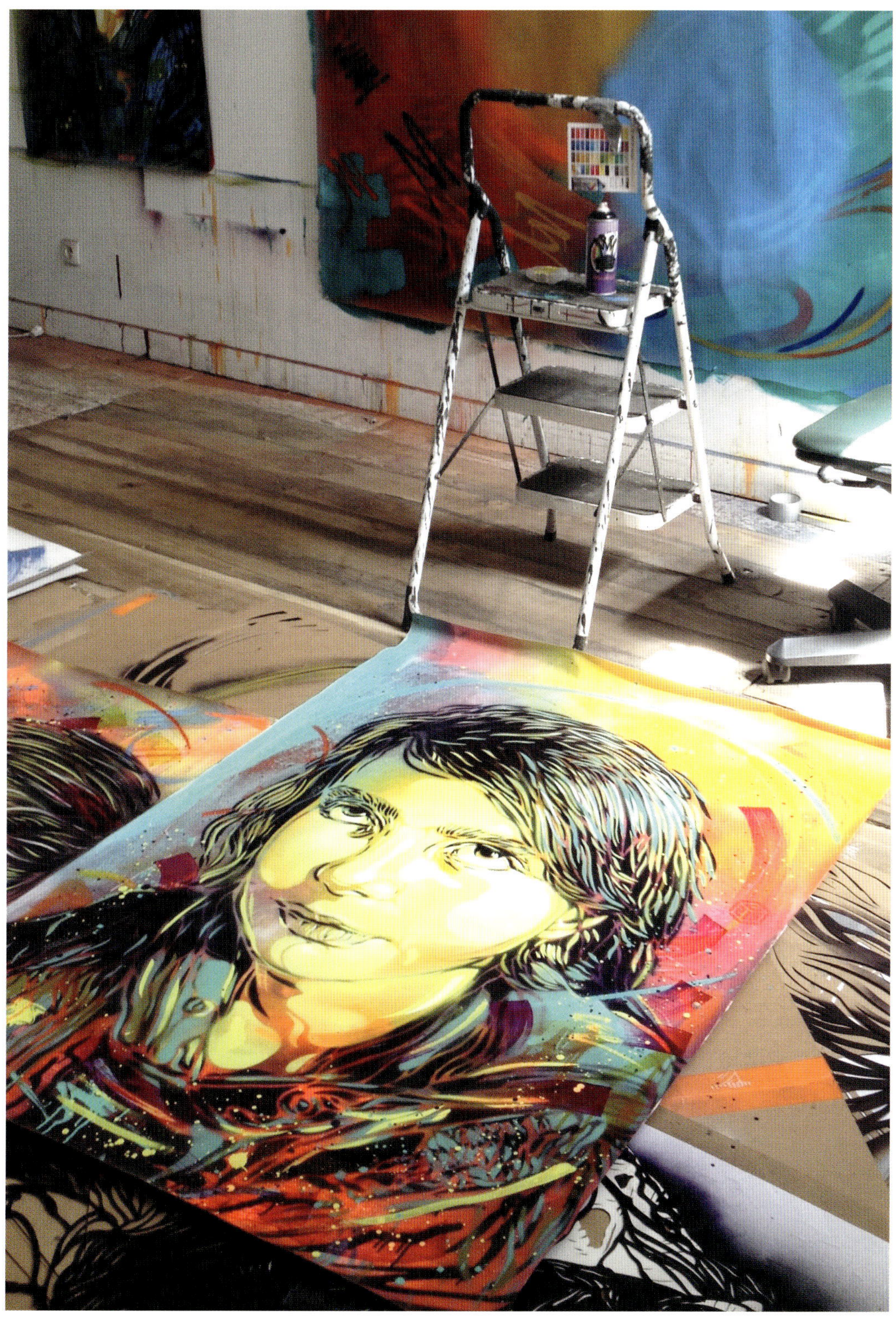

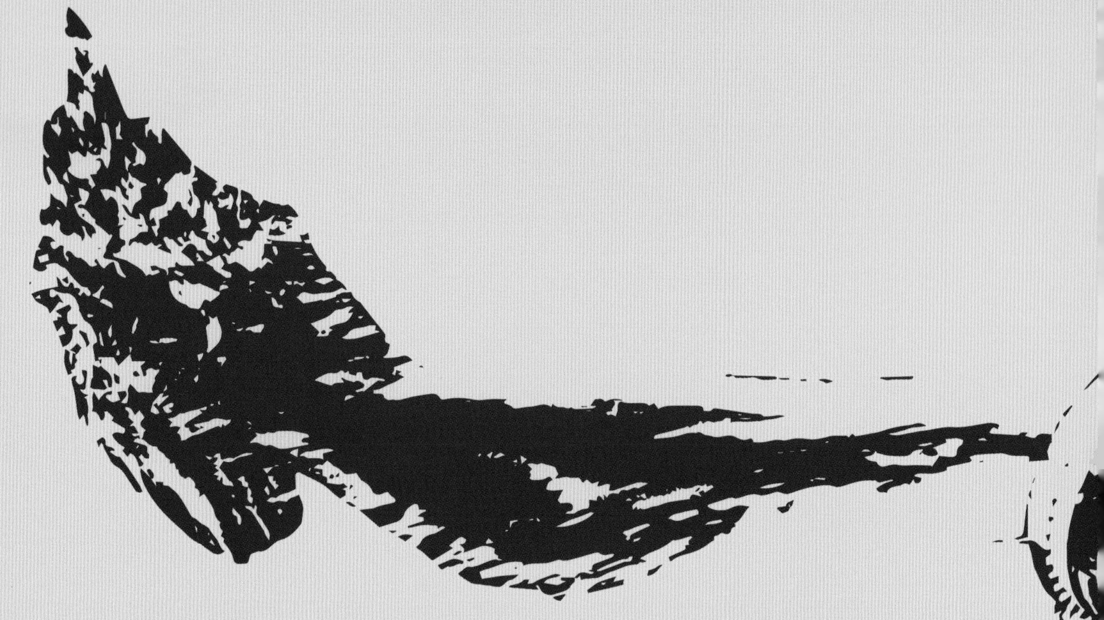

STENCIL PAINTING

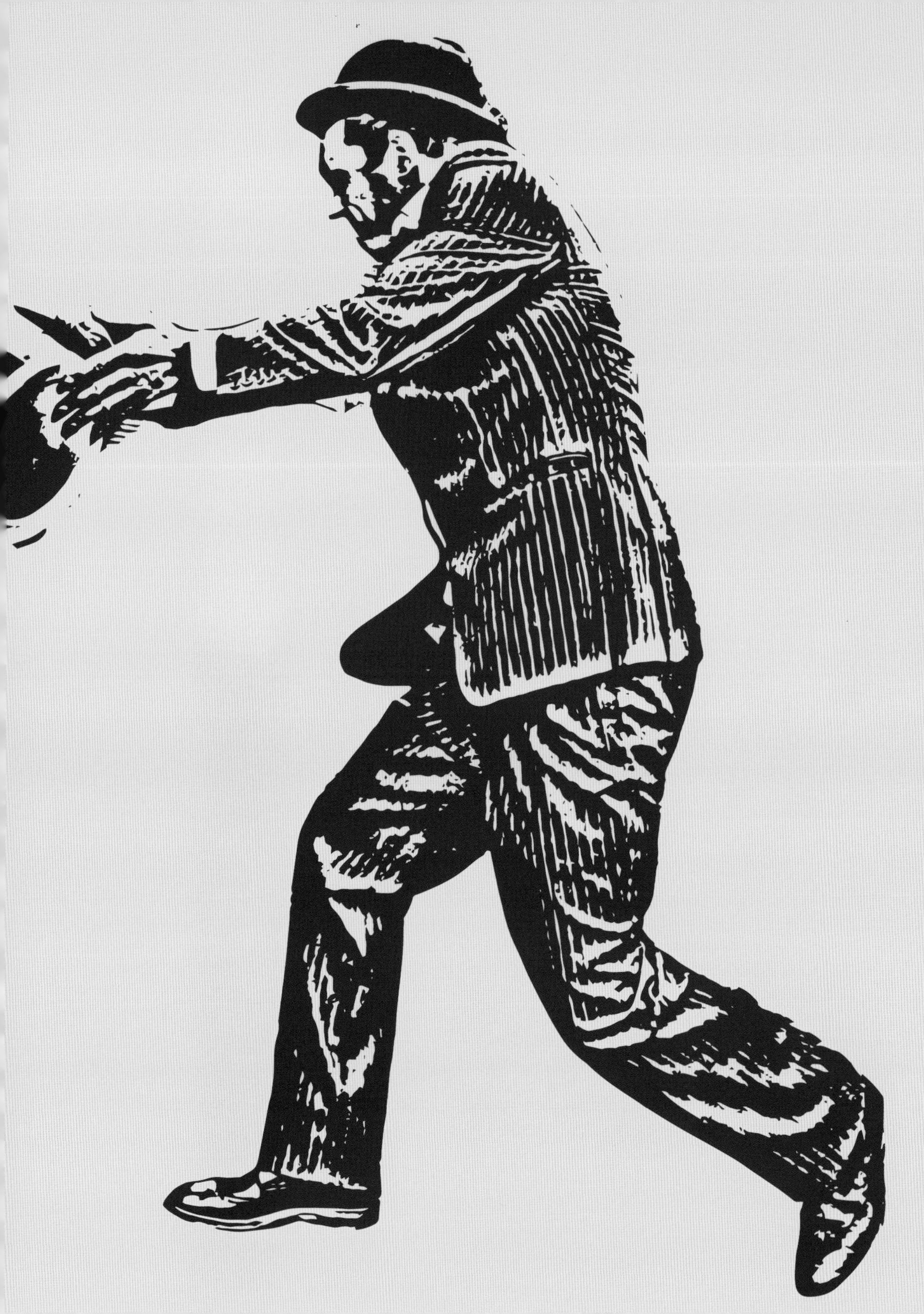

There are many ways to paint with stencils. Even if aerosol paint is generally used, various tools (spray, airbrush, stamp . . .) or filling methods (pencil, pastel, pencil . . .) can be used. You can also apply your paint and manipulate the stencil during painting in various ways.

1. Overview of supplies in my studio.

2. Various types of spray cans.

3. I use several brands of spray cans, taking advantage of their respective characteristics.

MATERIALS

While our ancestors projected natural pigments from their mouths onto the walls of caves to paint the silhouettes of their hands in negative (see photo, p. 10), the first stencils in ancient Egypt were used with charcoal. They were used by stonecutters to leave a trace of their designs. Charcoal remained the material used by artists and stonemasons alike to leave patterns until the modern age. In the Middle Ages, on the other hand, repetitive motifs such as fleurs-de-lis were already painted with paint applied with a stamp, which remained the main tool for applying stencils until the twentieth century. With printing and serial reproduction of printed images, stamps and brushes were used to colorize areas, as in the famous Epinal images. The stencil was then a strictly handcrafted tool. This reputation as a tool related to artisanship rather than art has long prevailed and still hovers over stencil creators today.

While the use of stamps for applying stencils was still dominant until the mid-twentieth century, this changed with the advent of aerosol paint in the 1960s. This portable tool makes it possible to spray paint through stencils without any contact with them. Almost all stencil artists use this type of paint. It goes without saying that it is absolutely necessary to wear a protective mask when using it, to avoid breathing in the toxic fumes.

Depending on the brand, some of these glycerol paints are more or less opaque. In fact, their composition, whose mixture of pigment, medium and solvent differs, leads to products with varied effects. Those with the most medium give better coverage, those with the most solvent dry the fastest, and the amount of pigment determines the intensity of the color.

For stencil painting, I recommend using brands whose paints dry quickly (therefore containing the most solvent), for two reasons. First, it is preferable, when applying several coats, that the underlayer is dry. Second, to store your stencils next to each other and archive them, it is better that the paint covering them is dry; otherwise they will stick and get damaged when you try to separate them.

Likewise, one should avoid overly thick paints; i.e.,paints that are essentially made up of medium, even if they give better coverage. By accumulating on the stencils, these thick paints will tend to create less sharp edges.

There were only glycerol aerosol paints until the end of the 2000s, but then industrialists developed ranges of water-based acrylic paints. These have the advantage of being less toxic. Their consistency is less volatile than glycerol, and the user inhales less gas. However, they have the disadvantage of drying slowly and therefore moistening the stencils, which damages them, and they can splay out or even run quite easily, which makes the result imprecise.

There are different types of nozzles, which make it possible to paint with a more or less wide or powerful jet.

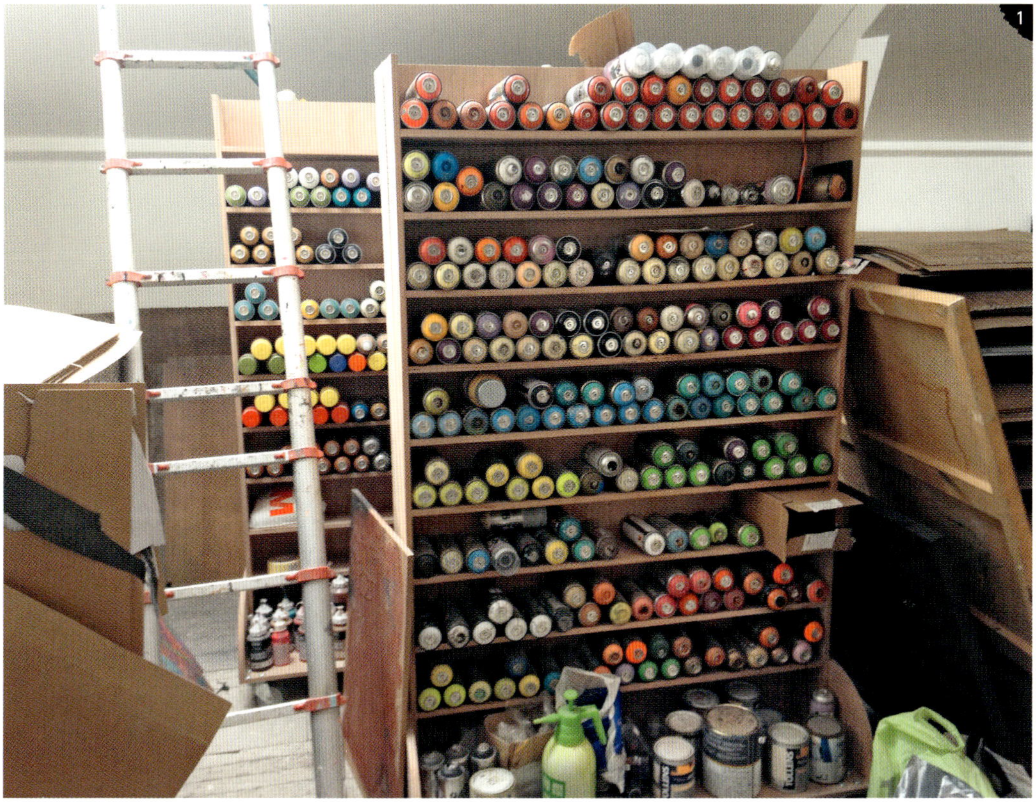

1

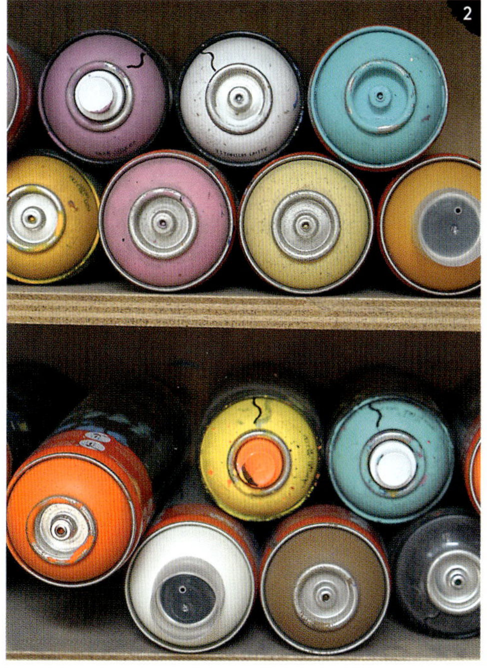

2

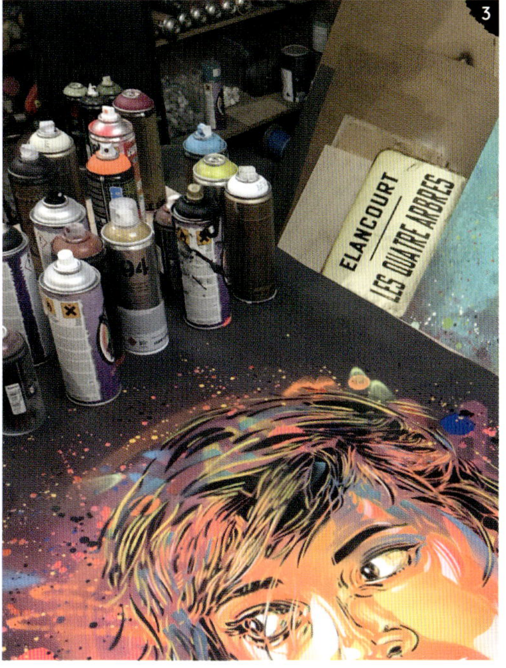

3

1. Stinkfish, *Berkeley Girl*, 2018 (detail). Notice how the flat paint stimulates contrast.

2. Ben Eine, *Create*, a monumental work of 17,000 square meters (55,774 square feet), London, 2018. (See his interview, p. 116.) Painted flat, these letters are extremely legible.

PAINT EFFECTS

Painting with a stencil doesn't necessarily mean filling the voids evenly. In this section we'll explore how stencil artists can play with different painting effects that make the result more complex.

FLAT

This is the most common and obvious way to paint a stencil, at least in the collective imagination. To achieve this, we paint vertically, at a certain distance, each of the areas that we want to color. To avoid drips and spills, it's better to make several thin layers than to apply too much paint. The closer you paint to the support, the more paint you load. I recommend that beginners use "skinny" nozzles, which have a light and moderately diffused spray pattern.

Flat painting doesn't necessarily imply monochrome; it simply means that the painting is uniform and without transparency effects. So it's possible to use different-colored sprays, each of which are used to paint different areas of the same stencil.

When I first started, I used only skinny nozzles, but they have the disadvantage of clogging up after each use. As time went by, my mastery of aerosol cans evolved and I started to "fat-cap," finding that these nozzles had a wide range of lines, from the thinnest to the widest, depending on the pressure you apply. They have the added advantage of never clogging up.

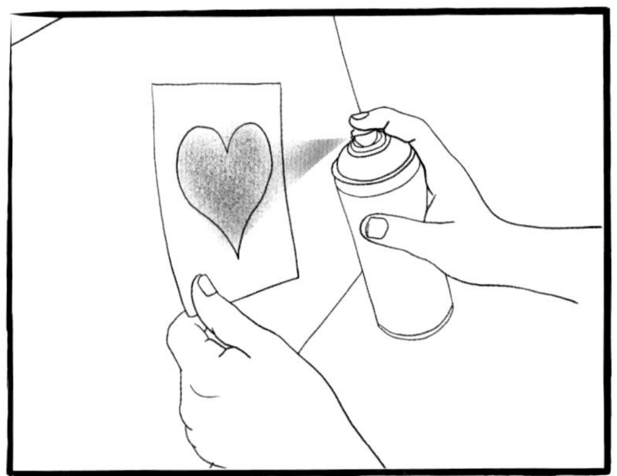

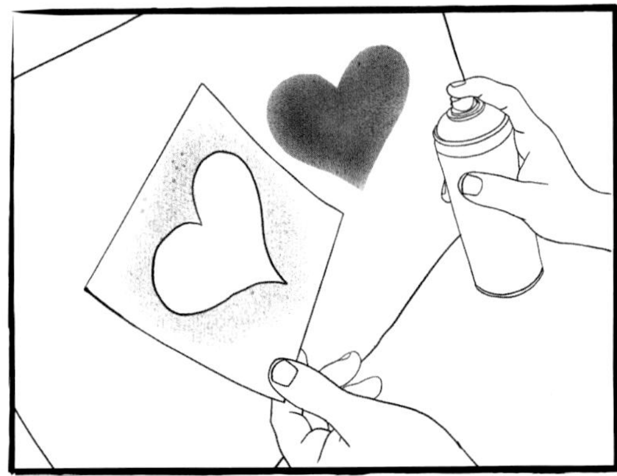

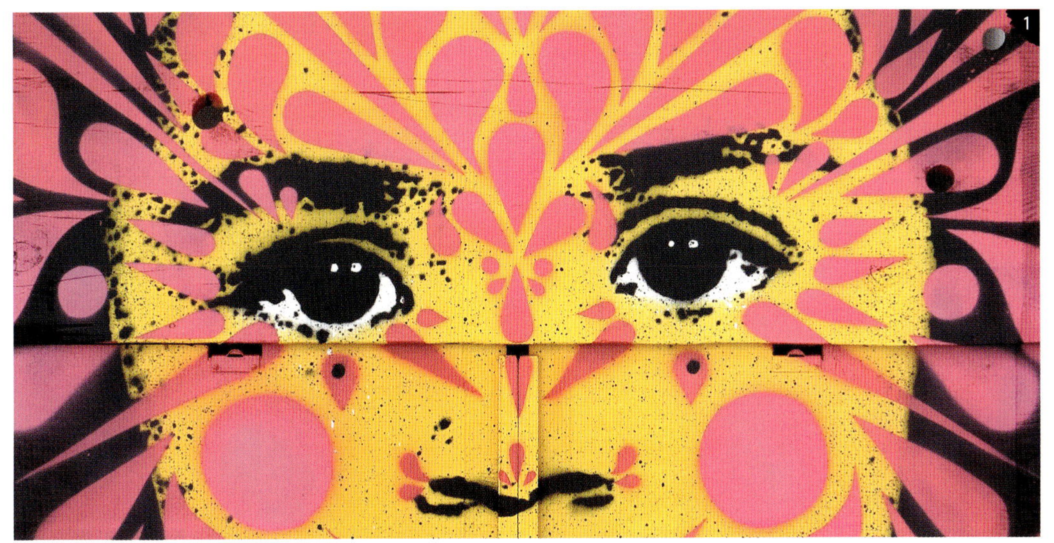

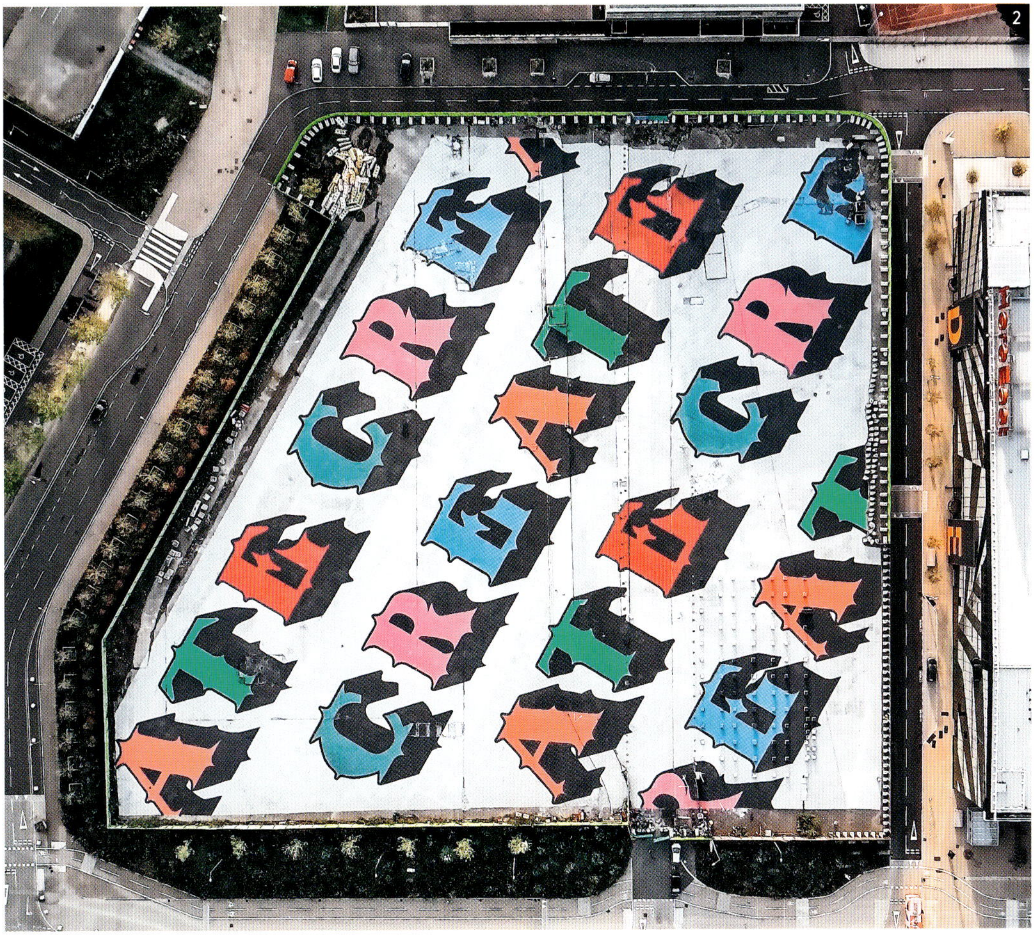

1. Working in the studio, Vienna, Austria, 2018.

2. *Delhi Girl*, 2018.

INTERVIEW WITH STINKFISH

Stinkfish is a Colombian artist very active in South America, but also an inveterate traveler. His work combines stencils and freehand paintings. His portraits are quickly stenciled before being extended with geometric motifs.

Site: stinkfish.tk

Instagram: @stinkfishstink

Why did you choose stencils rather than another painting technique?

When I decided on street art, I first did some test stenciling at home. My father always had some spray paint among his tools. So I started with a few spray cans, a piece of cardboard and a cutter, and the desire to do a T-shirt with the inscription "The Clash" on it. The same economic reason pushed me to paint in the street. I didn't have much money, and stencils allowed me to bombard everywhere with the same image, quickly and without anyone's help.

I worked for several years with different types of images, from books, magazines or the internet, then I painted portraits of people I photographed in the street. With stencils, I could faithfully reproduce the facial features from a photo, preserving the physical characteristics and proportions.

You have to of course take into account the work that comes before the painting—i.e., the treatment of the image and in particular the cutting—which offers the stencil artist an intimate moment with the image that he will then paint in the street.

How do you make your stencils?

My process begins with a photograph. I always carry my camera with me, to document places, moments, to photograph objects or people. From the selected photos, I make a digital image with Photoshop. I eliminate the background, I accentuate the contrasts; I adjust my image. I project the final result to the desired size. If necessary, I divide the image into several parts to enlarge it further. I generally use light, cheap paper that's easy to cut and transport. Once the image is projected on the paper, I cut it out, trying to keep the bridges wide enough to have a strong stencil structure. I then fold the cut elements to transport them.

The way I do it once I'm in place changes from wall to wall, but I always try to be quick. I use a single layer of stencil. I then paint the color details of my portraits with spray paint.

When I work in my studio, the process changes a bit, especially because of the small size. There I use a stencil for the colored details of my portraits. When the basic portrait is finished, I place translucent paper over it, on which I draw and then cut out those details. I then paint these small stencils onto the portraits.

How do you see the evolution of stencil techniques since you started out?

In essence, the technique is always the same: you need a support, a cutter and a color, nothing more.

But it's always interesting to see the new ways of interpreting this technique, depending on the time, the arrival of new materials, changes in formats.

More than an evolution, I would say that we are living a constant dynamic of experimentation, linked to working in the street and its multiple possibilities. Some artists make very complex stencils, mono- or multilayer. Others work on large walls or, on the contrary, very small surfaces. Some cut very complex

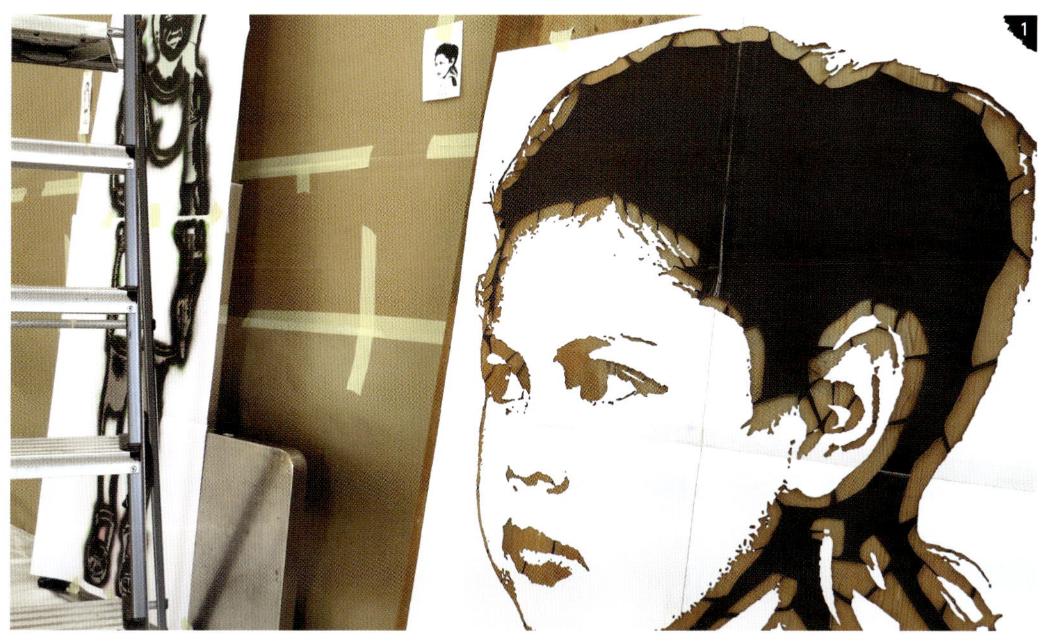

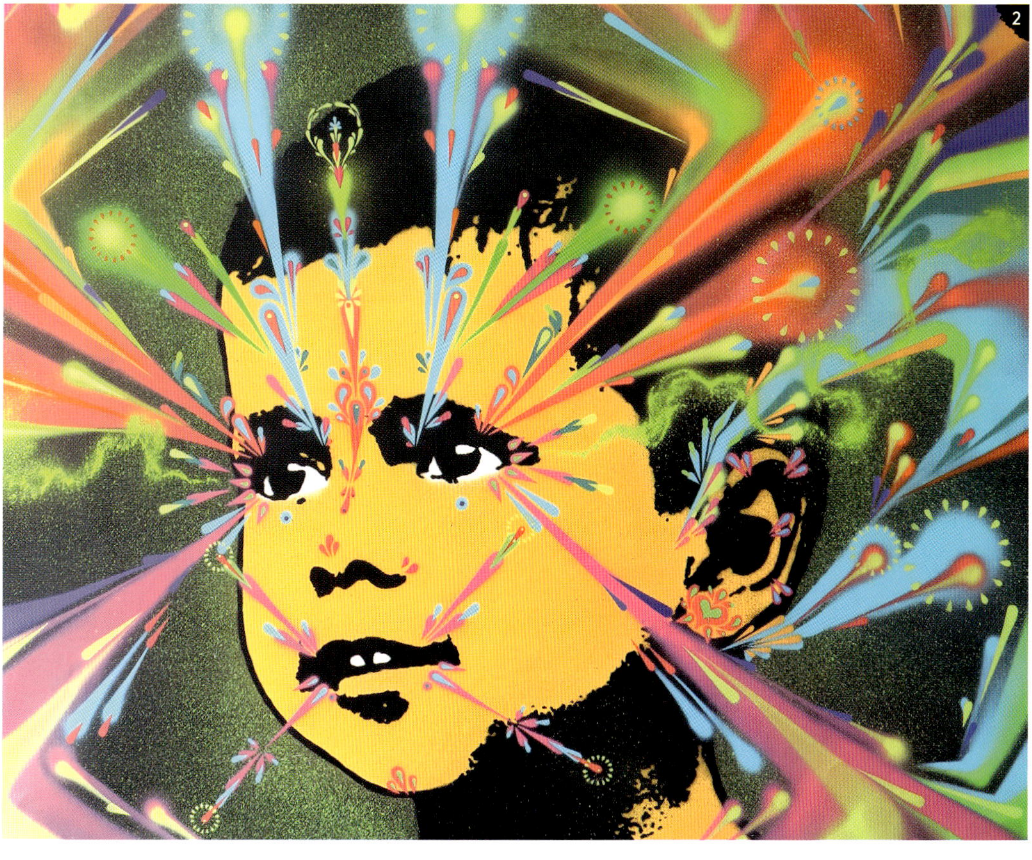

2

pieces for weeks in their studio; others do it directly on the wall.

Personally, I have completely detached myself from the idea of repetition, even though I deeply appreciate it. I paint the portraits I do in the street only once. The more I traveled, the more my stencils evolved in terms of practicality, becoming lighter, sturdier in their structure and easier to fold and carry. This meant that I could work anywhere outside my studio, in a friend's living room in Amsterdam or a small hotel room in La Paz. Then came the moment when I decided to paint each image only once and throw away the stencil, which was often deteriorated due to bad weather conditions or precipitation when I had to paint quickly.

Who are the artists who inspire you in your stencil work?

My main influence has always been the people who go out anonymously to bombard images in the street, stealthily, using small stencils. When I started painting in my city, Bogota, I was part of a nascent stencil scene that grew quickly. The stencils we painted represented different personalities in an era marked by political criticism and humor. Every time I find this type of stencil, in any city in the world, it reminds me of my beginnings.

Nazza Stencil, Hutch, Banksy and Btoy have influenced my entire career and continue to have a great influence on me. I could also name Himed & Reyben, Samina, Mando Marie, Empty Boy, Diseqtiva and Sr. X, who I believe are part of the great family of talented stencil artists.

What are the limits of stencils as a tool?

I believe that no technique has limits; everyone has a beginning and an end to what they do. Whenever a technique seems to be exhausted, someone manages to give it a new impetus. Personally, I think it's always possible to hybridize, to mix techniques and materials, which offers infinite possibilities.

For you, is a stencil a frame or a freedom?

Stencil is a technique, a means that allows me to concretize some of my ideas. I am not bound to one technique. Sometimes the best tool is a pencil, sometimes a stencil, or a roller at the end of a handle, a collage of posters.

Stenciling is without a doubt the technique that, from the very beginning, allowed me to understand and apprehend the street as a workspace.

Recently, with my two friends Diseqtiva and Empty Boy, we created Bogota's Cutting Institute, an imaginary institution to encourage the use of stencils in the street. We publish a free stencil fan-mag. The idea is to generate new initiatives based on this technique. This project stems precisely from the fact that we appreciate a technique that, regardless of the way of thinking and working, can bring people from different backgrounds together around a common universe: stenciling and the street.

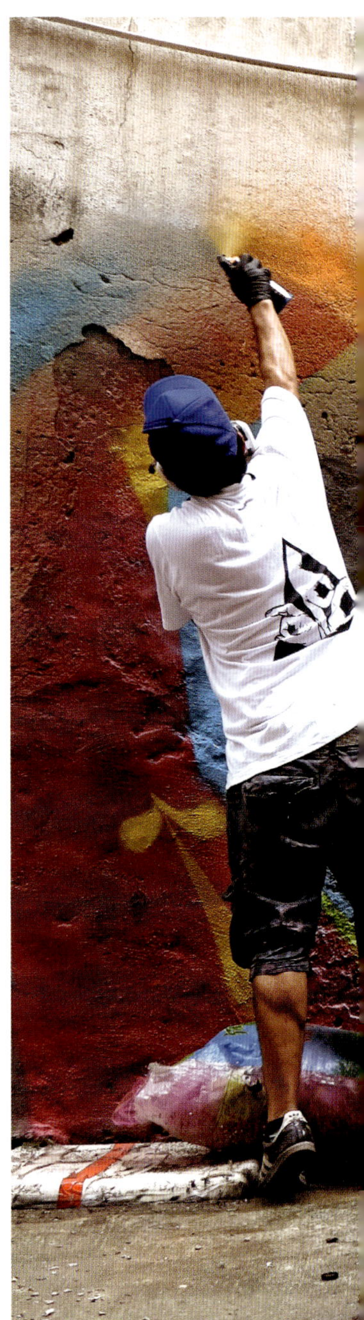

The artist at work, Hong Kong, 2015.

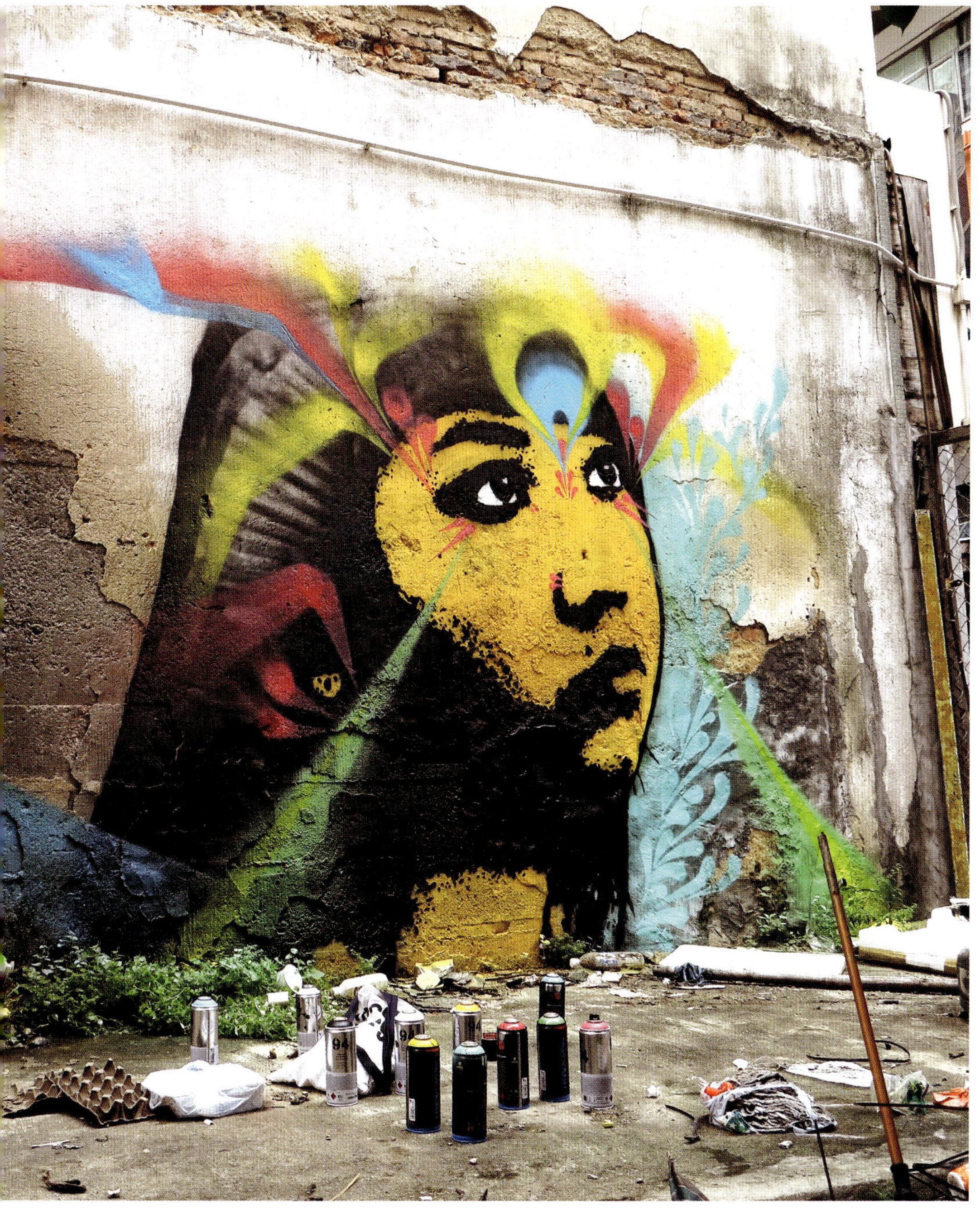

1. Bogota, Colombia, 2018.

2. Logo of the ATD Fourth World Movement that I have reinterpreted. Note the extensive use of gradient coloring in the heart of the single stencil.

3. Fading effects may even make sense.

Can you describe your studio for us?
It's a simple room in my house where I have a few tables, paint, paper and my tools. Ever since I started to travel a lot a few years ago, I work mainly far from home, in workshops, sometimes in galleries, but also in improvised spaces, guesthouses, inns, hotels. I always take my camera, my computer, my projector and my scalpel with me. The rest can be found in almost any city in the world: paint, paper, tape and walls.

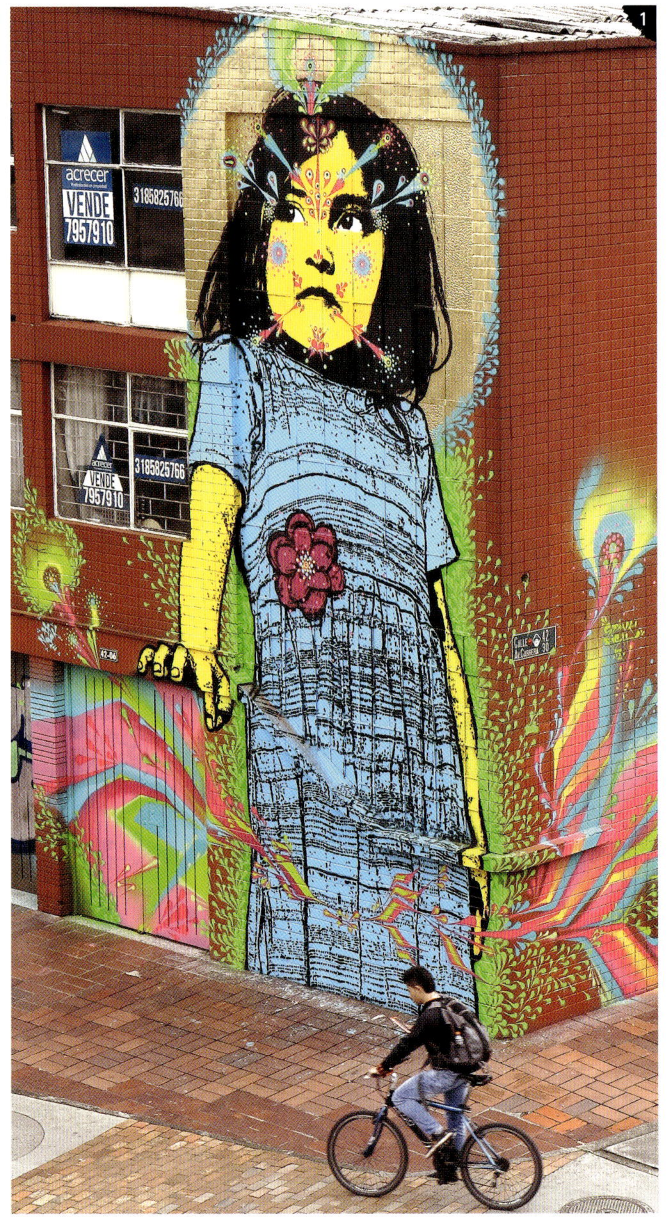

SHADING OFF

There is no obligation to paint each area of a stencil with the same intensity, or to paint it in a single color. For example, the paint can be applied in shades. There are two types: the fading of one color into another and the variation in intensity of the same color.

In a given area of the stencil, you can paint with several colors. With the lessening of the spray intensity of one or each of the colors, junction zones will form from the shading. The entire stencil could be painted like a rainbow. But with these effects, whatever you gain in style you risk losing in legibility if you don't maintain enough overall contrast with the support.

When you fade the paint in the same area, without filling it or reaching each of its edges, you obtain a gradient that moves from colored contrast to blend into the color of the support.

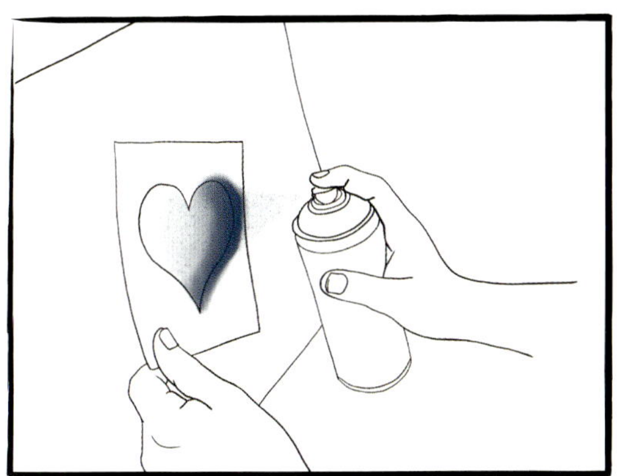

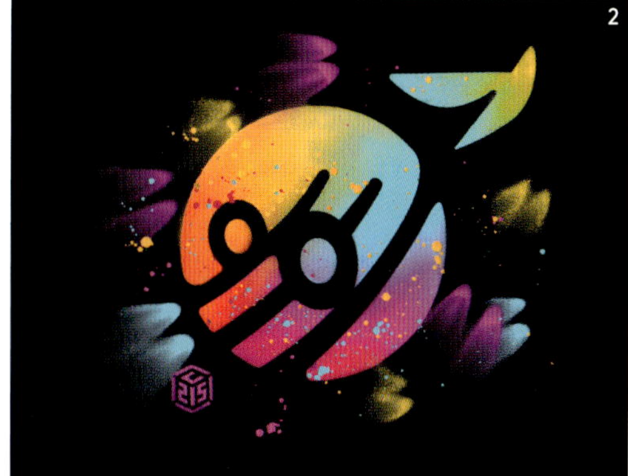

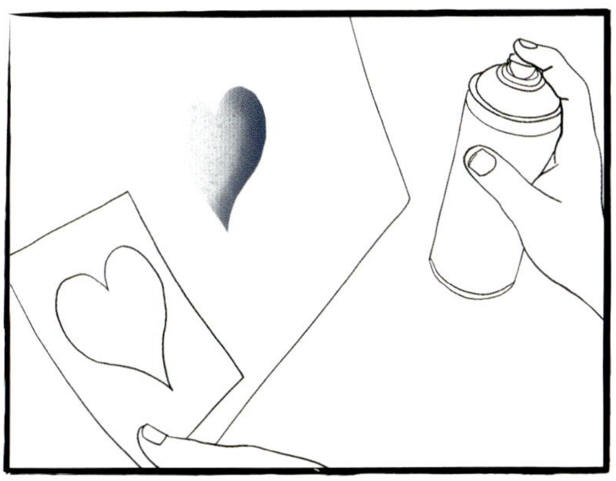

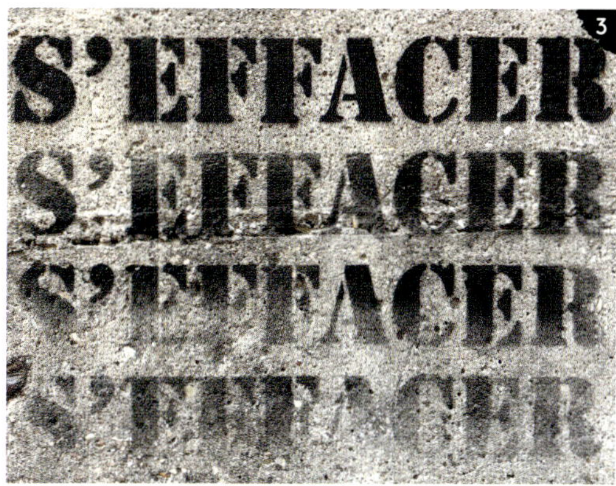

Three steps in the making of the *Vandal Paint Chucker*, 2016.

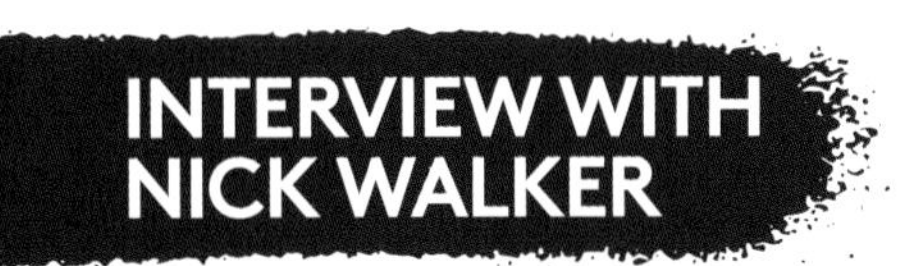

INTERVIEW WITH NICK WALKER

Nick Walker is a major artist of one of the most important scenes in the history of stencil, that of Bristol. Nick paints freehand as well as with stencils. Vandal, his alter ego wearing a bowler hat, is a facetious gentleman who distills love and magic on the walls.

Website: www.theartofnickwalker.com

Instagram: @nickwalker_art

Why did you choose stencils rather than another painting technique?

I'm not opposed to other methods. I started doing graffiti, freehand, inspired by the taggers who painted trains in New York in the 1980s. The first person I saw using stencils was a graffiti artist from Bristol called 3D. At first I thought it was cheating, but then I realized it was extremely visual. It was possible to print any image and explode it, turn it into something else. It was almost like making a photographic copy with an aerosol can while still retaining the spirit of the artist. I combine stencil with freehand when appropriate. My Erotica graffiti works, painted in the late 1990s and early 2000s, are an example of this. I wanted to make stencils of women but painted them freehand on a background that looked a bit like a Chesterfield leather sofa. I always liked the juxtaposition of the two techniques.

How do you make your stencils?

I first choose a subject, often a photograph I have taken. For example, when I use the Walker character of Vandal, I imagine a concept or scenario, my assistant takes a series of photos of me dressed as Vandal, then I choose the best photo and run it in black and white on Photoshop. I then have two options: cut out the black or the white of the image. I often choose to cut out the white, to make a stencil with two layers. I can also replace the white with other colors, silver for the watch, beige for the face or gray for the stripes of the suit. I change colors as I go along, avoiding using the same one twice in a row, but there are no real rules. You can create a work with many colors, making it look like there are several layers when you've used only two.

I started working with stencils at a time when street art wasn't very popular with the general public (especially the police). It seemed to me that it was easier to use this method on the street to be able to use several colors. The first step is always to paint the black silhouette of the character. Then I record the line and choose the colors I add. I like to cut my stencils by hand. It takes me a day if the image is simple and up to two weeks for those that are very detailed. It's tedious but, in my opinion, aesthetically better. In the end, it's your artistic choice that counts.

How do you see the evolution of stencil techniques since you started out?

In the beginning, stencil artwork looked a lot like the propaganda posters or punk band logos that young people drew on their jackets or bags. Things have changed a lot since then! The multilayer has profoundly transformed the practice. Before, you had to know your image well enough and paint it from a single layer. Now, some artists use up to ten layers or more. You can read the evolution and democratization of graffiti through the number of layers used to make a stencil. Some artists want to reproduce an exact replica of a photo. That's fine, but personally, I prefer to distort reality by introducing my own interpretation, by removing, adding or subtracting elements. It's crazy to see what each artist's imagination can generate from the techniques he uses and combines.

Who are the artists who inspire you in your stencil work?

3D was the first person I saw painting stencils in the street in Bristol in the 1980s. He started doing graffiti in the traditional way, like everyone else at the time. The first stencil I saw, I must have been eighteen years old, was a color picture of Margaret Thatcher turning into Marilyn Monroe. It immediately struck me as an interesting medium. It looked a little bit like Warhol, but of course with a completely different source of inspiration. It all got mixed up in my head.

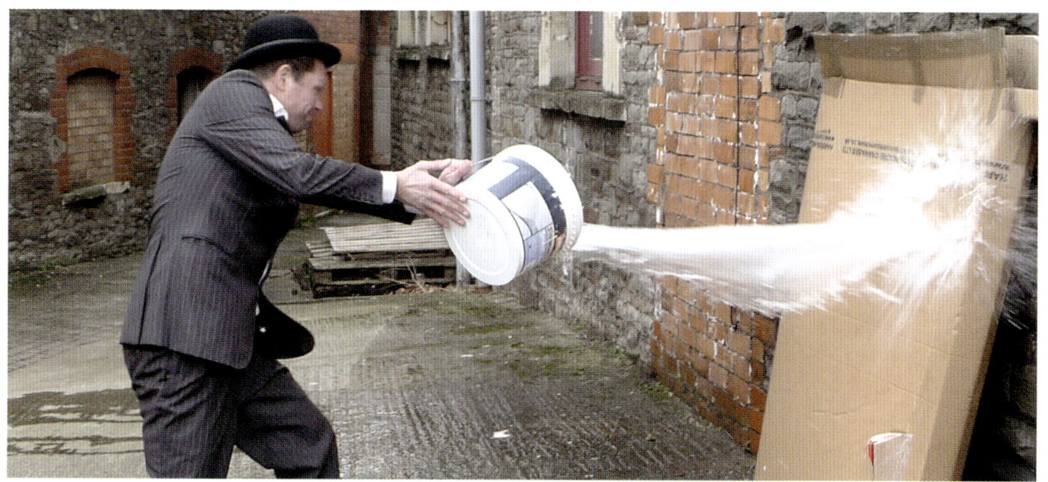

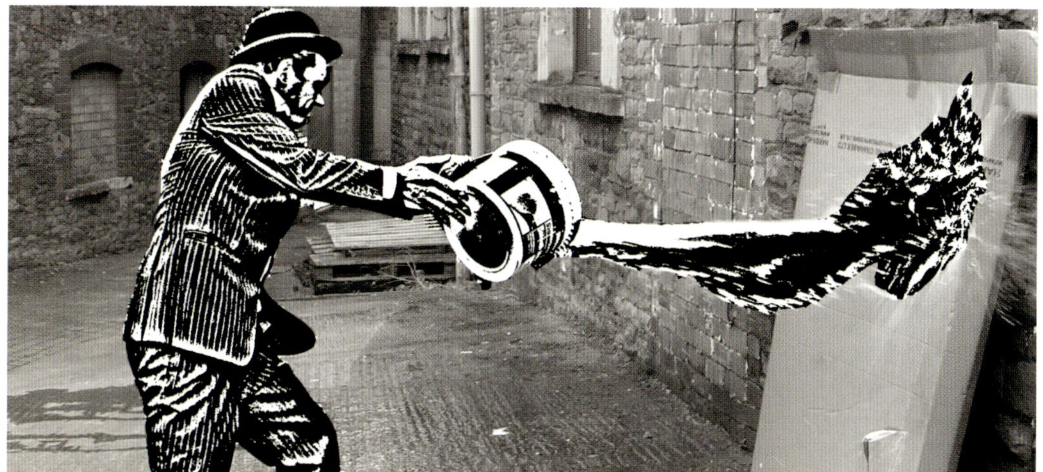

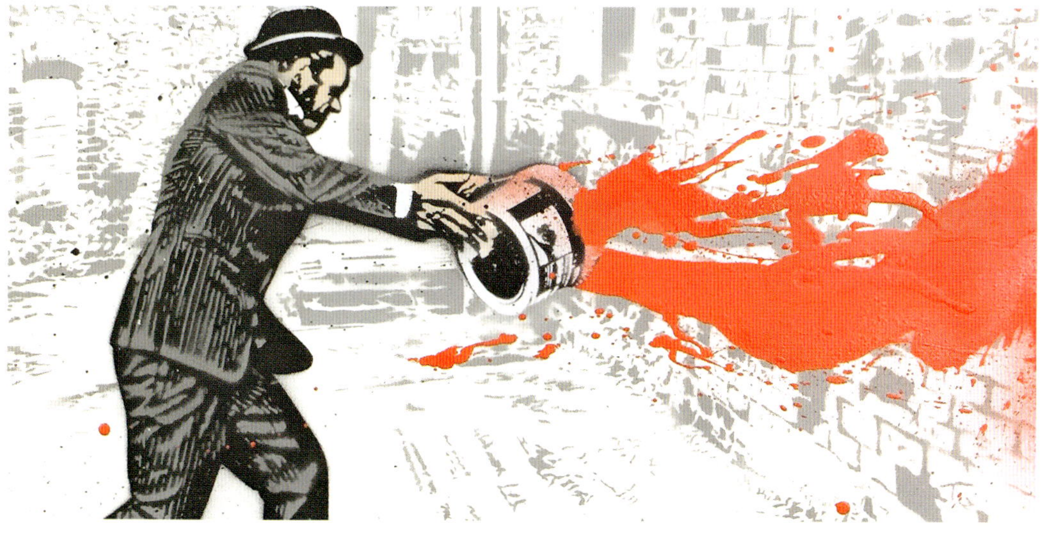

What are the limits of stencils as a tool?
There are not many of them. You can produce any image and cut it out. If you do it by hand, the only limit may be the time required. If you're painting outdoors, the weather can be rough and the wind can be a bit of a hindrance. If you are painting illegally on the street, you need to be prepared to give up your stencils; it's impossible to run with stencils floating around. You have to leave your smoking gun with the cops, so to speak. Anyway, they have no idea what they are seeing, and it's better than spending the night in police custody. I once had to watch cops tear a week off my job because they got stained from handling the stencils I had just used. They threw them in the garbage around the corner. Luckily, I was able to retrieve and repair them.

For you, is a stencil a frame or a freedom?
I don't really like being presented as a stencil artist. If you choose to do something, it's always about freedom. Art is simply freedom.

Can you describe your studio for us?
It is a place that allows me to cast out my demons, like a sanctuary. It's located in an old brewery. It has exceptional light and energy, which are the most important things. I moved there in 2008, and it has really been beneficial for me. This place allows me to find myself, to think. I want to be there even if I don't paint, just to enjoy that very personal space. At the front, I've set up a large table for my stencil cuts. The painting area is at the back so that I can concentrate completely.

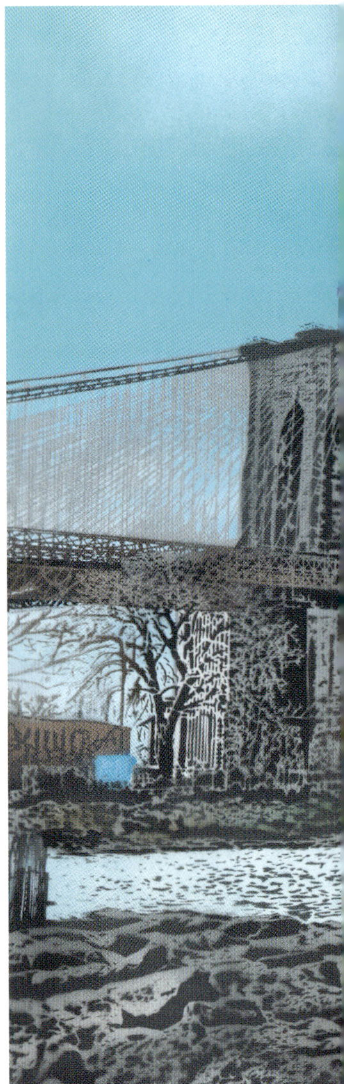

The Morning After Brooklyn, 2015.

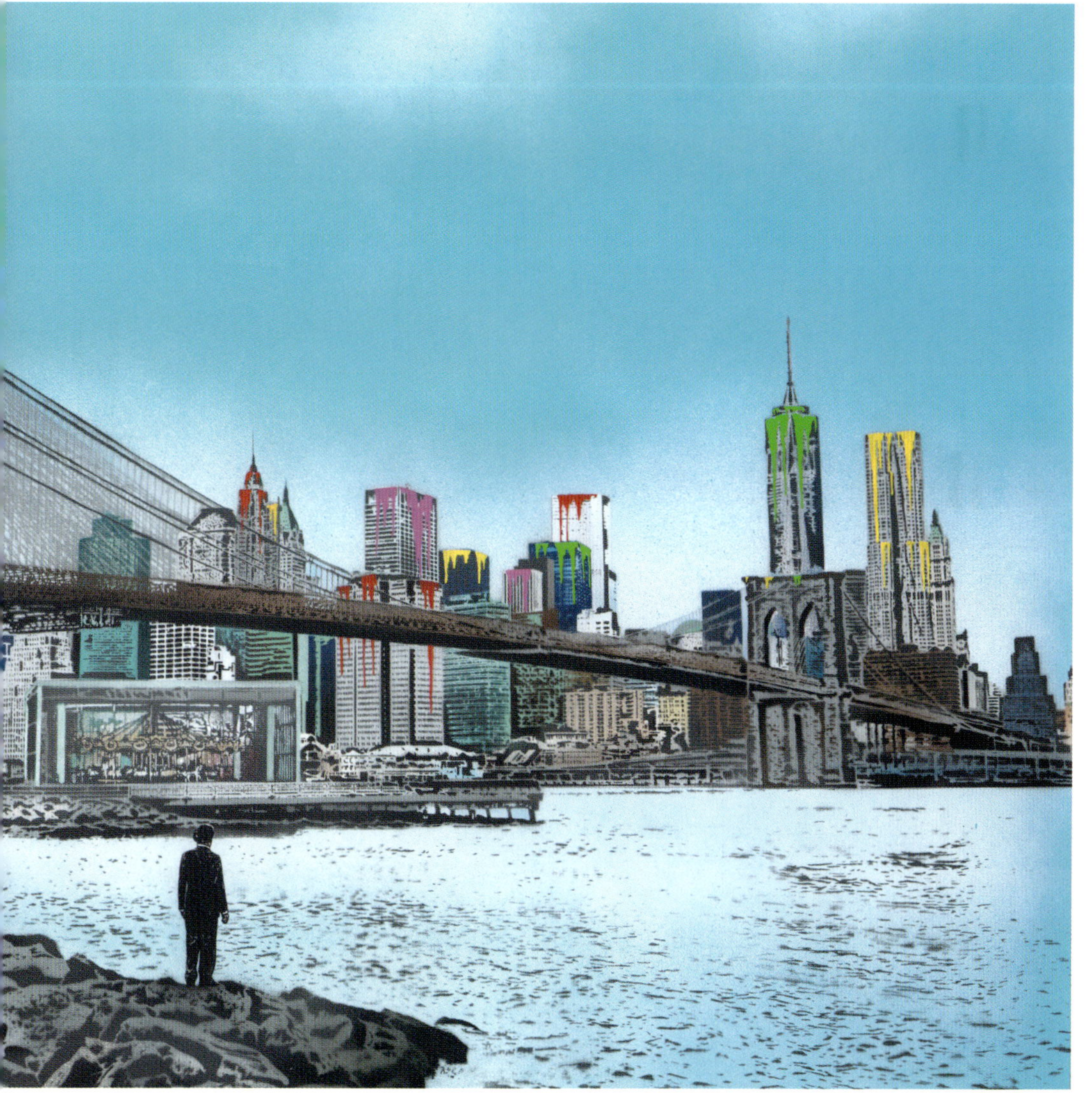

Jef Aerosol, portrait of Nina, 2012.

DROPLETS

Optical blending is a very important notion in stencil painting. Contrast effects, of shading but also of mixtures and separations of colors, are at the core of key artistic choices. Artists such as Logan Hicks or, following him, Fin Dac and Jef Aerosol are using subtle pointillist effects to paint their stencils. This approach has its origin in the pointillist painters such as Georges Seurat and Paul Signac. Logan's quasi-photographic rendering also reflects the grain of photographs taken with very high sensitivity film.

There are two ways of using spray cans for this purpose. You can press very lightly on the nozzle so that only a little gas escapes from the aerosol, so that the projection will be incomplete and diffused in droplets. For those who are less familiar with spray can use, it is possible to use the "needle" nozzles at a distance of up to a meter, which strongly sprays the paint in droplets.

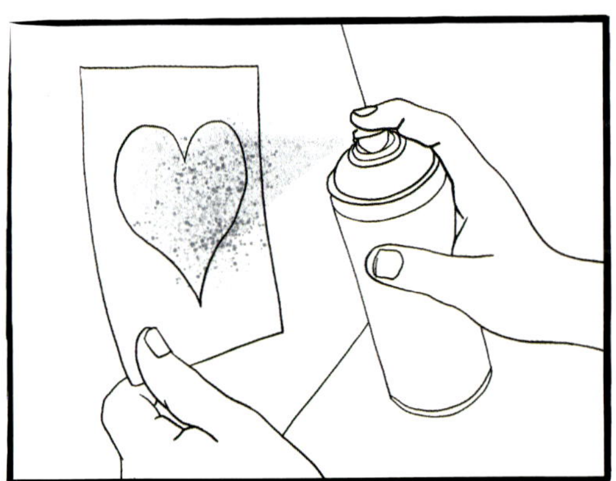

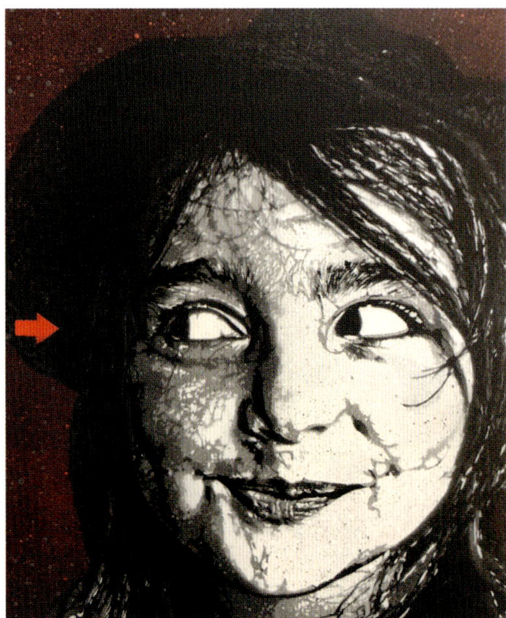

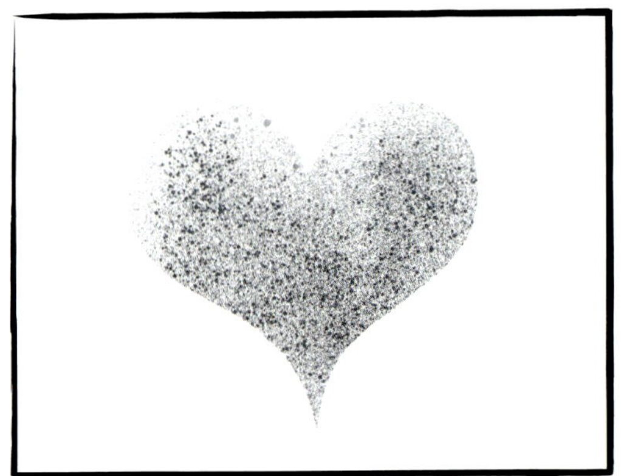

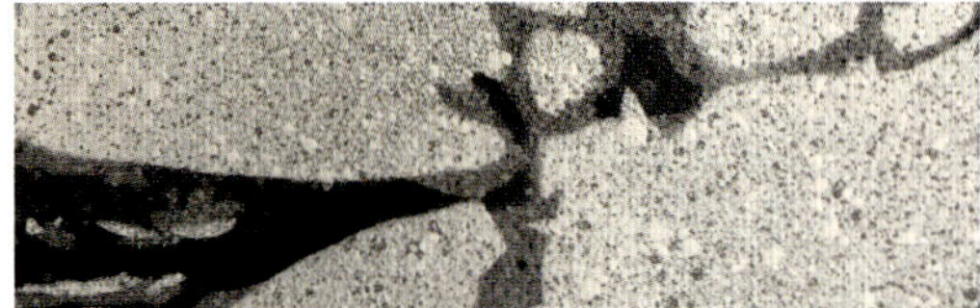

SHIFTED EFFECT

It is possible, from the same stencil or area, to create border effects. To do this, simply paint the stencil or an area of the stencil a first time in one color, then shift it slightly and paint it again in a second color that will cover the first one. This operation can produce various results, including relief effects: if you paint a black area that you cover with a lighter color or white, the border created by the offset will look like a shadow (*left sketch*). Conversely, if you create a white or light border that flanks a darker stencil, you'll obtain a relief effect (*sketch on the right*).

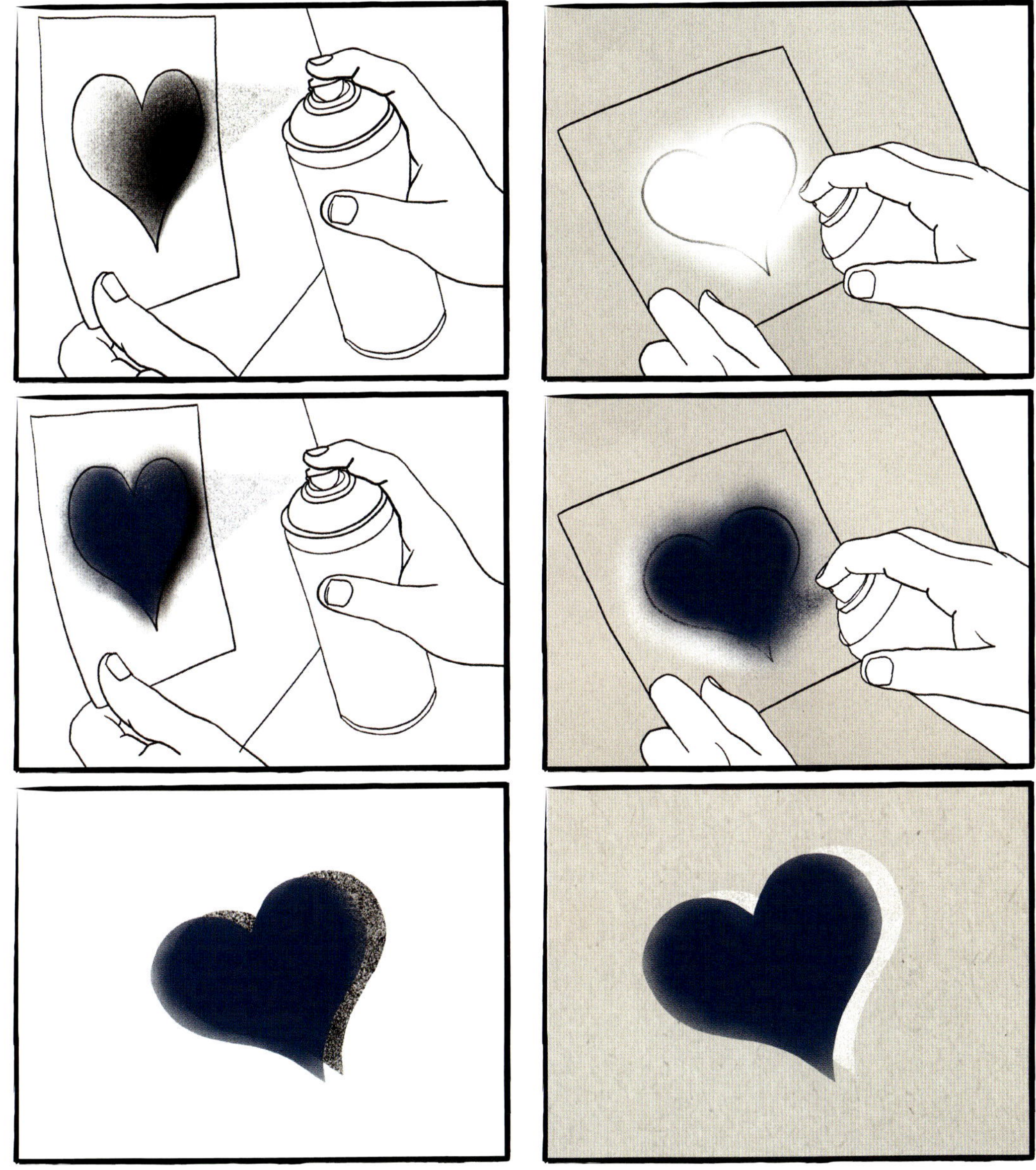

1. C215, 2016. By shifting several stencils designed to be superimposed, we create optical effects close to abstraction.

2. Epsylon Point, *Les marins génois* (detail), 2018. Polychrome composition with the same stencil shifting, in light and shadow.

3. *Loading* (detail), 2013. Acrylic and spray can on wood, flat screen, video.

The artist who, in my opinion, makes the best use of this register, to the point of abstraction, is called Epsylon Point (see his interview, p. 138).

An important and very interesting use of these shifting effects consists of painting, on a white background, a first time his stencil with transparent blue, then a second time, slightly shifted, with transparent red. You will obtain a spectacular three-dimensional effect that you can optimize by looking at your work with 3-D glasses, having one blue and the other red lens.

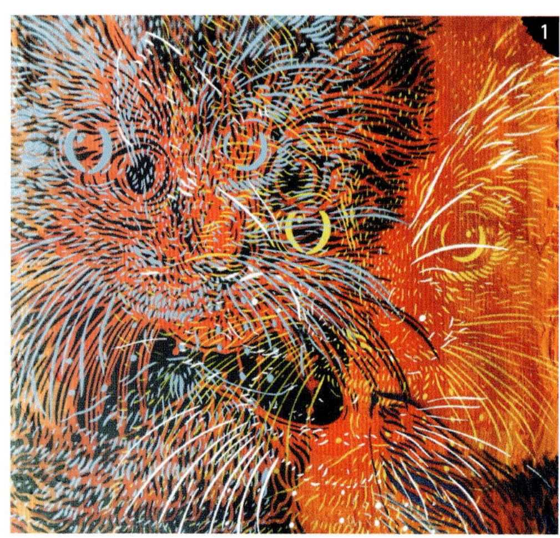

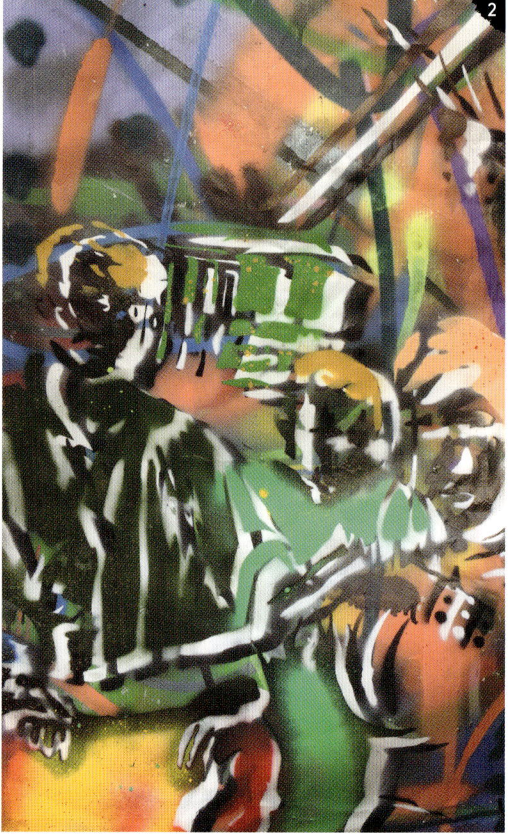

INTERVIEW WITH SPEEDY GRAPHITO

Speedy Graphito is one of the pillars of French urban art. This all-around artist is not, strictly speaking, a stencil artist. However, he has been practicing this art since the early 1980s. His sense of graphic design has allowed him to evolve the stencil approach on several occasions.

Site: speedygraphito.free.fr

Instagram: @speedygraphito

Facebook: @SPEEDY GRAPHITO

Why did you choose stencils rather than another painting technique?

I turned to stencil art when I started wanting to paint in the street. This technique allowed a fast and repetitive execution of my images. At that time, I had just finished my apprenticeship in art school. My paintings didn't interest the Parisian galleries. I had the idea to reproduce them in a simplified way with stencils and to expose them in the street.

How do you make your stencils?

In thirty-five years, things have changed. In the beginning, I used to draw on fairly thick cardboard that I cut out. My stencils were no larger than the standard "raisin format" paper size of 50 × 65 cm, which allowed me to carry them easily in a drawing box. When I wanted to make larger formats, I switched to a thinner medium, 300 gsm sheets of paper assembled and folded. I'm a fan of the monolayer stencil. I like to give a 3-D effect to my stencils by shifting the same image with a different color.

How do you see the evolution of stencil techniques since you started out?

The technique has become more sophisticated with the arrival of laser-cutting machines; there are more layers and the results are more and more photographic. The evolution of the tools (spray cans and interchangeable nozzles) has also contributed to more and more realistic stencils.

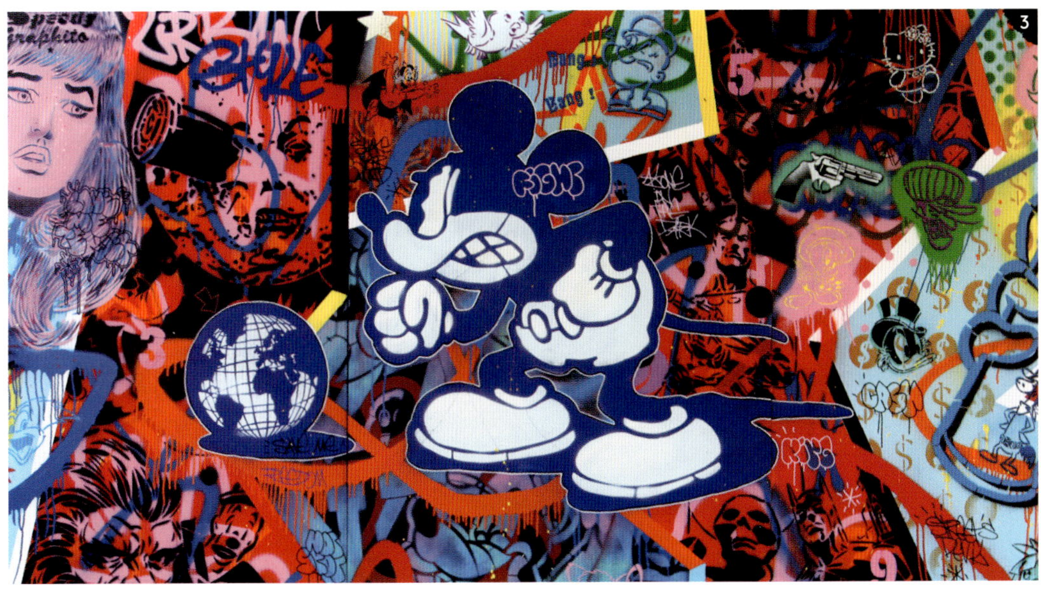

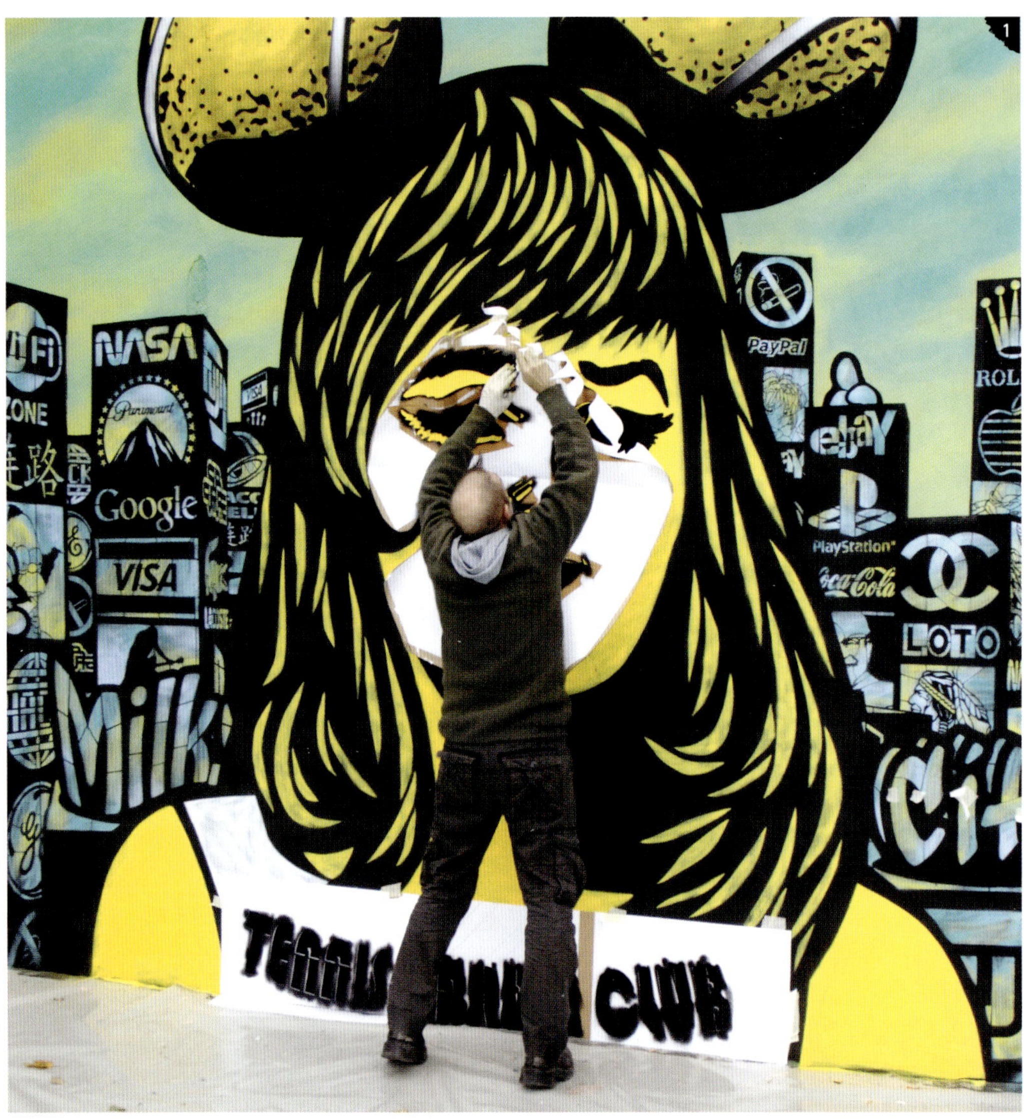

Who are the artists who inspire you in your stencil work?
None. When I started out, the only stencils I had seen were the ones made by alternative punk bands who wrote their band's name on the walls.

What are the limits of stencils as a tool?
The fixed size. To overcome this disadvantage, I often compose my frescoes from an assembly of several stencils of different sizes—wallpaper-style stencils that join to make large backgrounds, medium stencils for the main motifs and smaller ones to give detail.

For you, is a stencil a frame or a freedom?
Both! Hard to miss a stencil. I use stencils exclusively in the street and on the backgrounds of a few canvases when I want to give an "explosive" and "urban" effect.

Can you describe your studio for us?
It is multiple, because I live between Paris and Miami. It looks like a classic painting studio, with a large easel, painted walls and paintings stored all over the place.

1. *Tennis Barbie Club* (detail), Parc Suzanne Lenglen, Paris, 2010.

2. Epsylon Point, *Nostalgie d'un passé révolu* (detail), 2015.

3 and 4. C215, portraits of Mehdi Meklat, *La Mauvaise Réputation* exhibition, Openspace gallery, Paris, 2017. The same portrait painted in negative refers to the "evil double" of the character.

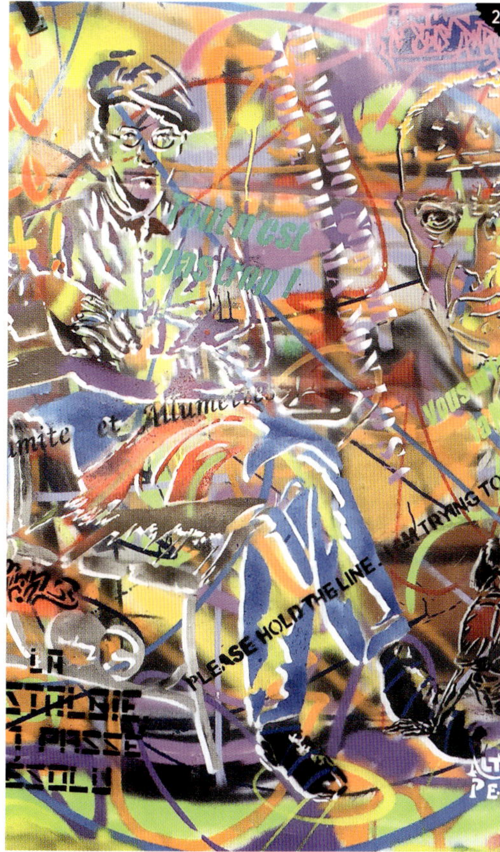

IN NEGATIVE

Nothing forces a stencil artist to use colors realistically, so some artists add a complexity to optical effects of their work by reversing the color ratios, painting certain areas in negative or using fanciful colors. The results are then very abstract, like the paintings done by Epsylon Point.

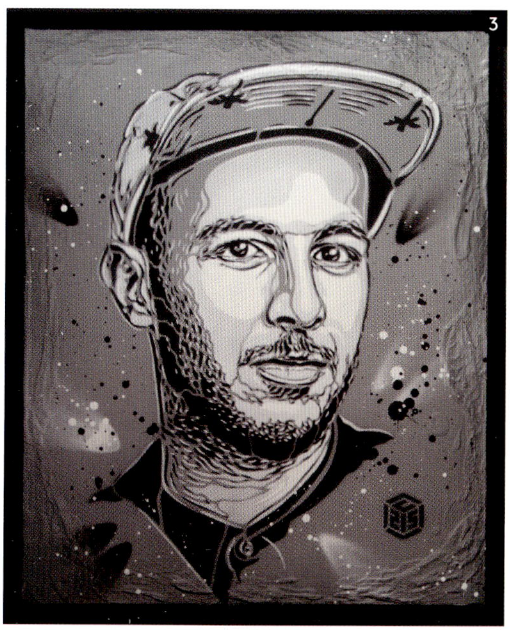

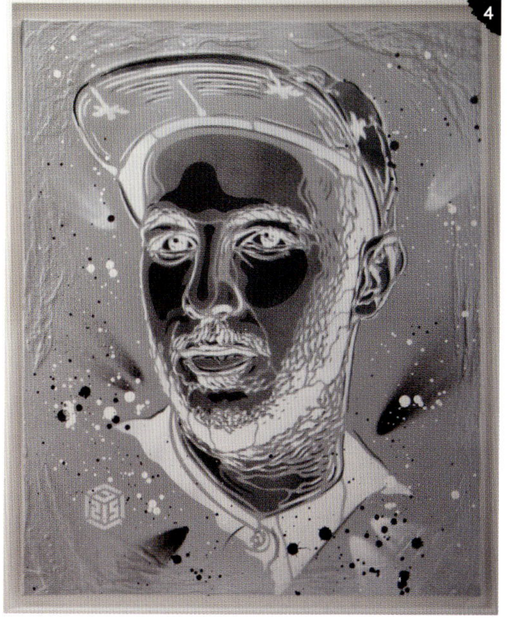

IN SYMMETRY

A fun way to use your stencils is to paint them by repeating them according to the principle of symmetry. This can be done on either side of a line, which produces a mirror effect (*sketches on the left*). You can also multiply the same stencil symmetrically around axes arranged in concentric stars, which makes it possible to create, for example, mandalas from a single stencil (*sketches on the right*). The often-decorative result—especially when the motifs are very elaborate, as with works by Speedy Graphito, Add Fuel or Obey—can give rise to works as aesthetic as they are significant.

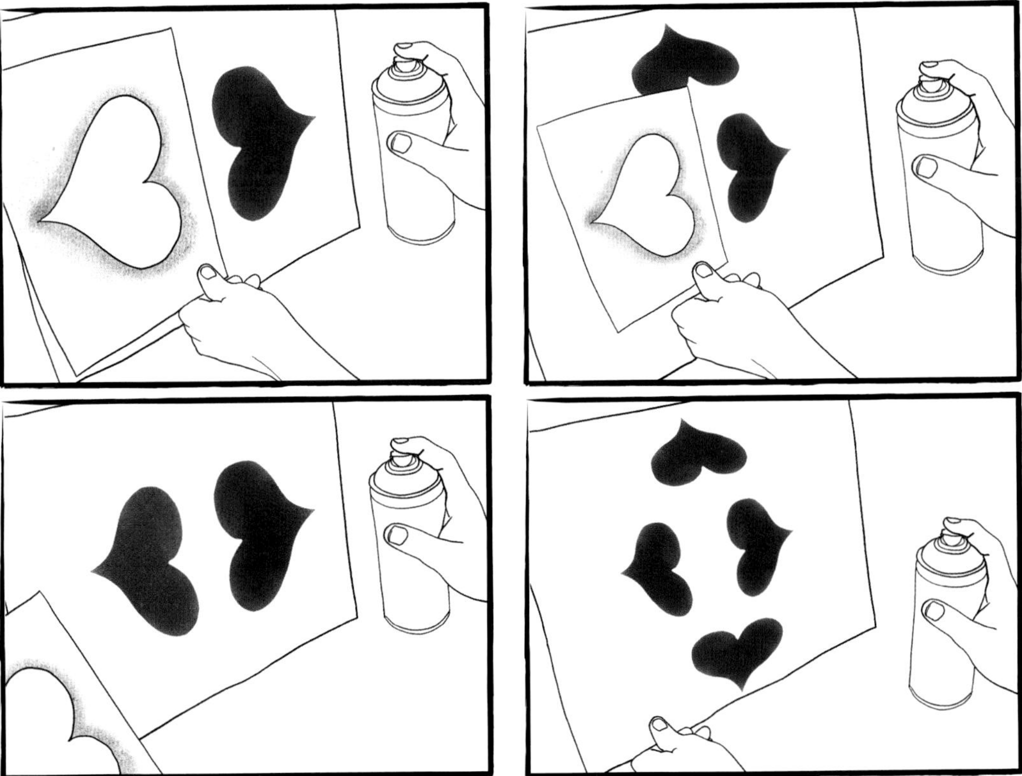

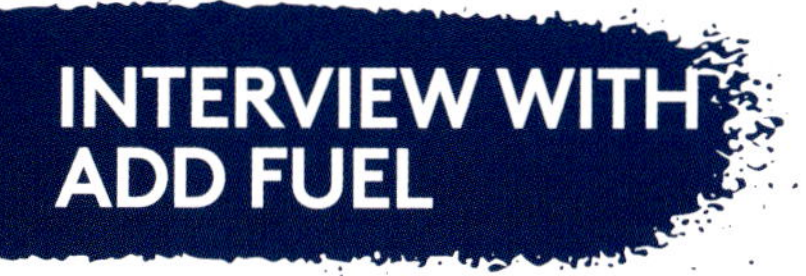

INTERVIEW WITH ADD FUEL

The artist using an acetate stencil, 2018.

The work of the Portuguese artist Add Fuel is inspired by a major cultural element of Portugal: decorated ceramic tiles called azulejos. He revisits their style by integrating resolutely modern motifs. To do so, he makes the most of the repetitive and symmetrical dimension of his stencils.

Website: www.addfuel.com
Instagram: @addfuel
Facebook: @addfuelune

Why did you choose stencils rather than another painting technique?

My work is based on the repetition of patterns. Thanks to stencils, I can reproduce them in a very clear and graphic way. Moreover, multilayering allows me to add a lot of colors, to create complex and colorful pieces without ever losing the regularity of the patterns, which are perfectly reproduced.

How do you make your stencils?

All my stencils start with a pencil sketch. I ink them first, then scan or photograph them, in order to get a digital version of my drawing. I then do a light cleanup on Photoshop to accentuate the contrasts between black and white. I perfect the shapes and add details using Illustrator. I use that software to deconstruct the future stencil into a certain number of layers, depending on what I imagine the final result to be. Once the vector files are ready, they're laser-cut in cellulose acetate. This material allows me to paint several times with the same stencil without soaking it with paint, which would happen with paper or cardboard stencils. I make new stencils for each new mural painting.

How do you see the evolution of stencil techniques since you started out?

Nowadays, access to laser-cutting machines and cutting plotters is very easy. The digital process of creating a stencil is much simpler than a few years ago. When I started out, I used to cut several multilayer stencils in cellulose acetate by hand. I now use laser cutting. Since the technology exists, I use it with great pleasure.

It allows me to save cutting time and focus on artistic creation, to make more artwork. I am not what many people consider a "stencil purist," and I don't agree with those who consider

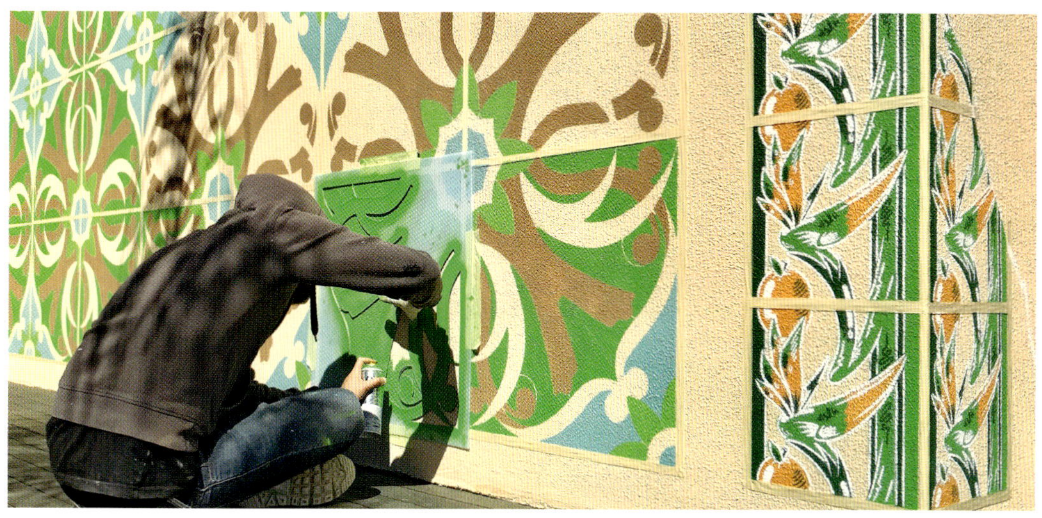

it imperative for an artist to manually cut his stencils. I would say that stencils have evolved since my early days. In the beginning, they were simple works of art, of a single color, even in black or gray. They have become complex pieces, with a lot of depth, color and movement.

Who are the artists who inspire you in your stencil work?

When I started experimenting with this medium, I didn't know many stencil artists. The development of my technique was based on trial and error, as well as my knowledge of screen printing. In fact, the preparation of files to create a silkscreen print is quite similar to the design of multilayers to make a stencil. I met other stencil artists only after I gained confidence in my technique.

Anyway, I really like the dynamic way C215 uses stencils, sometimes by adding hand-painted elements to a multilayer composition, other times by cleverly elaborating a piece from a single layer stencil with several juxtapositions and embellishments by hand. I love Evol's extremely precise technique, his use of scales and the way he uses shadows to create depth. I also appreciate Yellow's playful and iconoclastic approach, the way he plays with context in a way that makes his work (almost always) perfect.

What are the limits of stencils as a tool?

They can be complicated to travel with. I tend to use large stencils cut out of cellulose acetate. They can be very heavy, which means I have to travel with a huge and bulky suitcase! On the other hand, the stencil is a "closed" tool. You can't change its dimension once it is cut. This sometimes makes it a challenge to paint some murals. I always try to get the right size for each wall beforehand, so that my stencils fit the support as well as possible, but that's not always possible. But actually, I enjoy solving these kinds of problems, and that's probably one of the reasons why I like this tool.

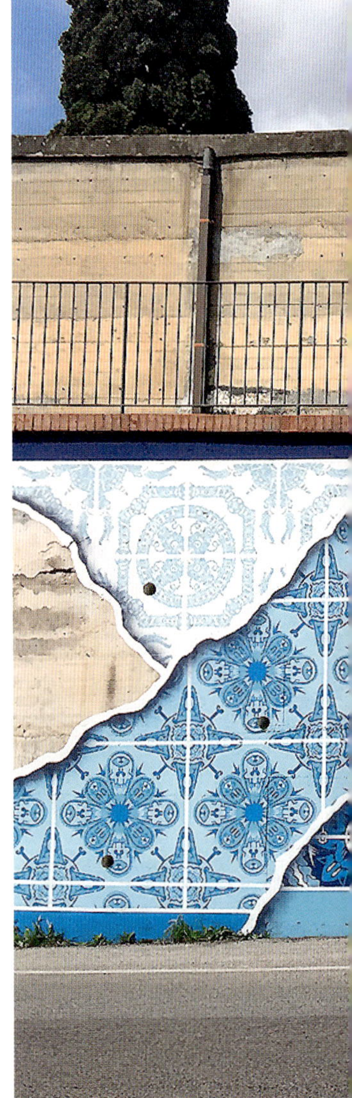

Darkless, Maranola Cemetery (Italy), 2016. As part of the Memorie Urbane Festival.

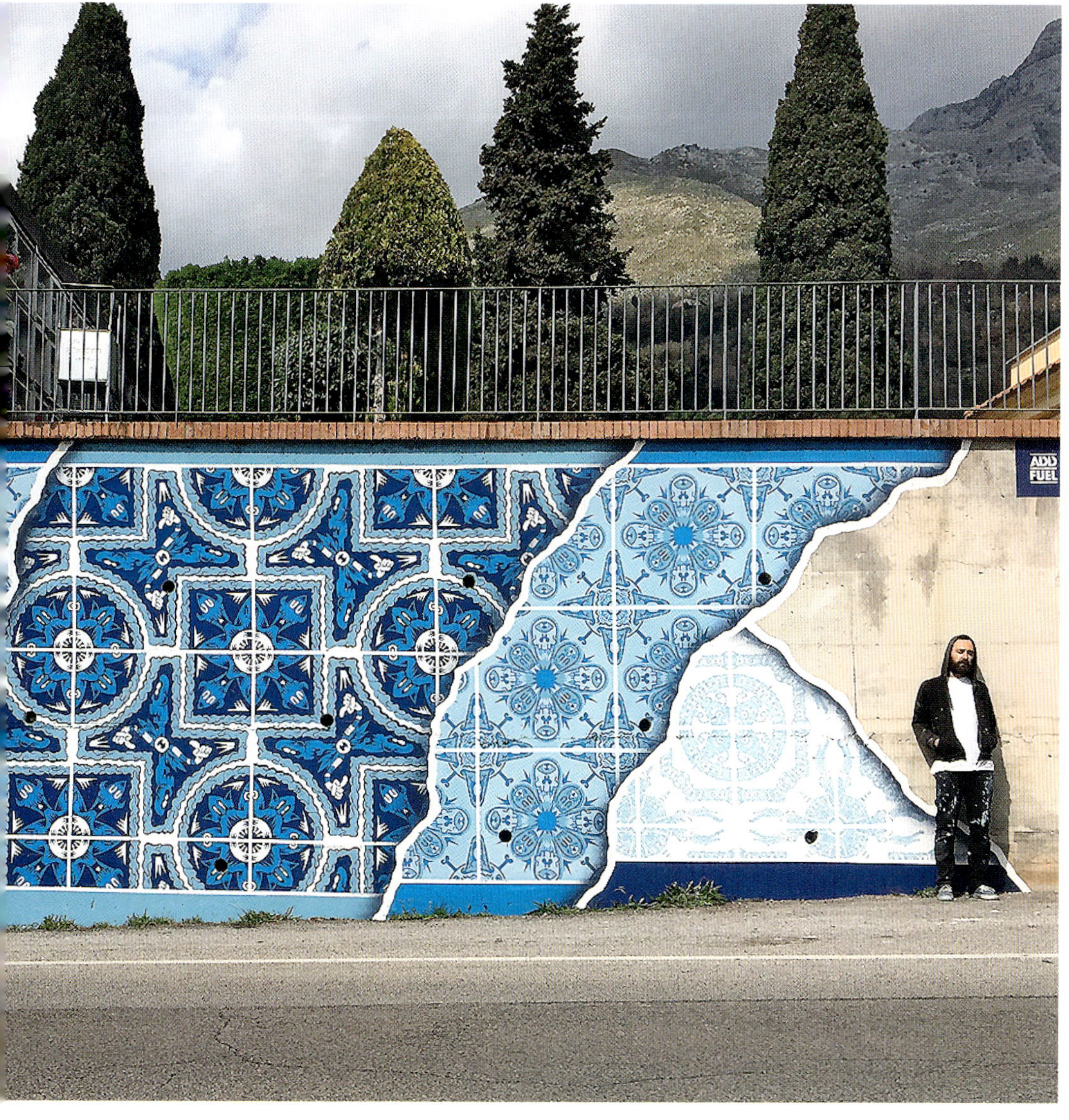

For you, is a stencil a frame or a freedom?

I would say freedom in a cage. The good thing about a stencil is that it allows you to repeat patterns, work quickly and create multicolored compositions with relative ease. On the other hand, its size and form are fixed and the number of colors is defined. It can therefore constitute a frame. But in the end, it's all in the creativity we show and in the solutions we find to go beyond our own limits. This creates freedom.

Can you describe your studio for us?

I have tables and shelves to store my documents, a desk and my computer. My studio is also very oriented toward the creation of my ceramic tile pieces. I have a kiln, lots of unglazed tiles, inks and varnishes suitable for high temperatures, as well as all the necessary equipment for making tiles. But lately, I've been painting more and more on canvas with stencils. So I use a structure on trestles to paint horizontally. There are small stencils everywhere, lots of spray cans and tape, not to mention the big pile of stencils from all the murals I've done, because I keep them all.

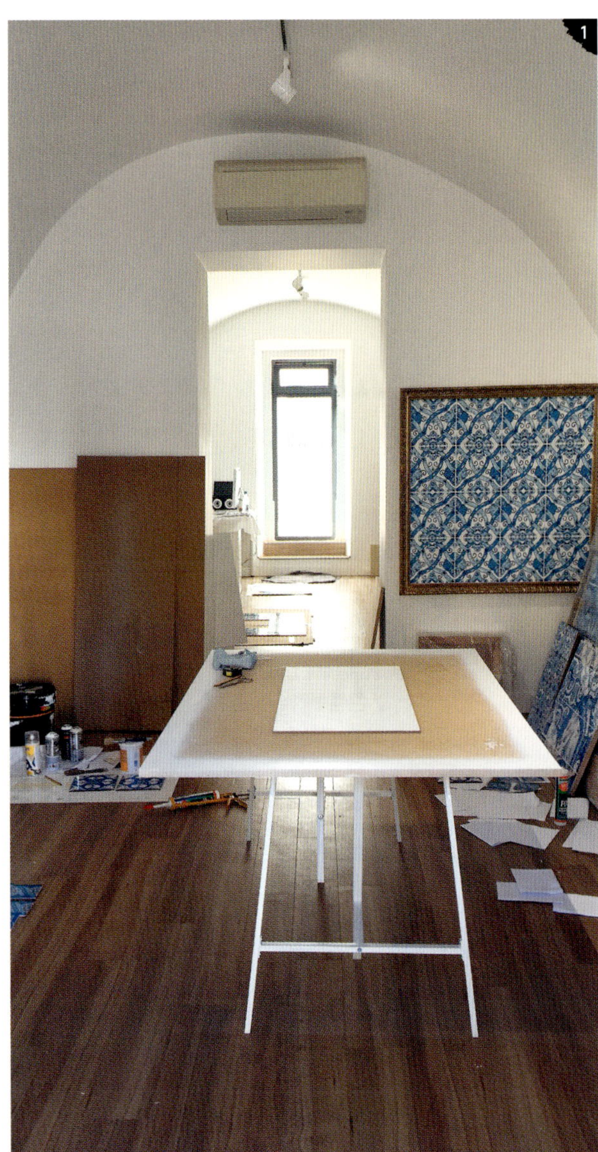

1. View of the studio.

2. Details of a stencil.

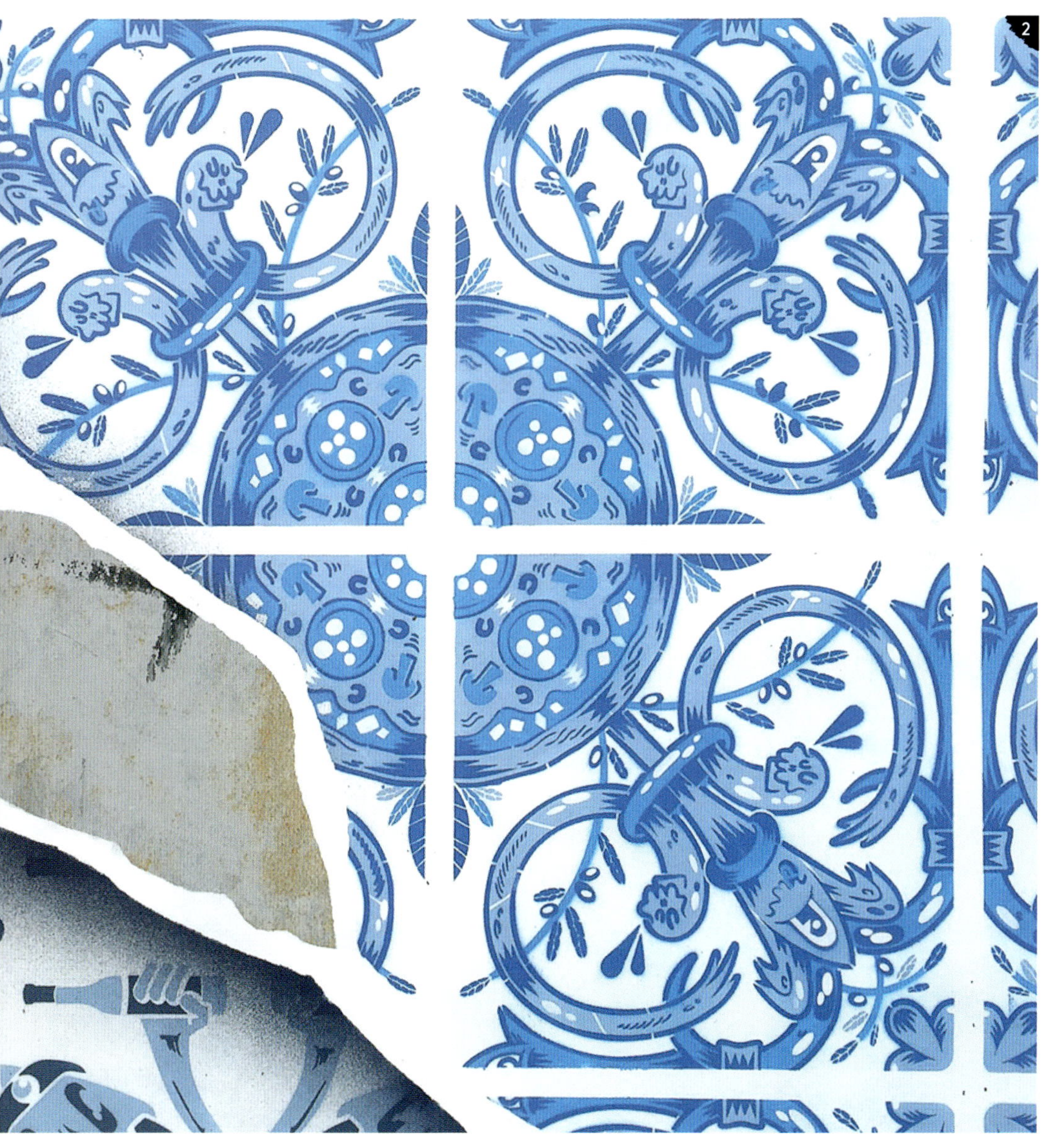

SLIDING

Some artists, such as Jef Aerosol in his self-portraits, slide their stencil with one hand while they paint it with the other, creating an interesting effect of sliding movement or distortion.

1. *Réglez le siège à la hauteur désirée*, 1987. Free canvas.

2. *Quatre poses*, 1987. Wood panel.

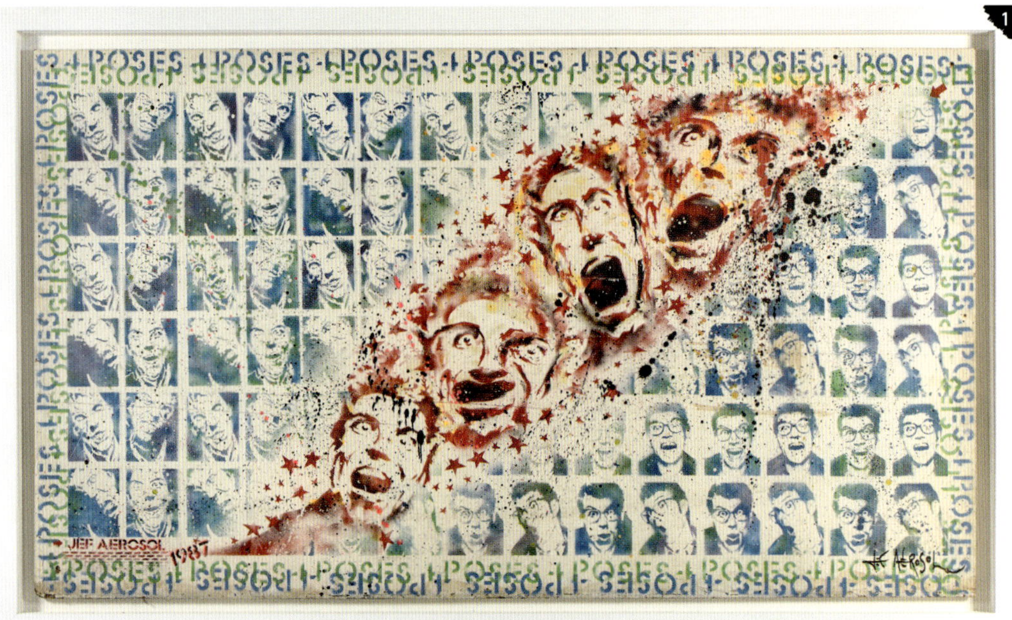

INTERVIEW WITH JEF AEROSOL: SLIDING STENCILS

Jef is one of the pioneers and pillars of stencil in France. While the years have seen his plastic evolve from manual cutting to digital creation, he has left in my memory iconic works on the theme of music but also a large number of incredible self-portraits, some of which were inspired by photocopies that he painted in motion.

Website: www.jefaerosol.com

Instagram: @jefaerosol

How did you start out?

In the late 1970s and early 1980s, I had several jobs as a night watchman in factories, offices and businesses. That's when I started having fun with photocopiers! The copiers at that time were of course not yet digital and ran on toner, a printing powder then composed of carbon black and iron oxide. The photocopier couldn't reproduce the shades and gradations of the originals and automatically turned them into black or white areas—the toner either deposited or did not deposit.

I really liked these "stylized" photos from the machine. This photocopied imagery had become the trademark of the punk movement in 1977: fanzines, record covers and visuals that used and abused photocopying and its cheap effects.

Plus, the very fact of making art with a tool that was not intended for that was totally part of the punk spirit.

In 1980, a number of artists and galleries turned the photocopier into an artistic tool in its own right, calling this technique copy art, electro graphics or xerography. One of the leaders of this movement was Christian Rigal, alias Cejar. He was there at the beginning of the exhibitions, books and articles of this movement, which spread internationally, and which had actually started to emerge in the 1960s when the first photocopiers appeared on the market.

I totally joined this movement and I "copied" over and over again, trying to push the photocopier to its ultimate limits. I put various materials on the glass, photocopied photocopies, etc., until I obtained interesting results. The textures and alterations of these successive copies captivated me. I loved the random, somewhat psychedelic and very experimental dimension of the process.

Of course, I also placed my face on the glass, moving it, turning it to follow the movement of the light tube and thus obtaining totally incredible deformations, elongations, slides and stretching of the image that were totally unique. For example, I've made self-portraits showing both my two profiles and my face from the front, like a flattening, like a planisphere. In the early 1980s I participated in several copy art exhibitions and mixed my practice of photo booth art with electro graphics.

What made you turn to stencils?

The important use of photocopying in the punk iconography of the years 1976–1977 went hand in hand with the use of stencils. In fact, the cheap and industrial side of this imagery found itself in total harmony of spirit with stencil lettering, a detour from industrial and military typography and signage. It wasn't yet a question of making stencil images, but only words and sometimes very simple logos. Members of the Clash, for example, wore shirts and jackets covered with stenciled text. The Crass group diffused its logo through stencil curves. These three practices (photo booth, electro graphics and stenciling) combined and matured in my mind to lead to my first try at stencil art in the street in 1982.

The final trigger was undoubtedly the Clash concert at the Mogador Theater in September 1981, during which the New York graffiti artist Futura 2000 was at the back of the stage, armed with spray cans and painting a large canvas while the musicians were playing. I had never seen anyone use a spray can for artistic purposes, and it was a real revelation.

A year later, in the fall of 1982, after leaving Nantes (my hometown) for Tours, I took the plunge. From a self-portrait taken in a photo booth and enlarged with a photocopier, I cut out my first stencil and sprayed it on the walls of old Tours. The fact that photocopying transforms the most nuanced photos into high-contrast images helped me considerably in the development of my stencils.

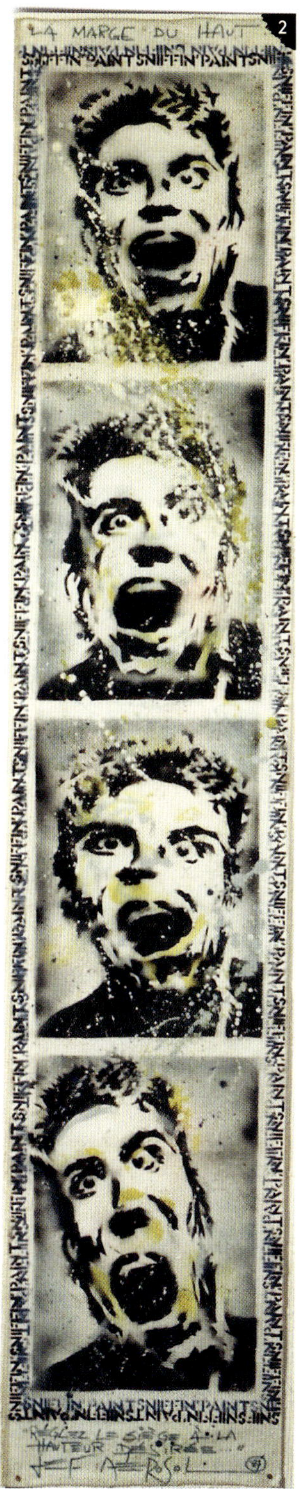

How was the sliding-stencil technique born?

It didn't take me long to try to reproduce the deformations and stretches in my cuts that I obtained with the photocopier. These attempts proved unsuccessful because the stencil froze and "stiffened" the dynamic movement of the electro graphic. So I gave up the idea of cutting out the "slides" that I could do with copy art. One night, I found myself with a self-portrait stencil in my left hand and a can of paint in the other, as usual. I don't know how the idea crossed my mind, but I began to slide the stencil while spraying and I realized that I had found a simple and obvious way to reproduce on a wall the effects that the photocopier allowed me to do. My sliding-stencil technique was born. I practiced it a lot throughout the 1980s and early 1990s, but then I got a little tired of it and moved on to other images and more sophisticated stencils, but I didn't give it up completely.

I also continued my copy art practice through much of the 1980s, at exhibitions, publications and performances where I was supported by brands such as Canon and Rank Xerox who lent me copiers. The advent of color photocopying also opened new perspectives. Later, when traditional copiers gave way to digital machines and scanners, the results were different and less interesting, and I detached myself from electro graphics. I now rarely use a sliding stencil, but it still happens to me from time to time . . .

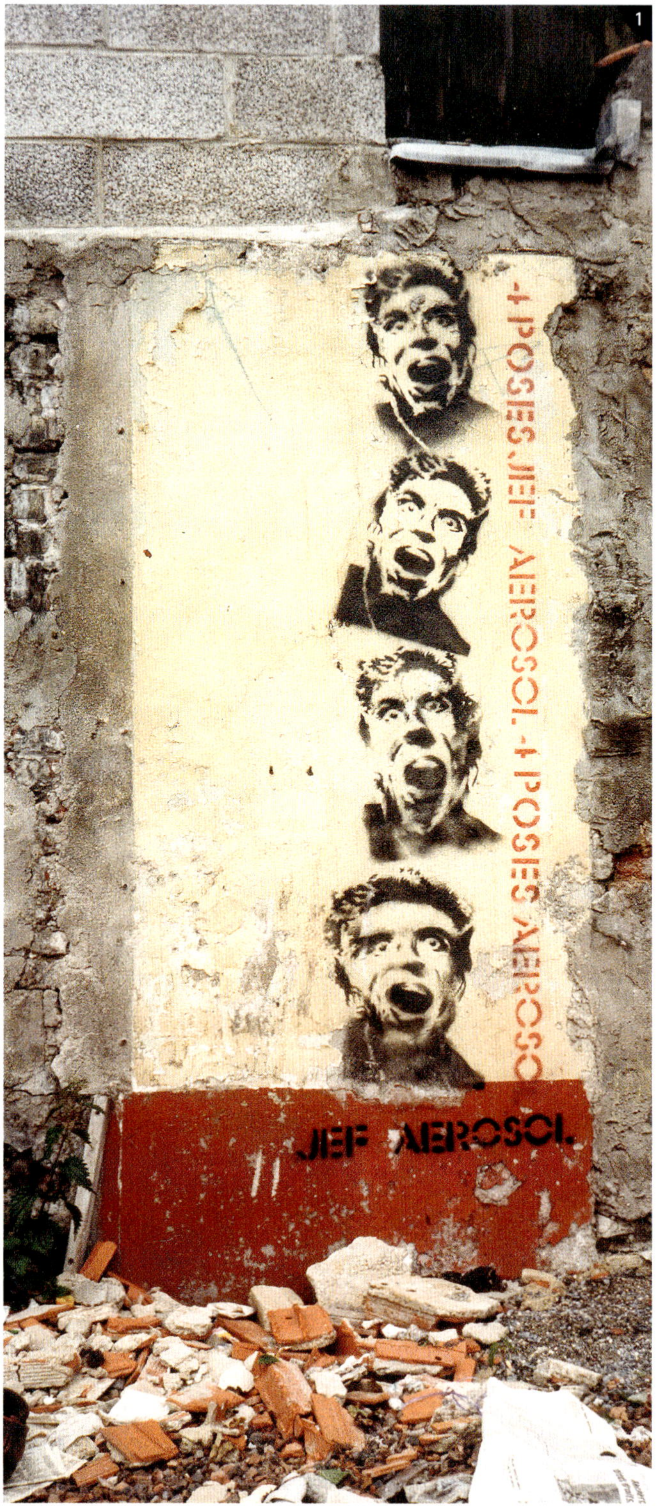

1. *Quatre poses*, wall in Lille Wazemmes (France), 1984.

2. Add Fuel. Applied and cut out of the support, then removed, using masking tape; the same technique as traditional stenciling.

3. Aletaïa, creation of a constellation, Vanves (France), 2019. Lines created using masking tape.

MASKING TAPE

Building painters frequently use tape as a masking tool. The logic is the same as that of a stencil artist: mask the reserved area, paint over this masking and when it's removed, the unpainted area is revealed. But care must be taken to ensure that the tape is adhered to the support along its entire length, since otherwise the paint will penetrate underneath and overflow.

Many graffiti artists use masking tape in their work, especially to create straight lines or to obtain a perfectly accurate separation of areas. The most well-known French artist working this way is most certainly L'Atlas, who makes his lettering by affixing rectilinear adhesive tapes, on which he paints. Once removed, they reveal cryptic labyrinthine writings, directly inspired by those of Tania Mouraud, who has been using this process since the 1970s.

Abstract artist Felipe Pantone creates beautiful multicolored optical works with this technique, which allows him to quickly obtain straight lines and perfect area separations.

By taking advantage of tape art, an artist can create extremely complex designs, figurative or abstract. This method is currently one of the least exploited in the field of stencil art.

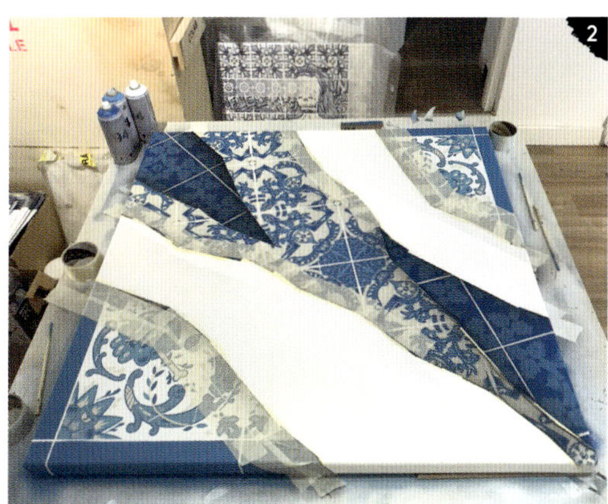
2

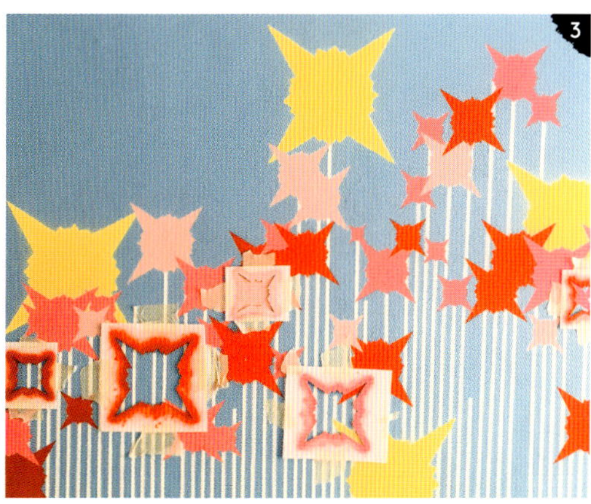
3

INTERVIEW WITH ALETEÏA

Aleteïa is a Parisian artist who has been practicing her art for almost fifteen years. Using adhesive tapes and stencils, she deploys her dreamlike universe through participatory projects in which she lets children paint.

Website: www.aleteia.fr
Instagram: @aleteiagram
Facebook: Emilie Aleteïa Garnaud

Why did you choose stencils rather than another painting technique?
In my case, it was what I wanted to achieve that made me turn to stencils and masking tape. To draw constellations, you have to draw long, straight lines. Using tape was immediately obvious. Likewise, as I repeat the same star shape, which has become my signature, making stencils of them means I can be quick and efficient, which is important when you choose to paint in the street. I also like the very precise rendering of the tape and the way it blends into the sprayed stencil, which is more blurred.

How do you make your stencils?
I use several very simple techniques. For large formats on the ground, I make stencils of stars that are sometimes very large, 16 feet (5 meters), by assembling sheets of foam core. This allows me to fold them and store them in a cardboard box. It's a little like a magic box from which I take out giant stars and lengths of adhesive tape. From this rudimentary material, I can make large-scale works such as the *Paramour* fresco on the courtyard of the Centre Pompidou. I really like the idea of making large formats from a very simple and space-saving material.

In addition, I use the masking technique. It consists of applying tape, painting over it and then removing the tape, which reveals the drawing. This lets me make my works very quickly, with precision and little material. I precut stars in tape and use tape of all sizes to create the lines. What interests me with masking is the reappearance of the raw wall or an intact color through the painting. It's a very enjoyable technique. When you remove the tape and the drawing appears, there's a twist that I like very much.

How do you see the evolution of stencil techniques since you started out?
For me, stenciling and especially masking with tape are, above all, effective methods. There's been a great evolution in the materials, and especially in the tapes that can be found today in all widths and materials. This has given me a great freedom of supports and formats that I didn't have at the beginning.

Who are the artists who inspire you in your stencil work?
I don't really have stencil artist references. I discovered the different uses I could make of tape with L'Atlas when we first started out. Artistically, I feel rather inspired by the work of Felice Varini or Georges Rousse, for their way of thinking about space, color, geometry, meaning.

What are the limits of stencils as a tool?
Its precision, which removes a little grace and emotion compared to paintings done directly. It's colder, less vibrant; it has a technical side. I try to compensate for this effect by the meaning I give to my work and the fact that my constellations, or celestial trees, are all different, unique, adapted to the spaces and taped directly on site. That's also why I never have a complete shape precut out of tape, for example. What interests me is to make the drawing in situ, and I draw directly with tape as if it were a pencil.

Imaginary constellation *Écouter/Regarder* in progress in the rue du Théâtre-Français in Marseille, 2019. As part of urban art project Le Premier, Quartier des Arts.

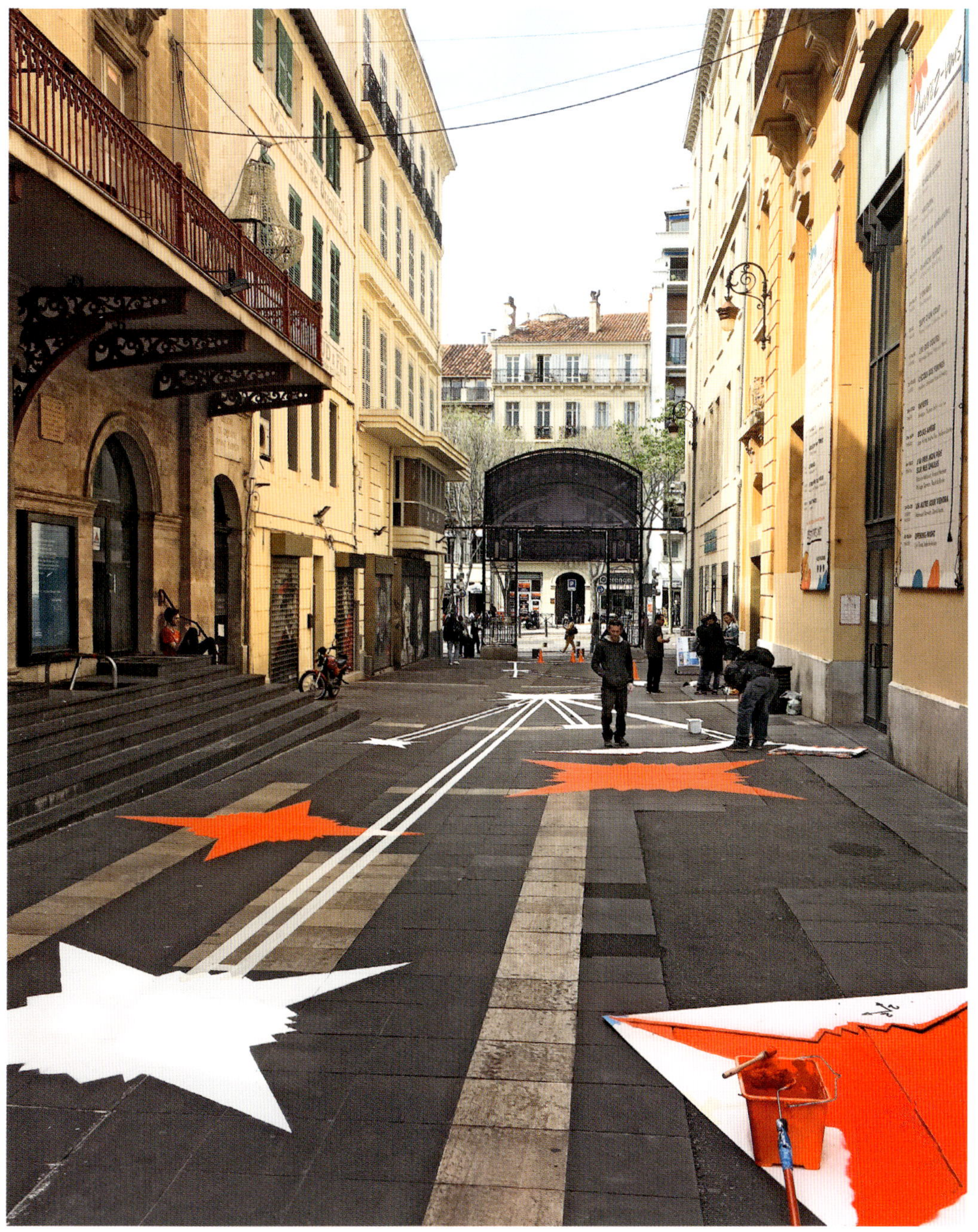

Can you describe your daily life as an artist?
I alternate between institutional commission projects and participatory project editing, and I continue to paint in the street, alone or in a group. I work with associations such as the Constellation or Art Azoï to set up institutional projects. After a few years in Paris, I set up my studio in La Grande Borne, in the Parisian suburbs. I found it more interesting to paint in a city whose spaces are conducive to street painting. So I make the journey, the connection between the city and the suburbs. I try to make that relationship come alive, to map it. I set up some projects to invite other artists to paint in La Grande Borne. It's a subject that interests me, this round trip that's so complex even though it is so short a distance. This kind of journey in the socio-sphere seems more complicated to undertake than going to the other side of the world! In the same way, I work around the notion of public space: how to reappropriate it with the residents through painting projects. I explore the place of the poet walker in these areas of flux.

For you, is a stencil a frame or a freedom?
It is a clever mix of both. It's a frame that makes it possible to create drawings in the street more easily. It means you can paint with others and therefore compensate for the mistakes that people who are going to paint for the first time with a spray can will make. I often work in a collective or participative way, and I invite people, often children, to paint my stars. Stencil art offers a freedom in painting that can be easily shared.

What is your studio like?
I'm not there very often, but it is an essential place, a refuge that shelters a large part of my brain! It's a real space for reflection and preparation. At the moment I'm almost exclusively producing in the street; I hardly do any canvas, but that's slowly changing.

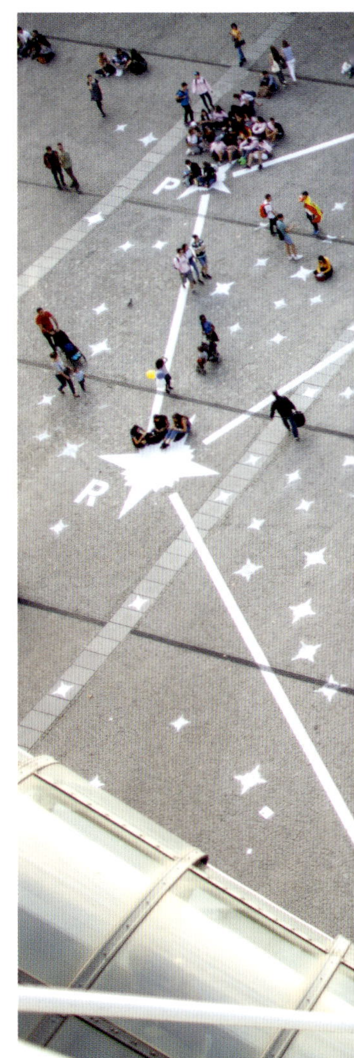

Constellation *Paramour, la famille nouvelle*, collectively created in the courtyard of the Centre Pompidou, Paris, 2017.

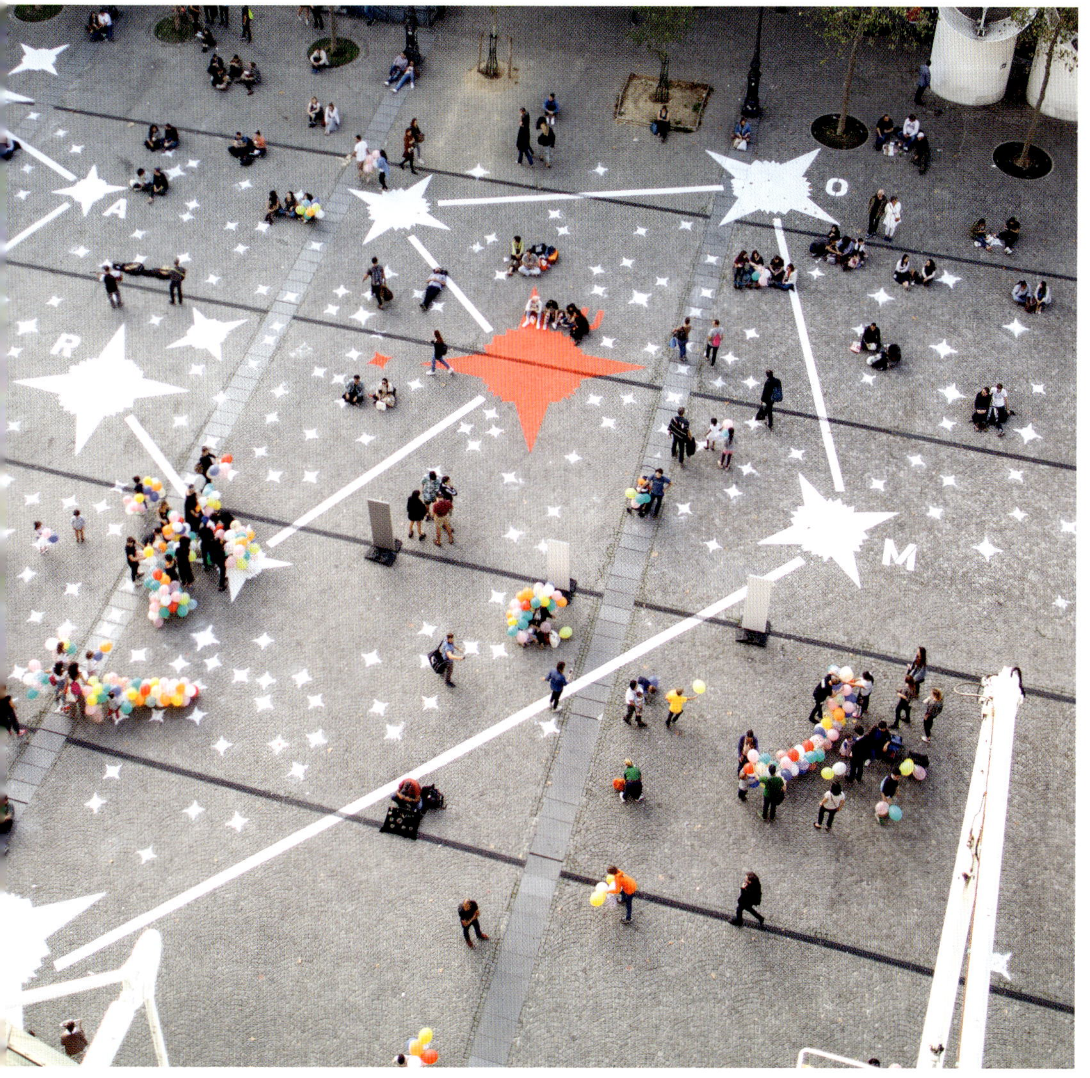

STAMPING

A stencil and its voids are generally used to paint through, but some stencil artists, such as Epsylon Point or Stew, realized that it's possible to apply the paint-coated stencil to the support surface, as one would do with a stamp. In this case, you're painting a positive image. The carved-out part does not appear on the work; only what has been painted over is visible. A very useful trick when you want to rid your strongest stencils (acetate or thick cardboard) of an accumulation of paint and have it be a stylistic approach in its own right.

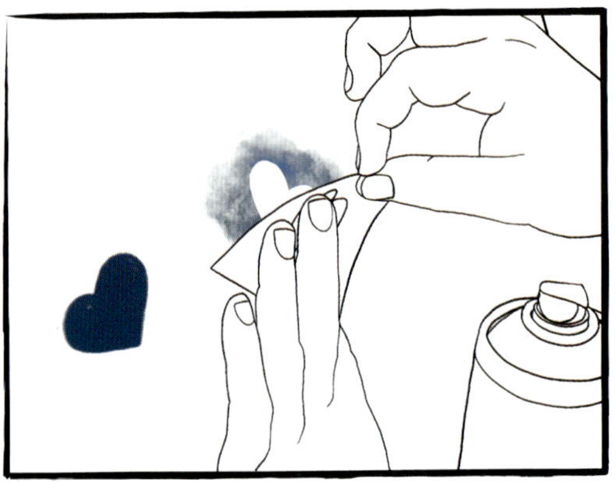

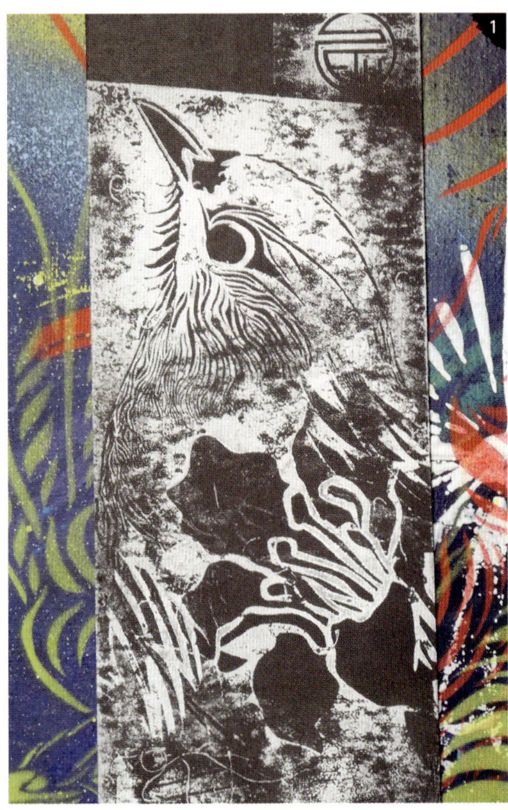

SUPPORTS

Painting makes sense only in relation to the support that lies beneath the painting. In general, if you want to obtain a clean rendering, it's important to paint on a smooth surface without irregularities.

However, the notion of flatness is relative: for those who paint a large brick wall, the unevenness caused by the brick joints will be only slightly visible if the painted areas are large. Generally speaking, the smaller and more detailed the stencil is, the more it will require a perfectly flat surface. Conversely, the simpler the stencil and the larger the area, the less it will require a flawless support surface.

On the other hand, the support's relief elements and the blurring effects they cause are an integral part of the work if they are mastered and integrated into its design. A work of art doesn't necessarily consist only of clear and perfectly delimited areas.

If you choose to paint on a rough or irregular surface and you want to obtain a clean rendering, there are two solutions. The first method is to compress the stencil at the exact place where the paint is being applied, moving along progressively, to make it adhere to the support. The other approach involves using a very thick stencil and a powerful spray can. Directed at right angles, the paint spray will accurately adhere to the support, whatever its roughness. The same principle applies when working on a curved surface.

1. Stew, 2016. Artist's proof made with a stencil used as a stamp.

2. C215, Brooklyn, 2008. Sometimes the form of the support is integrated into the design of the work.

3. C215, Vitry, 2010. On an irregular support, placing the important parts on the flat surfaces ensures they are perfectly legible.

4. C215, Vitry, 2009. Example of a metal curtain; a powerful nozzle was necessary for this work.

5. C215, Mouans Sartoux (France), 2018. In the frame area, the paint is less clear. It's important to place the stencil skillfully.

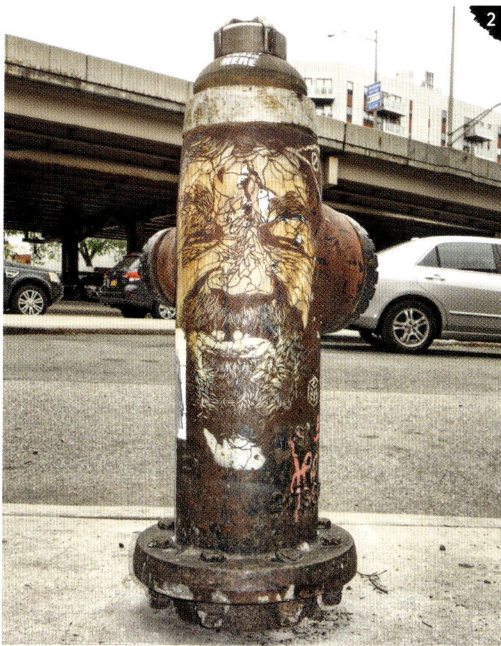

2

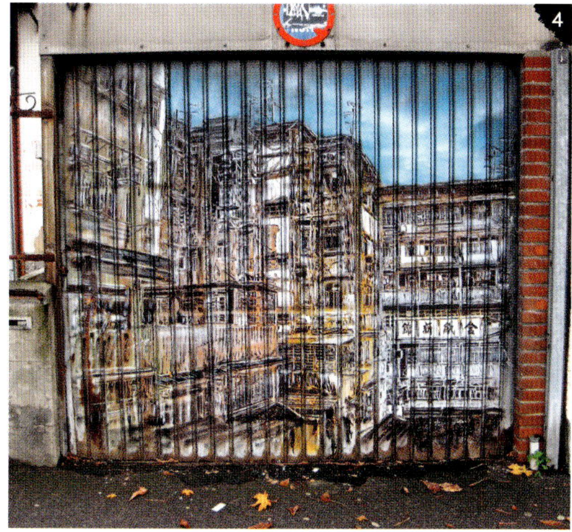

4

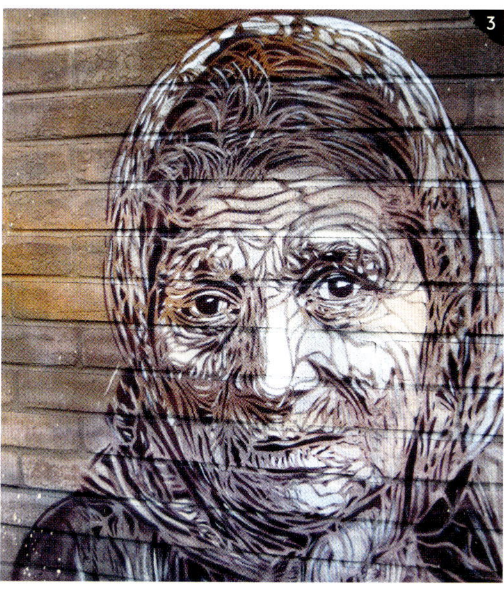

3

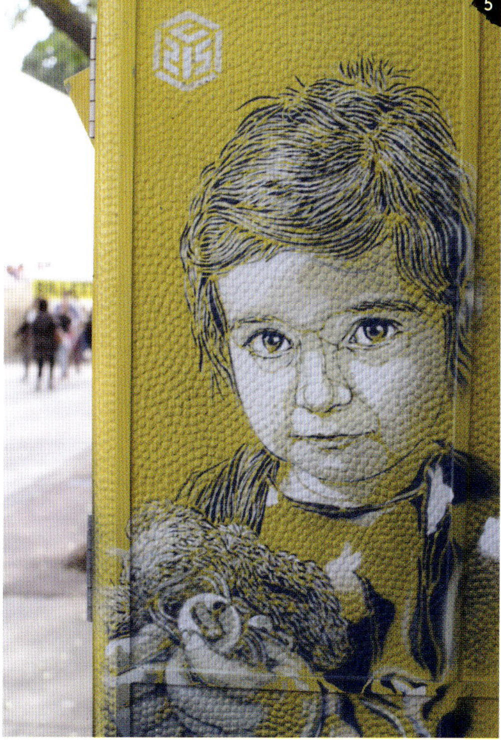

5

PAINTING COMBINING MEDIUMS

Nothing about a given stencil defines the manner in which that stencil will be used, or the painted result. Everyone is free to apply different effects, to invert, slide, stamp, partially paint the stencil, or paint it on any type of support . . . nothing predefines either the use or the result of the tool. This is why what the stencil offers, in my opinion, is freedom—much more so than limitation.

Each stencil can be put to extremely varied uses, which the artist applies as they please. Masking effects, retouching during the intermediate stages, mixed-media techniques, the choices of inks, varnishes, powders, tracing effects. The only thing that affects a stencil's potential is the artistic bias of the user.

Mixing mediums offers unlimited options. There's no cardinal rule to follow. With the exception of what's already been seen and done, everything remains to be experienced and discovered with stencils.

I can, using the same portion of a stencil, reproduce only the contours of the area with a pencil, paint only a part of it, apply a partial gradient, reverse the stencil or rotate it as many times as I like. Any experimentation is good and any attempt is acceptable! So I'm optimistic about the future of stenciling because the souls of artists always strive for creativity, originality and innovation.

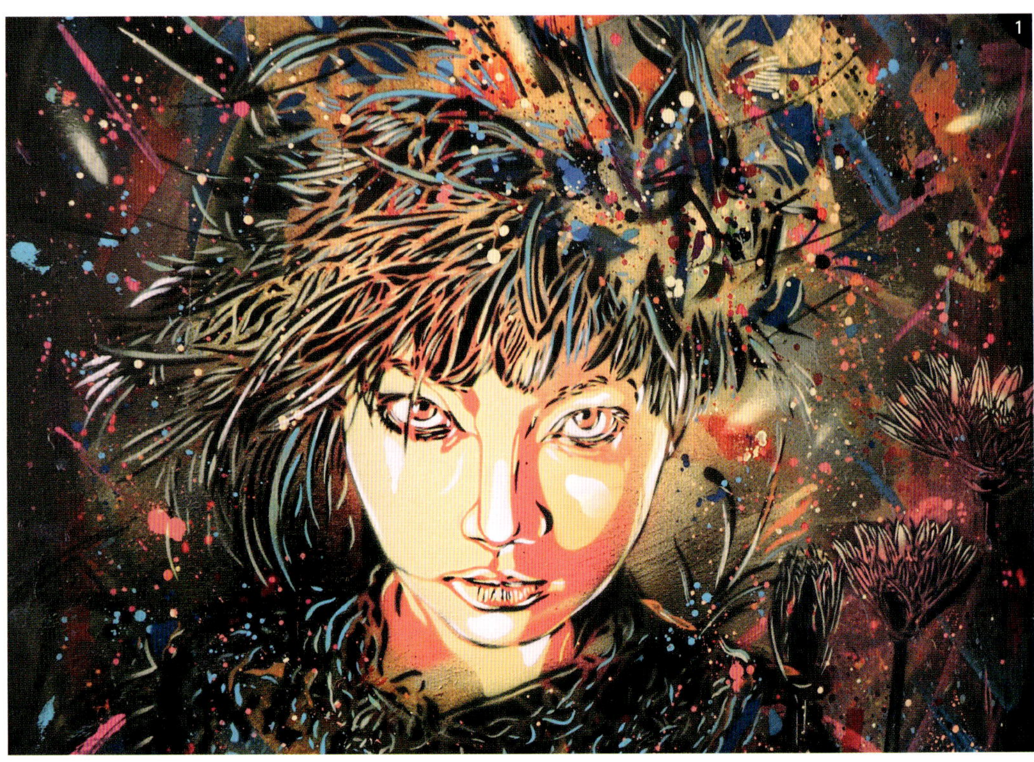
1

1 and 2. C215, 2013. Works created in mixed techniques, combining aerosol paint with stencil and acrylic.

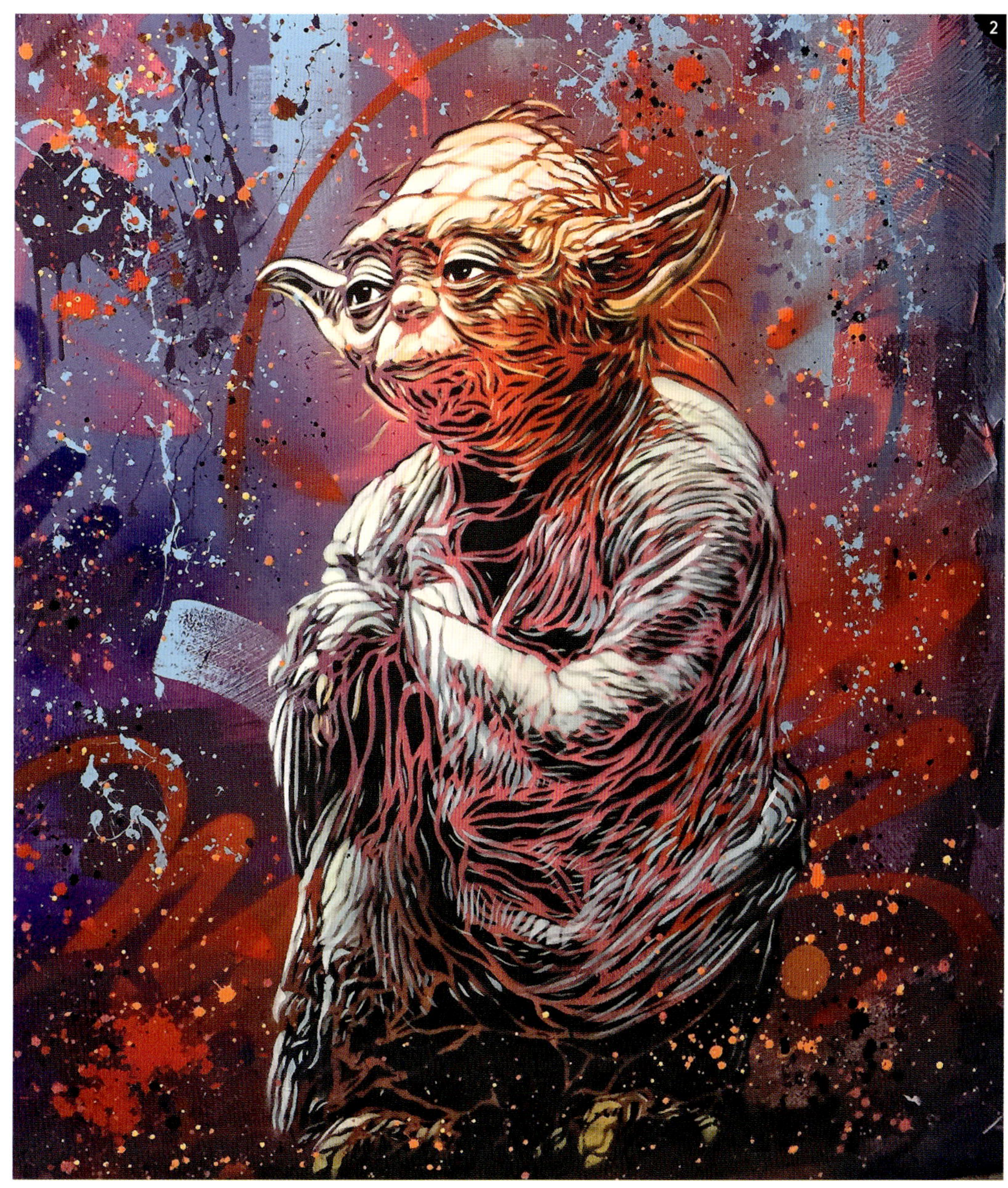

MAIN SUBJECTS

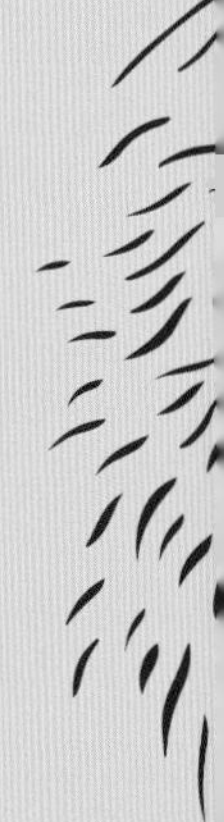

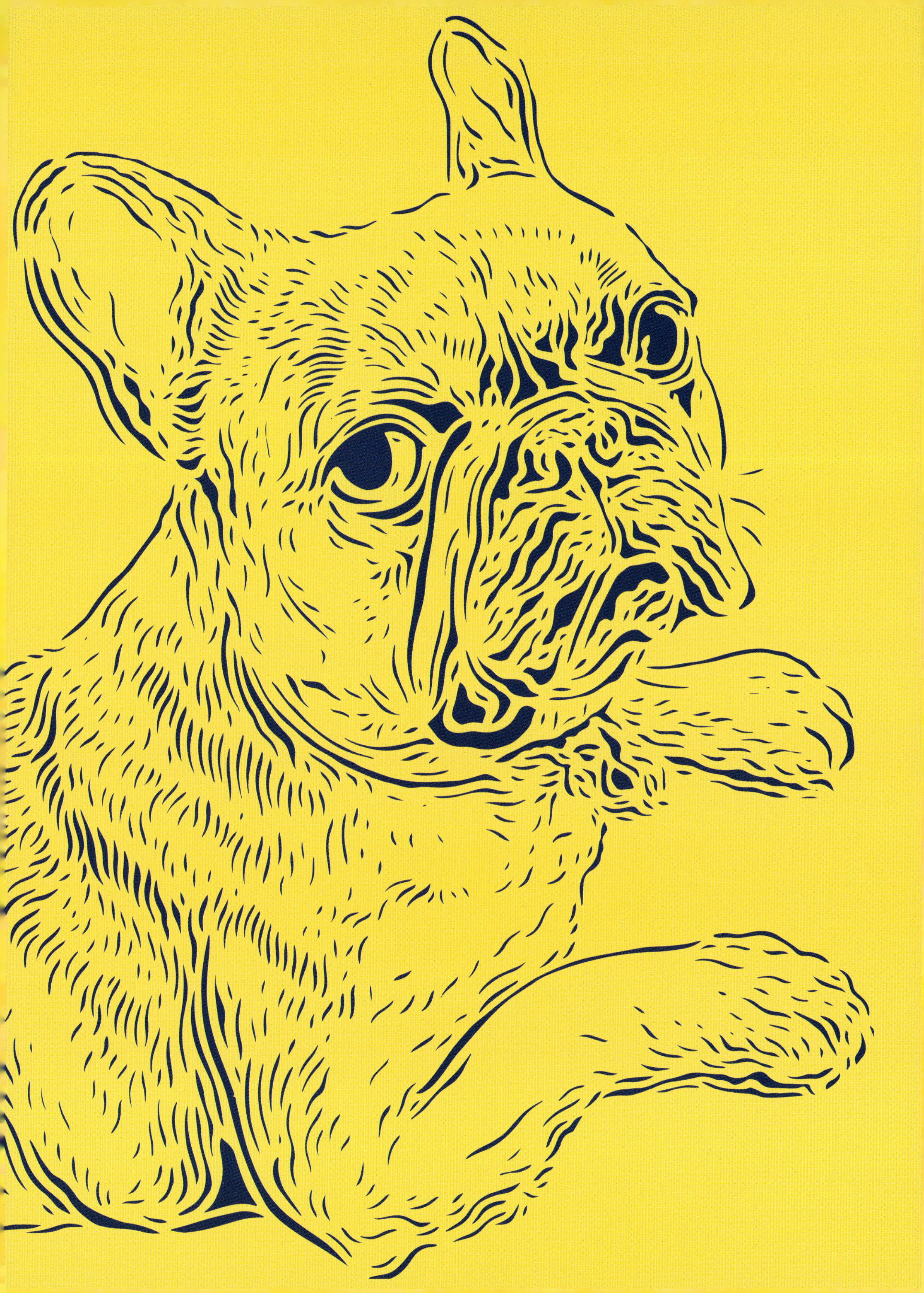

1. Portrait of my mother, Patricia Bonnefon (1960–1979), by Logan Hicks, 2018. The crackling of the paint drops is reminiscent of the graining of old photos.

2. Stinkfish, *Black Thorns Kid*, 2011. Portrait in tribal style.

PORTRAIT

Today, most artists starting out or using stencils choose portraiture, but this hasn't always been the case. When I started out in 2006, it was a minor genre, represented in France by Jef Aerosol, in Italy by Sten & Lex and in the United States by Swoon. In fact, most of the stencils you saw in the streets at the time were inspired by Banksy and showed off standing characters and logos, for satiric and protest purposes. Starting in 2007, stencil artists began to really focus on portraits, refining and making their cutouts more complex to make their subjects more realistic. Since then, many portraitists have emerged, such as Fin Dac and Snik, and it seems that portraiture has become the most nourished genre in the stencil world.

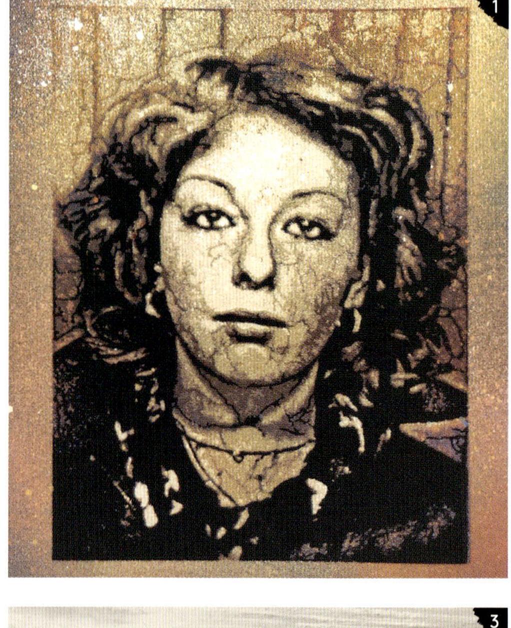

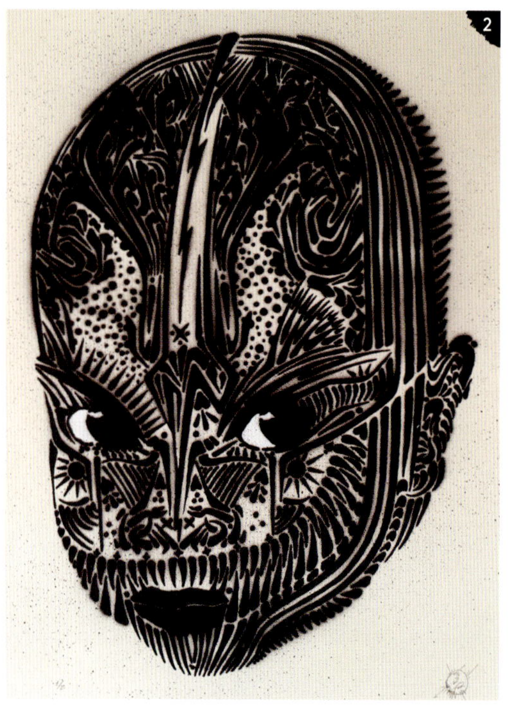

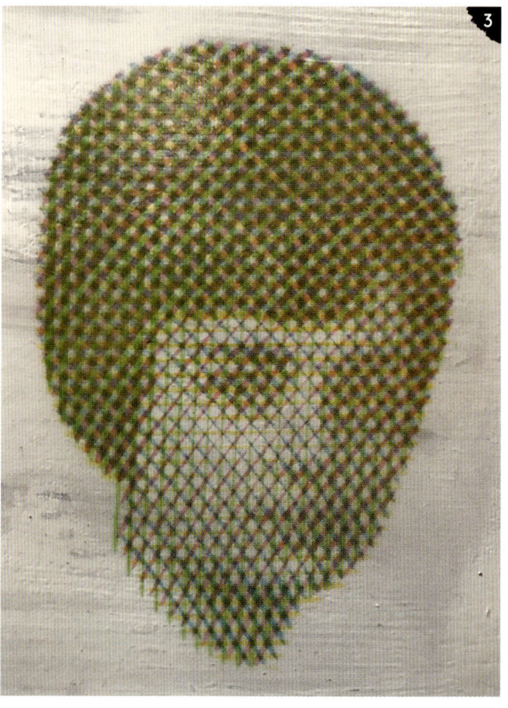

3. Sten & Lex, 2008. Portrait made in offset-inspired geometric lattice.

4. C215, Paris, 2018.

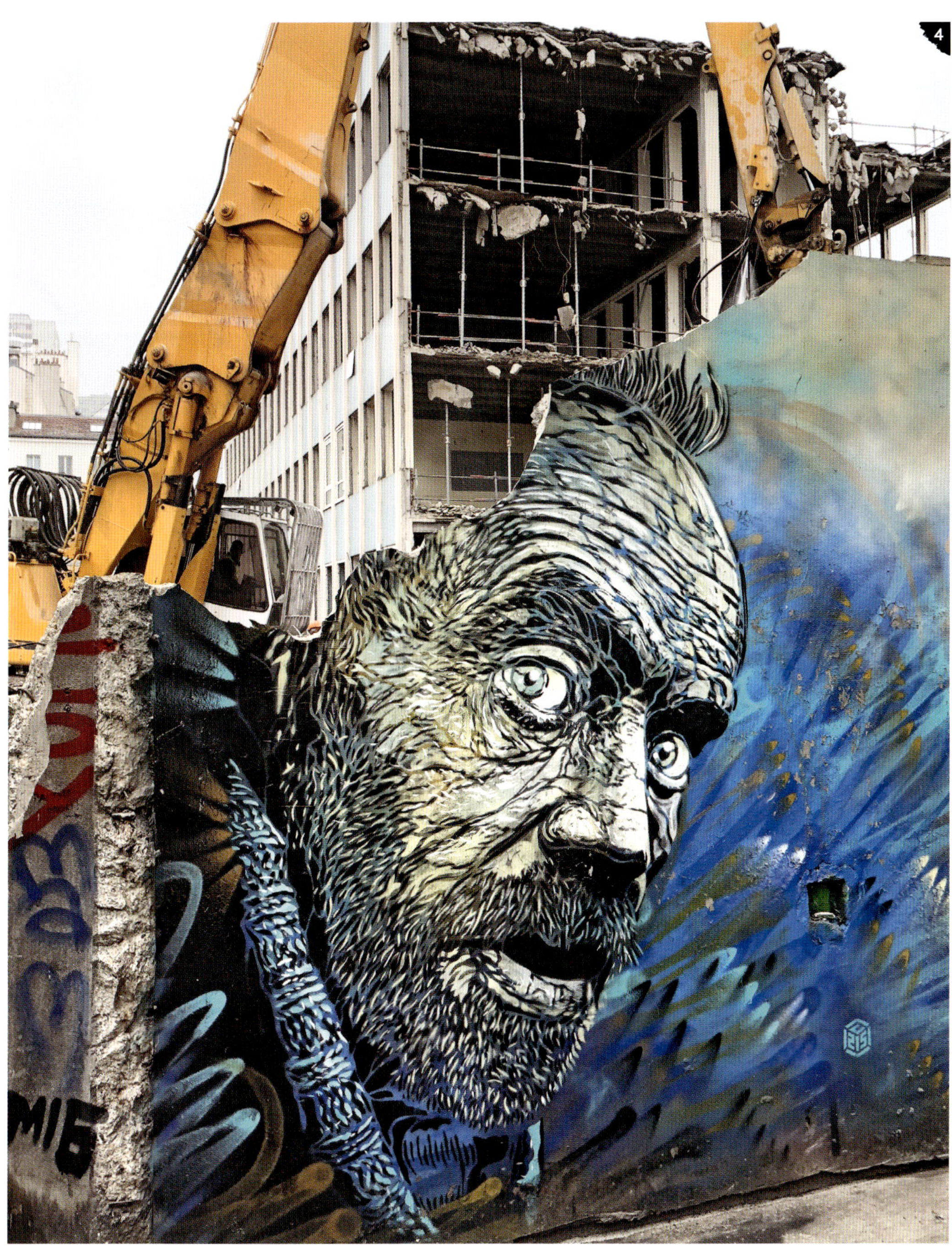

1. Wrdsmth, London, 2016.

2. Ben Eine, *A–Z (Red Glitter)*, 2018. Polychrome typography created from several stencils.

3. Banksy, New York, 2013. A typical example of typographic art with aesthetic interest stemming from its placement and the meaning of its message.

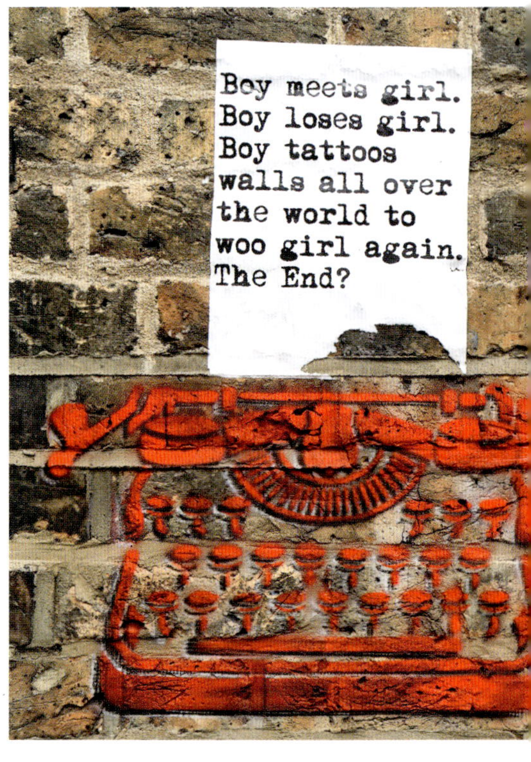

TEXT

When painting text, contrast and legibility go hand in hand. This is why it's important to ensure that the colors used for the text and the colors of the support are sufficiently contrasted so as to facilitate reading.

Ever since the Industrial Age, text has been marked using stencils, leading to today's stencil typographies by graphic designers. You can find them in the Stencil category of the online typographic database www.dafont.com.

Some stencil artists have especially distinguished themselves in typographic art. Many cultivate strong messages by focusing not on consideration of form, but on great contextual relevance, such as Wrdsmth or Banksy. Others, like Ben Eine, have developed a whole body of messages and slogans, designing their typography with an extraordinary aesthetic sense.

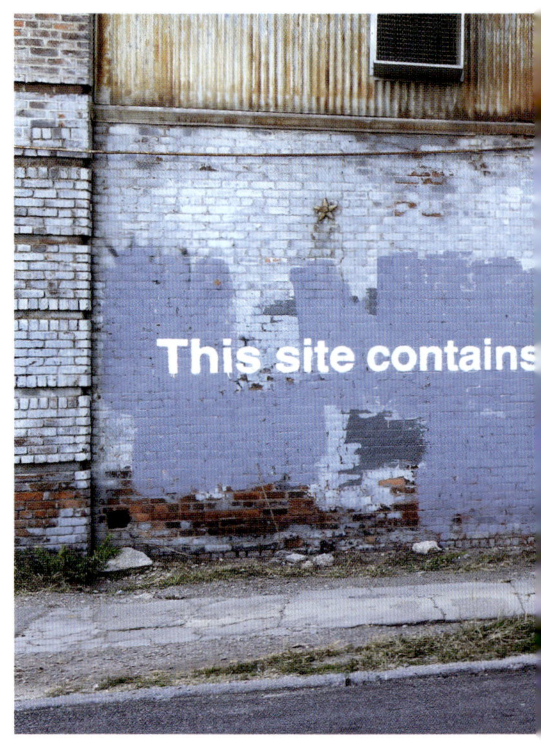

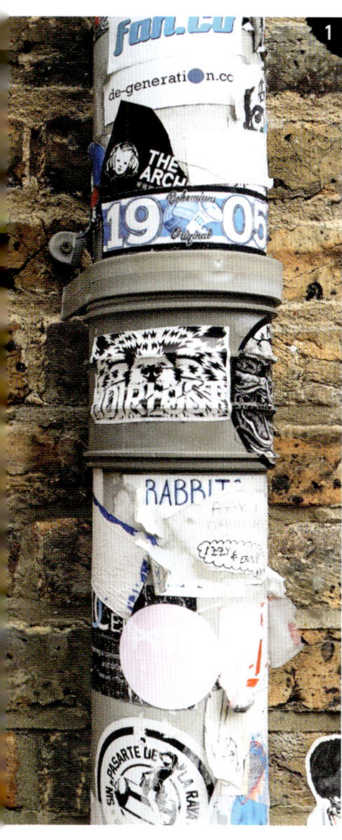
19 05

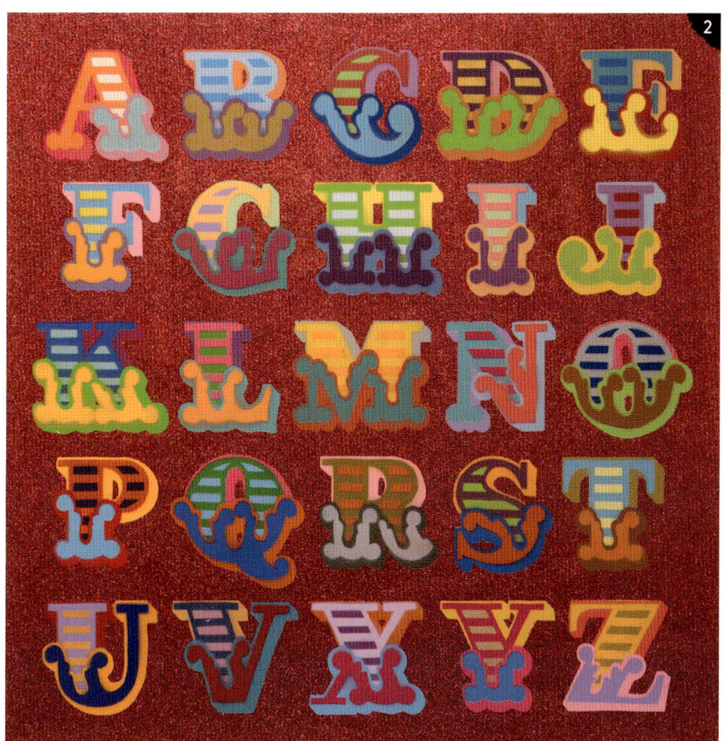
ABCDE
FGHIJ
KLMNO
PQRST
UVXYZ

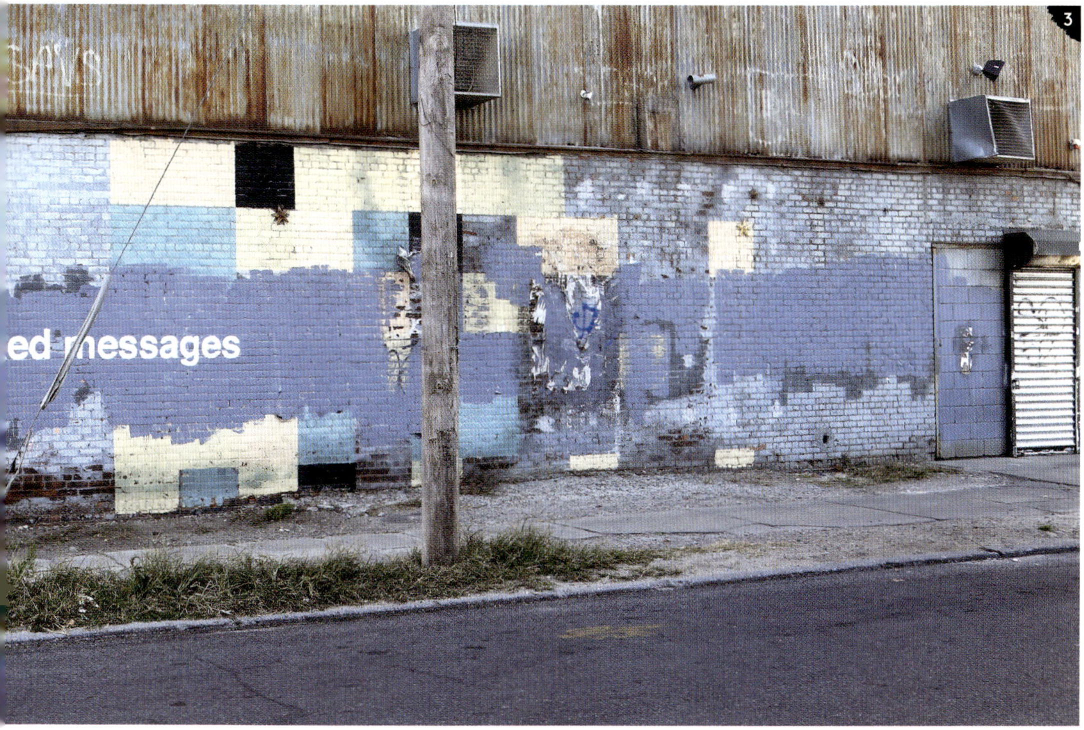

INTERVIEW WITH BEN EINE

Since the late 1990s, Ben Eine has been recognized as the undisputed master of typographic stencil art. In London and around the world, his large frescoes hammer words such as Amazing or Scary, which comment on both a social context and a notion.

Website: www.einesigns.com

Instagram: @einesigns

Why did you choose stencils rather than another painting technique?

Stencils lend themselves to a particular type of paint, the spray can, which is the type I prefer. They allow me to create and add more complex and detailed elements to my work. Passersby rarely believe it, but my creations are done freehand. I use stencils only for the horizontal stripes in my letters. Thanks to stenciling, I can re-create them identically over and over again. *Stop Knife Crime* is a good example: I painted fourteen letters in my NewCircus font on a 69-foot-long (21-meter) wall on Old Street. Stencils usually allow me to control the details of my work.

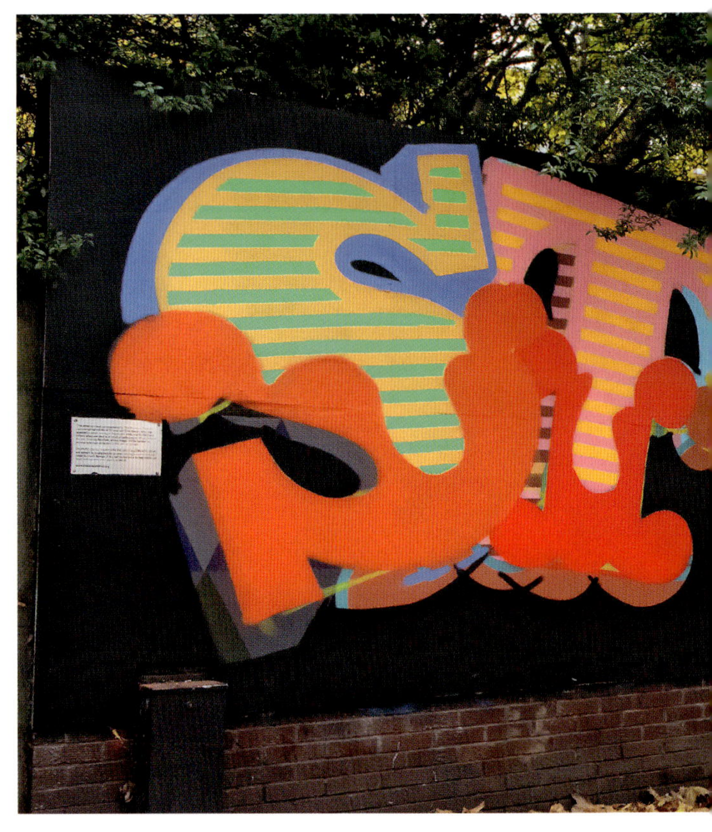

Stop Knife Crime, London, 2008.

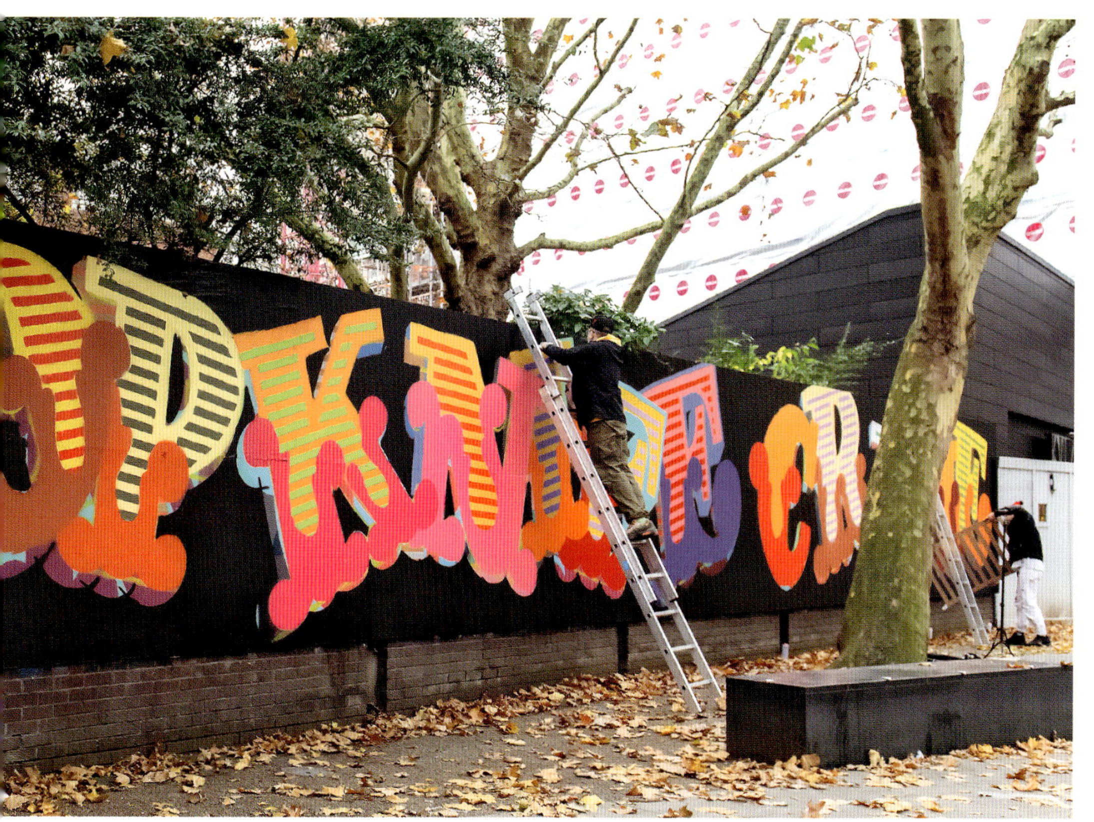

1. *Dance to the Radio (Teal) (Black Glass)*, 2018.

2 and 3. Work in progress: *Working Class Hero*, stencil on canvas, 2017.

How do you make your stencils?
I draw the image freehand and scan or simulate it digitally. Then I scale it, print it or project it onto a sheet of paper. I choose the thickness of the paper according to the type of surface I'm going to work on. Then I cut it with a utility knife.

How do you see the evolution of stencil techniques since you started out?
I would say that digitization has advanced stencil technique. Digital tools have allowed artists to create more complex stencils, separating an unlimited number of colors and elements.

Who are the artists who inspire you in your stencil work?
Banksy, Shepard Fairey, Logan Hicks and, of course, our French master, Christian Guémy, a.k.a. C215.

What are the limits of stencils as a tool?
There are not many of them. Just as with silkscreen or block printing, you can reproduce an image with extreme precision. Digital tools allow you to achieve the level of detail required, and when it comes to dimension, methods such as laser cutting offer the possibility of creating huge layouts that can virtually cover soccer fields. For example, my *Create for Zippo* piece (see p. 75) in East London, where stencils were used to make the details of the contours sharp, covers 57,415 square feet (17,500 square meters). It's one of the largest paintings in the world. Even when complications come up such as bad weather or uneven surfaces, stenciling is no problem as long as you take into account the material from which the stencil's made.

For you, is a stencil a frame or a freedom?
Certainly a freedom. I'm not strictly a stencil artist, but I think it's a powerful tool, and I use it a lot to get the rendering I want. My brand-new font, Keyline, recently used for the *More Than Words* mural on the Great Eastern Art Wall in London, is one of my most complex fonts to date. It integrates up to a hundred colors in a single piece, which would be impossible without the stencil technique. It's a question of when and how to use it. It's not a wise decision to limit yourself to one medium or method; it's better to master several skills.

Can you describe your studio for us?
Organized chaos. There are objects everywhere, all my materials and lots of paintings, ideas and things that inspire me stuck on the wall.

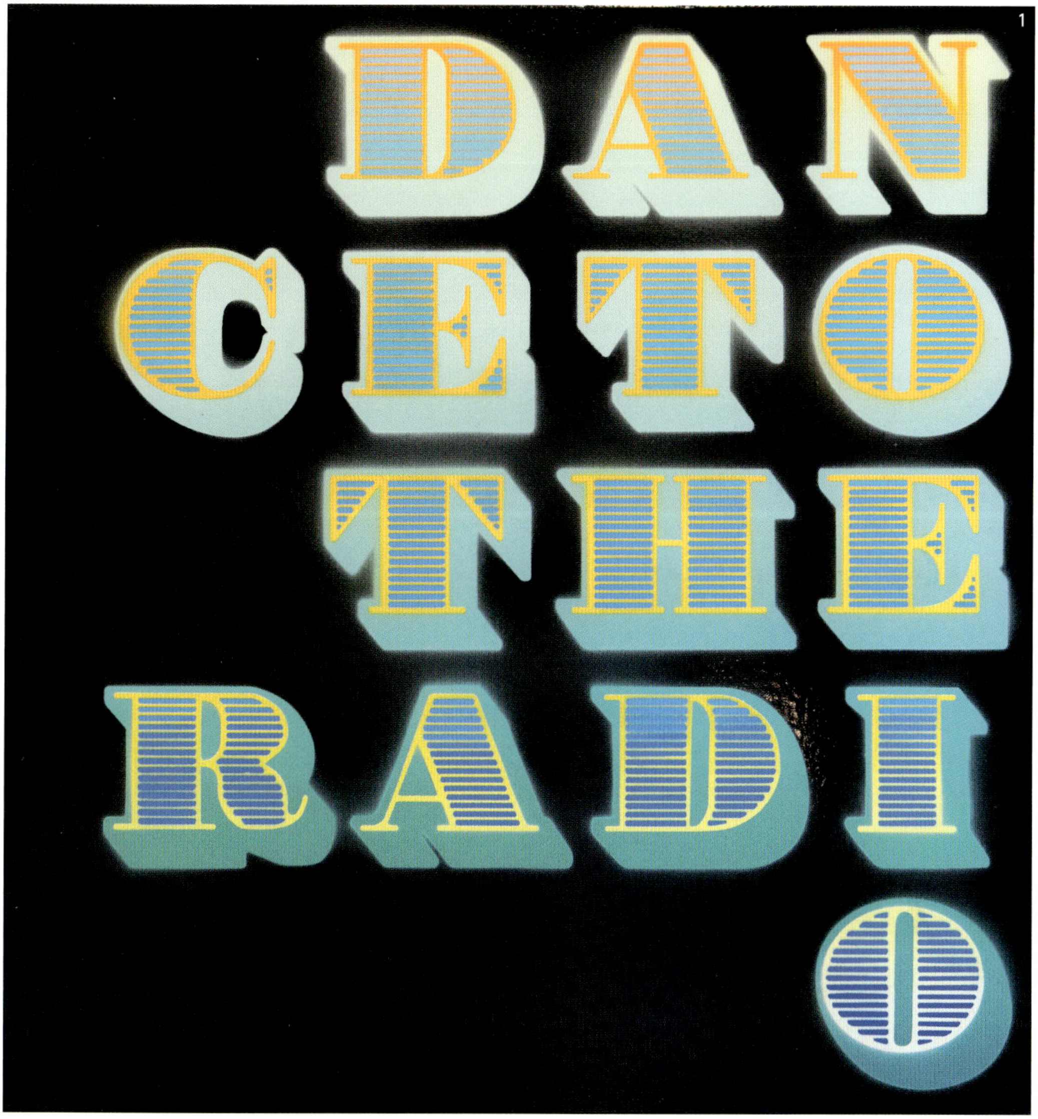

1
DAN
CETO
THE
RADI
O

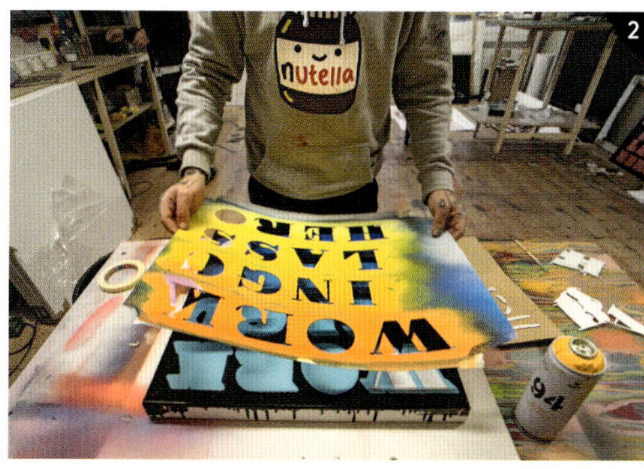
2
nutella

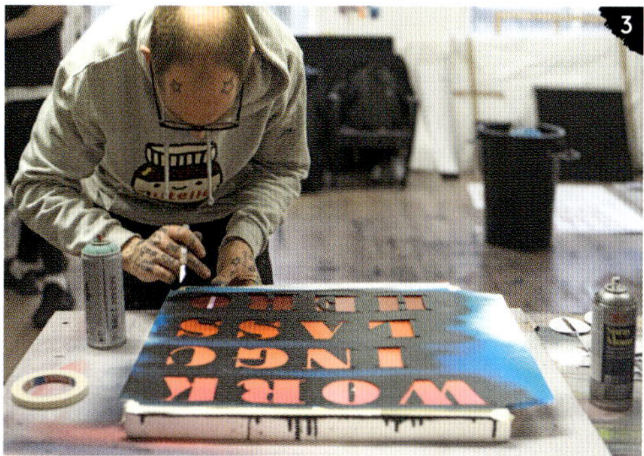
3

1. Stencil matrix, *Assignée à résistance*.

2. Working in the studio.

3. Street stencil, Paris, 2017.

INTERVIEW WITH MISS.TIC

Miss.Tic has tirelessly marked the history of stencil art just as much as she's marked Parisian walls since the early 1980s. Her feminist and poetic aphorisms, which adjoin her monochrome creations, most often female portraits, are an integral part of the identity of Paris.

Site: missticinparis.com
Instagram: @missticofficial
Facebook: @missticofficiel

Why did you choose stencils rather than another painting technique?

When I started working on the walls of Paris in 1985, the first urban activists used several painting techniques. At the time, the term "street art" had not yet been invented. Some hijacked posters from acrylic billboards, and others worked with a paint pot and a brush, like Jérôme Mesnager. Most people were using spray paint and stencils.

Seeing these young artists at work gave me the idea to use this medium to express myself through drawing and words. Stenciling proved to be the simplest method to print the same subject several times.

How do you make your stencils?

After drawing a character, usually on A3-size paper, I photocopy it to the size I want—I enlarge or reduce it. I then glue this reproduction onto either a sheet of 300 gsm paper (when the stencils are designed for the studio), or 1-millimeter-thick cardboard (when they're matrices intended for the outside). Then I cut out the drawing with a cutter and blades. Same process for my quotations; after printing the text, it's glued on the cardboard and cut out.

How do you see the evolution of stencil techniques since you started out?

In the beginning, for the same image there was often only one or even two layers of stencil. With the use of computers and drawing software, stencils are getting closer and closer to the aesthetics of photography and the airbrush technique with several stencils.

Who are the artists who inspire you in your stencil work?

My first two influences were Ernest Pignon-Ernest and Gérard Zlotykamien.

What are the limits of stencils as a tool?

All tools have limits; that's why it's not against the rules to use more than one medium.

For you, is a stencil a frame or a freedom?

A stencil is not a frame; rather, it's a technique within a frame, and if one chooses to use it, it must be in complete freedom.

Can you describe your studio for us?

My studio isn't very big, because I made the choice not to relocate to the suburbs, and staying in Paris is very expensive! The lack of space forces me to tidy up often and to tidy up well . . . I spend two-thirds of my time in my studio. I've put in a bunk there to be able to take naps, because it's difficult to be there from dawn to dusk.

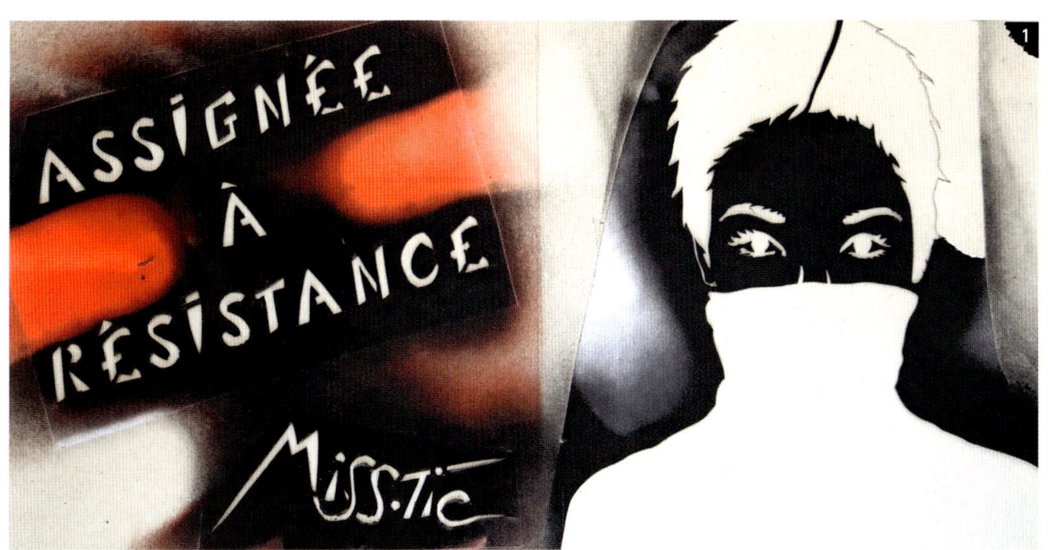
1
ASSIGNÉE
À
RÉSISTANCE
MISS.TIC

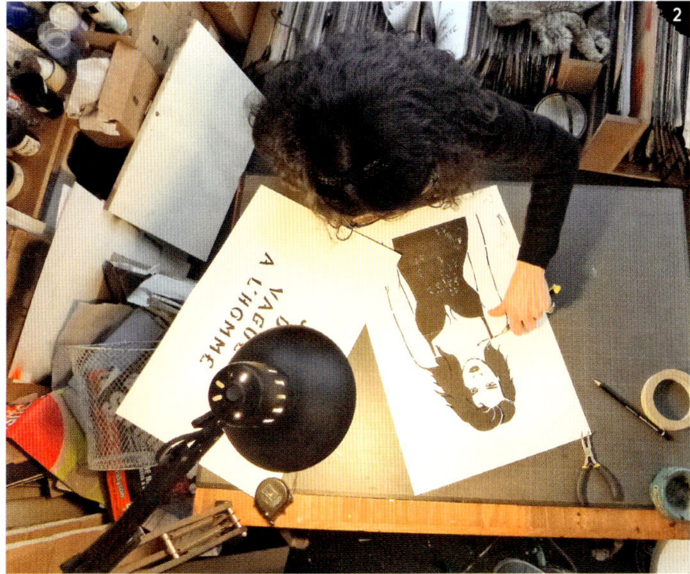
2

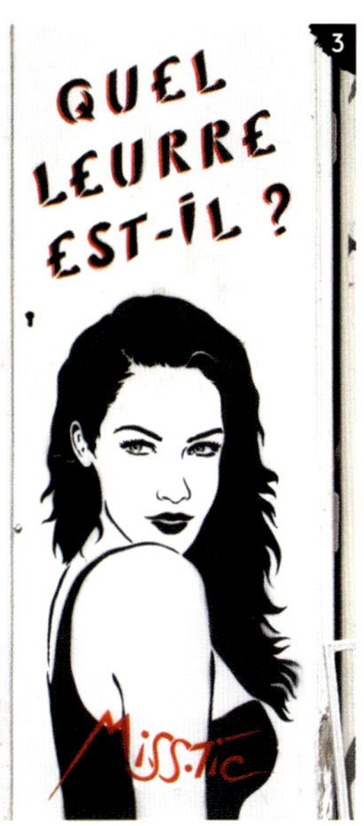
3
QUEL
LEURRE
EST-IL ?
MISS.TIC

ARCHITECTURE

A certain tradition of urban stencil refers to the representation of architecture. I tried it myself from 2008 to 2010. It is a genre in its own right, which could be compared to landscape drawing. While some have produced urban views with virtuosity, such as Logan Hicks, now considered the undisputed master in the field, others have sought, using elements of "urban grammar" (windows, doors, etc.), to reconstruct, in miniature versions, buildings on street furniture. Evol is a brilliant example of this mise en abyme of the city.

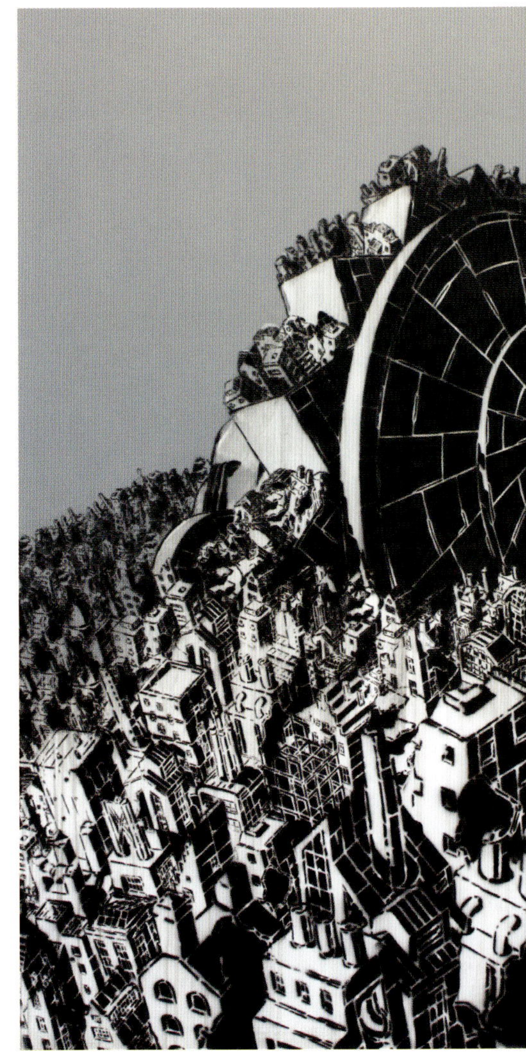

1. M-city, 2008. Composition on canvas made from architectural modules.

2. C215, Istanbul, 2009. An example of an architectural mise en abyme.

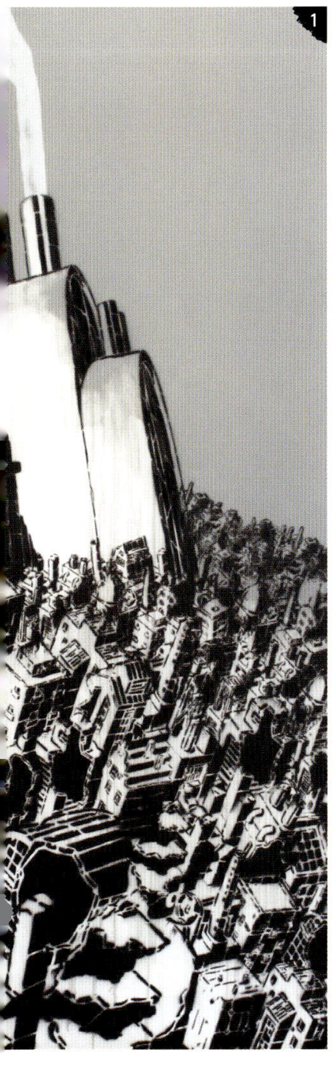

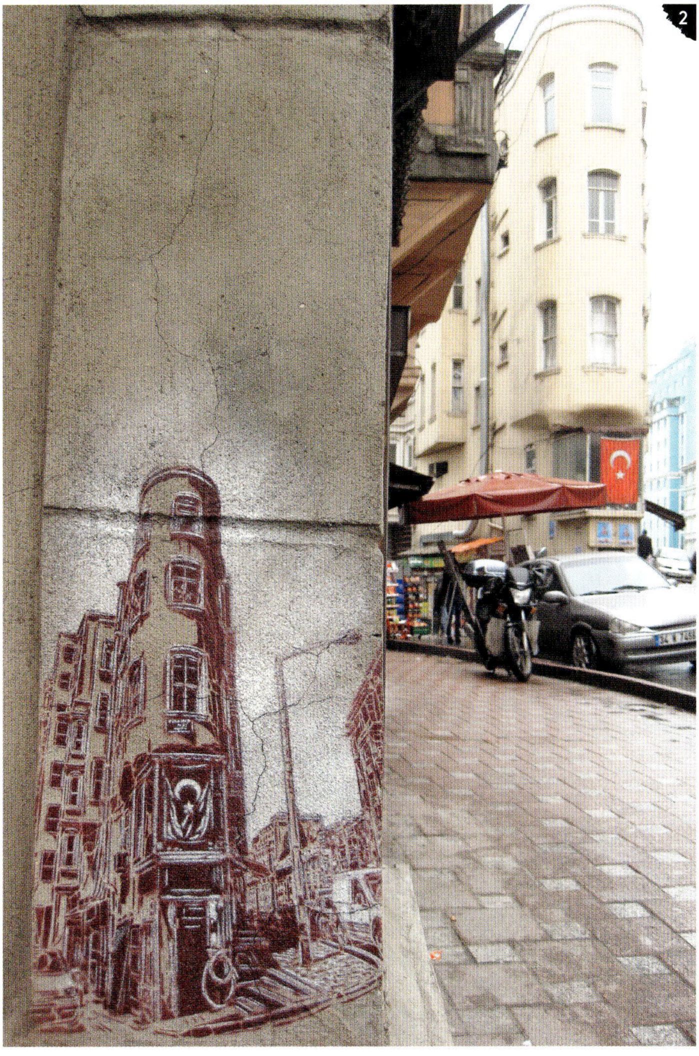

INTERVIEW WITH LOGAN HICKS

Checking the *No End in Sight* stencil before the third coat of paint, 2013.

The American artist Logan Hicks is one of the first to have created artwork by superimposing layers of different colors. Trained as a serigrapher, he has become a key figure in stencil art. Also a photographer, he is one of the rare stencil artists who paints without simply applying the flat layers. The nocturnal, electric atmospheres of his work are among the greatest classics in the history of stenciling.

Site: workhorsevisuals.com
Instagram: @loganhicksny
Facebook: LoganHicksPage

Why did you choose stencils rather than another painting technique?
Stencils are the mirror of what I think. For years I wanted to be the kind of artist who could just take a jar of paint and a blank canvas and turn it into a work of art, but that's not the way my brain works! I see the elements in layers: I can see the good and the bad, the easy and the complex, the ugly and the beautiful at the same time. Stencils have so many different layers, which means I can process all the thoughts that go along with my artwork. I feel like every painting I produce is four works of art in one, because of the amount of thought I put into each layer.

How do you make your stencils?
There are four steps to making a stencil. The first step is to take a picture. I travel a lot and take pictures all the time. I can go months without making a "physical" stencil, but I don't stop working because I know that every picture I take has the potential to become a stencil.

The second step, probably the most annoying but also the most important, takes place on the computer. Once I have determined which photo could be converted into a stencil, I work on the image to match my vision. From there, I break down the image into high, medium and low contrast and then proceed to make the bridges. This connecting process keeps all the details together once the stencil is cut. The first layer always contains the most detail and will be the darkest color. I start on a black background and build the layers by painting directly on the previous one; this helps to build the colors. The last layer usually represents only the highlights of the piece and contains as little detail as possible. On my screen, everything is in black and white. I don't care about the colors at this stage; I only look at the amount of detail and if everything reads well. If a piece doesn't look good monochromatically, it won't be better just because I add color. I've used up to twenty layers for a single stencil, but I usually limit myself to five.

The third step, cutting out, takes place once the image has been prepared, cut into layers, and I have been able to visualize on my computer how things will unfold. If I'm working on a mural, I separate the stencil into pieces. If it's a smaller painting, I print it right away. Depending on the size and complexity of the stencil, it can be cut by hand or by machine. Once the stencil is cut, almost all the work is done. The last and most fun step is spray painting. This is where the color comes in. With the stencil being a rigid support produced according to very precise steps, I leave myself a certain freedom of interpretation with the paint. I try to paint the world as I see it rather than as it is. Sometimes it can look like the original photo. Most of the time, it doesn't.

How do you see the evolution of stencil techniques since you started out?
When you start making stencils, the technical limitations are enormous. In the beginning, I spent much of my time trying to match the stencil to the vision I had in my head. It's frustrating to have an image in your head but your hands can't make it happen!

Creativity is a language that has no clear direction. Art tries to speak a language that is not written down. I spent years looking for a way to speak the language that was mine. Once I learned it, my motivation was to try to understand what I wanted to say.

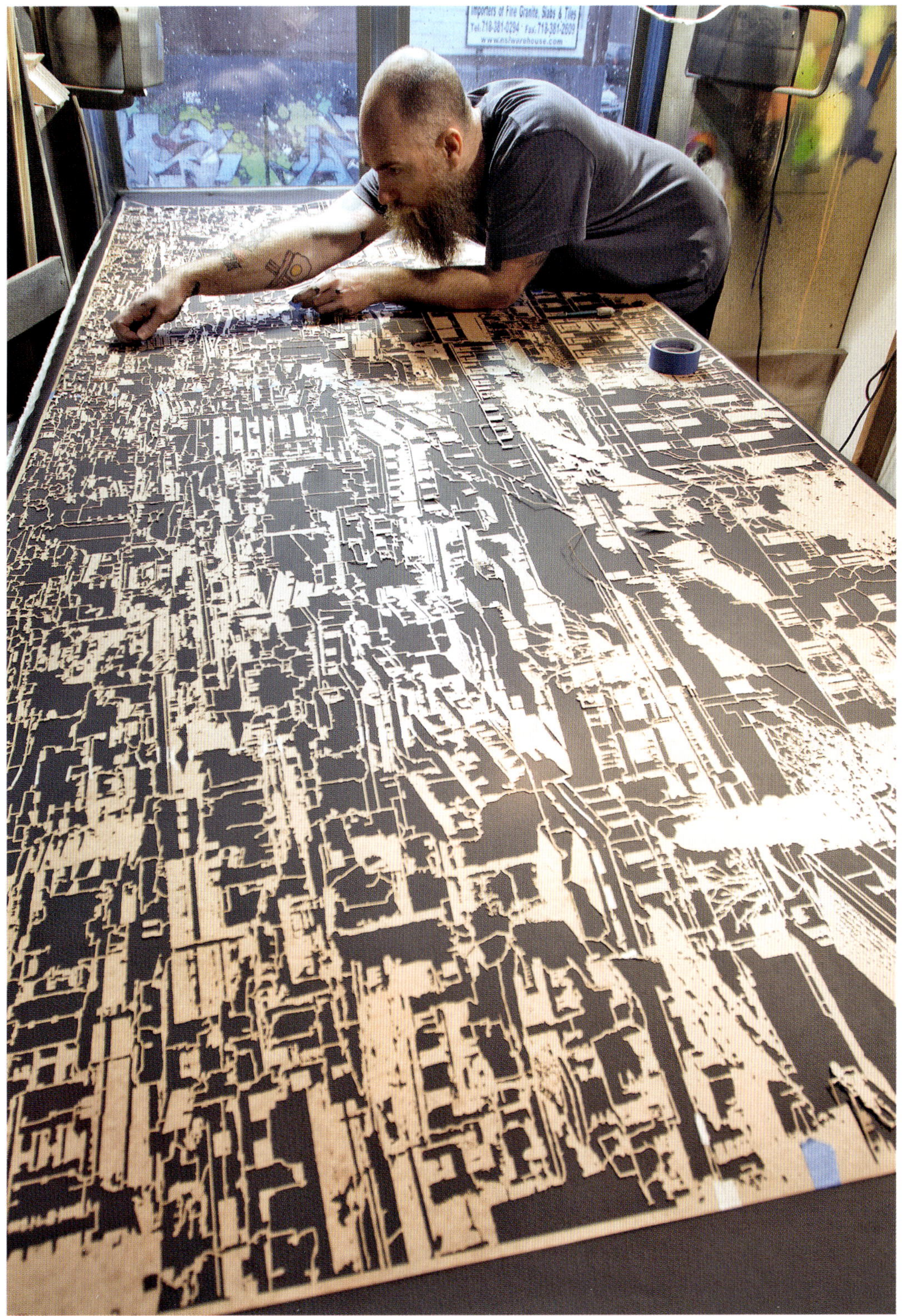
Importers of Fine Granite, Slabs & Tiles
Tel. 718-381-0294 · Fax: 718-381-2609
www.nslwarehouse.com

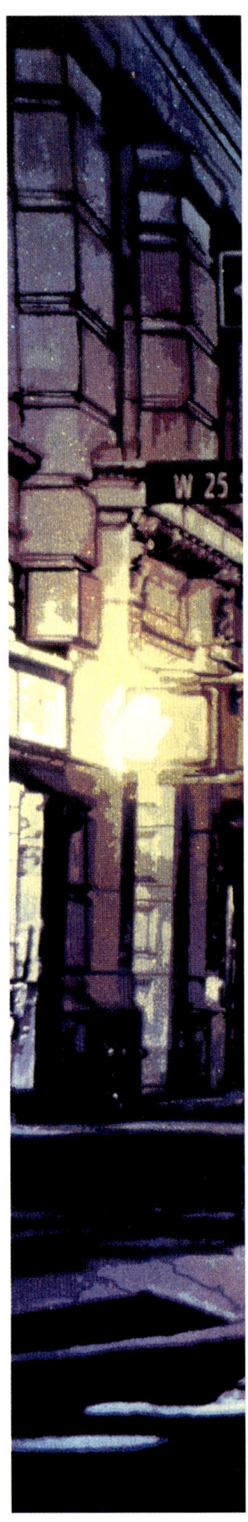

Travel North, 2018. Spray can on canvas.

It took me almost eight years before my technique matched my ideas. Then I started to explore other limitations such as the use of color, different layers, sizes, subjects. Ten years after my first attempts, I managed to reach my goal: to use my stencils to paint the ideas I had in mind.

Who are the artists who inspire you in your stencil work?

I tend to be attracted to artists who work with their hands as much as with their brains, the "intellectual working class." The first two stencil artists I met in the mid-1990s were Chris Francis and Chris Stain. It was in Baltimore, Maryland. Chris Stain's work was about minorities and workers, Chris Francis' work was about the struggles of people who were precarious or disenfranchised. Both were critical of my initial exploration of stencils. Christian Guémy had a great influence on me because of the subjects he treated in painting and his mastery of color.

People who influence me do not do so because they use stencils, but because their artwork offers a vision and representation of the world.

Shepard Fairey is the one who originally inspired me and pushed me to pursue my art after my studies. When I graduated from university, I felt out of touch with the art world. Shepard visited me in Baltimore in 1996. Seeing his approach to art, with posters and artwork that were more affordable and easier to understand, I decided to leave Baltimore for California and pursue the stencils I had started.

Many other artists inspire me and push me to surpass myself, such as Miya Ando, who has a very fluid approach and whose work appeals as much to the emotion as to the intellect, or Joe Iurato, who uses stencils to speak an authentic language, in line with his experience.

What are the limits of stencils as a tool?

I've been drawing stencils for decades, so I see fewer limitations than before, but they still pose problems. The slightest mistake can derail a painting. If the stencil is misaligned, it destroys a piece; it's the same if the layer lifts when you paint; if you cut in the wrong place; if you step on the stencil; if you drop it or if it gets stuck on something, it will tear; if you don't have the right tips; if you don't shake the paint long enough; if the material in which you cut your stencil is too thin or too thick; if you use the wrong color; if you paint a surface that is too rough; if the Scotch tape that holds the stencil sticks to the paint and tears when you remove it; if the stencil sticks to the surface of the painting . . . There are so many possible technical problems! Producing a beautiful work of art with stencils is like threading a needle in the middle of a storm.

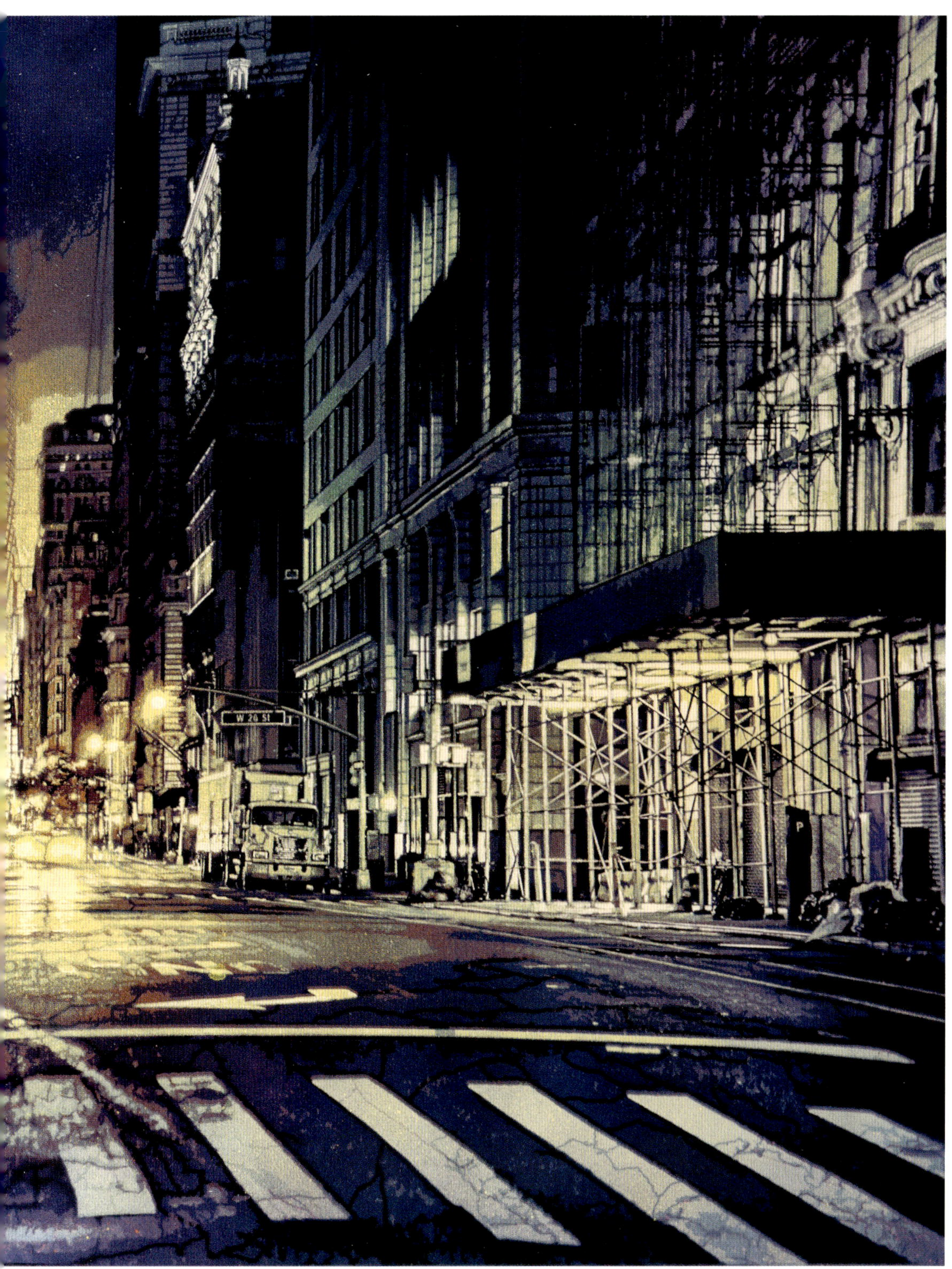

For you, is a stencil a frame or a freedom?

It is neither one nor the other; it's simply a necessity. I need something that allows me to create art and stencils. Making art is like having a conversation: the materials talk to you, the stencils tell you the details to capture, the paint tells you how to capture the light, your hands show you how precisely you can follow your idea. Stencils are just one of the many things you'll use to build that conversation.

Creating stencils takes a lot of time. It slows me down, helps me think and visualize the work I want to do. I come from a working-class background, blue collar, so working with my hands has always been part of my accomplishments. Even if you don't think stenciling is a physical job, it can be. Especially when it comes to painting a large format. I can usually tell if I'm happy with the work I've done based on how exhausted I am at the end of the day: if my body is tired and my mind is numb, it means that I've devoted myself entirely to the work in progress.

Can you describe your studio for us?

My workshop is small, but extremely organized. I have all the colors in the Montana paint line, although I probably use only about 20% of the shades. I like being able to visualize the full spectrum; it reminds me that anything is possible. I keep the stencils I use, so they cover my shelves, wrapped in kraft paper, with their names on the outside. Every brush, canvas, spray can, power tool and book has its place. When my studio is messy, it drives me crazy and I usually stop working to tidy it up. My stencils and space reflect my meticulous approach to creating.

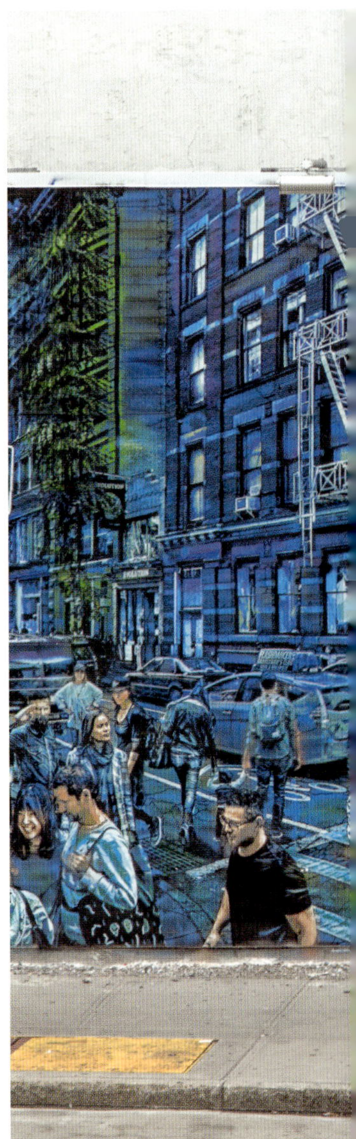

Story of My Life, Bowery Wall, New York, 2016.

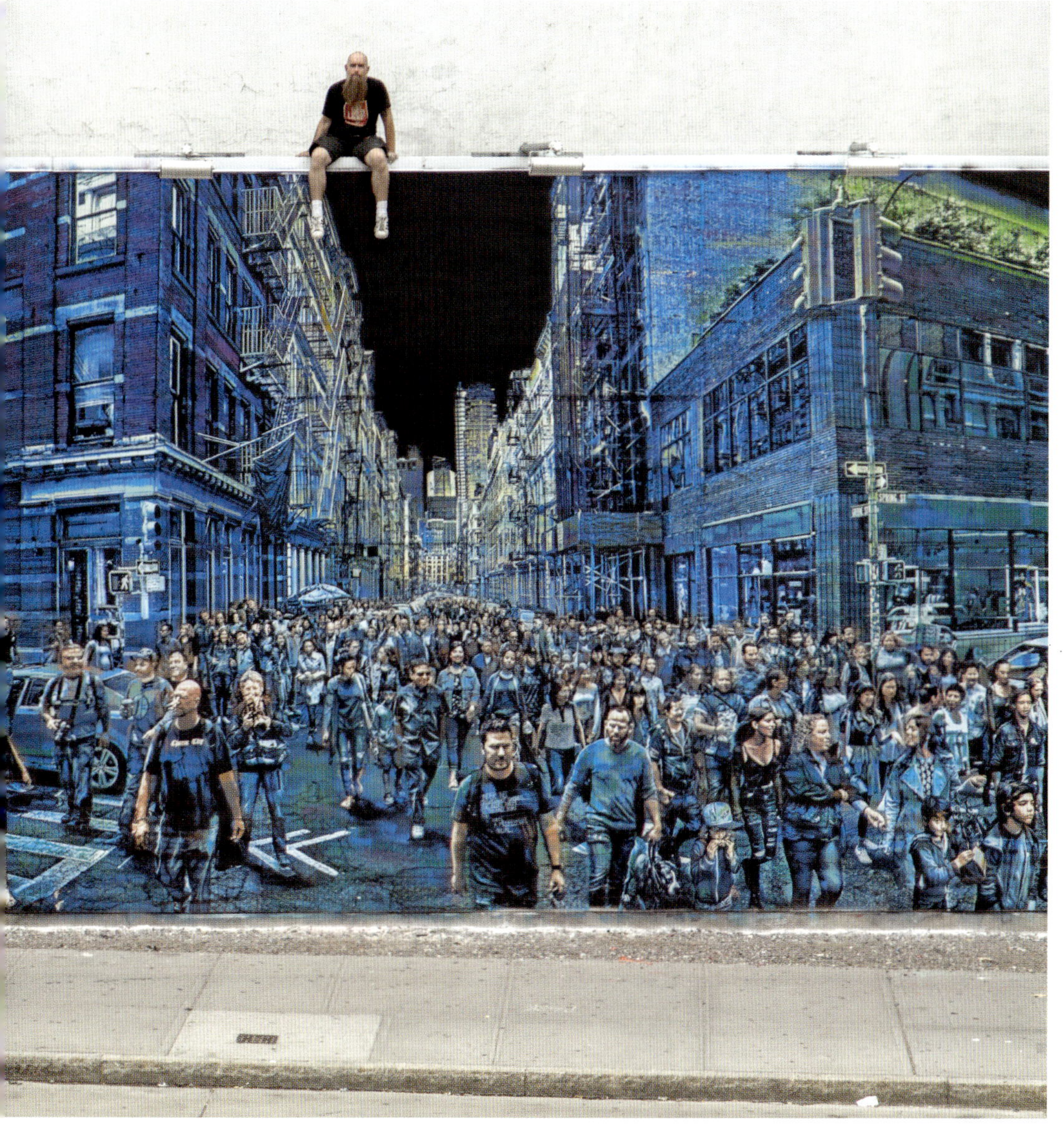

INTERVIEW WITH EVOL

Evol is a Berlin-based artist known for his work in miniaturizing modern architecture on street furniture. He reproduces a multitude of windows and facades by reducing them to the sides of electrical boxes or on cardboard boxes, going so far as to create true trompe-l'oeil. He succeeds marvelously in converting his digital work into a visual work of art.

Site: www.evoltaste.com
Instagram: @rinkveld
Facebook: EVOL.ct

Why did you choose stencils rather than another painting technique?

Even though I always drew a lot, I never really liked to paint with brushes: mixing colors, cleaning the supplies . . . it wasn't for me. Thanks to spray cans, I discovered graffiti. For me, it was a way to draw on a large scale, quickly, with premixed colors, and easy to use on many surfaces. Painting outdoors was also a defining experience.

Two reasons pushed me to experiment with stencils. First, I love the quality of the painted surface, totally uniform and flat. Previously, printing was the only way to obtain that result. But unlike screen printing, which requires a lot of technical equipment as well as time to carry out the different steps, stenciling is much simpler and faster! All you need is paper or plastic, a sharp blade, a little patience, a spray can and you're ready to go. You can reuse the cut stencils, experiment easily with colors, etc. The second advantage of the stencil is that it is flexible and quick to paint once cut. For a complex illustration, the creation of the stencil can be done without time constraints, at home. Then you can paint it very quickly wherever you want.

How do you make your stencils?

After all these years, the process of creating my stencils has definitely changed a bit. It's now very rare that I draw directly with a blade. Most of the time, I create a digital vector illustration from drawings or photos I've done. This allows me to then adapt them to the desired dimensions. I obtain the photorealistic results I want to achieve thanks to a layering technique and the use of transparencies. Thus, in my creative process, I decide on the printing order of each layer, each color. These choices arise from the particular needs of the design. There isn't really a standard procedure: sometimes it's better to go from dark to light or from light to dark, sometimes to have a combination of both. Thanks to the computer, you can check the result beforehand and predict, for example, the number of transparent layers. It sounds complicated, but it's still a little crazy! When I finish the illustration, I feel like I literally hand-drew every hole in the stencil set, even though it was all done digitally.

The next step is to produce the stencil. For many years, I printed on paper, assembled and glued the pieces on thicker paper and then cut each hole by hand with a cutter. Since this part of the process took as long as the creation of the illustration (up to a week or more), it became more economical to let a machine cut out the holes for me. I use paper for shop work and thin acetate, which is stronger and more durable, and it doesn't matter if it gets wet when I'm working in the street.

How do you see the evolution of stencil techniques since you started out?

The principle remains the same, but my practice has become much more refined over the years. In the beginning, I mainly used one color per layer, and the paint was fairly evenly distributed. The more you master your technique, the more freely you can use it. I've experimented with mixing shades within a layer, applying colors in blurred, light shades, etc. I have also experimented with using a combination of shades within a layer. I started to lift the stencils partially or totally to soften the edges, to give a blurred look, like a false depth of field.

Gold Is the New Grey, Vladivostok (Russia), 2017. Transformation of an electrical box into a modern building.

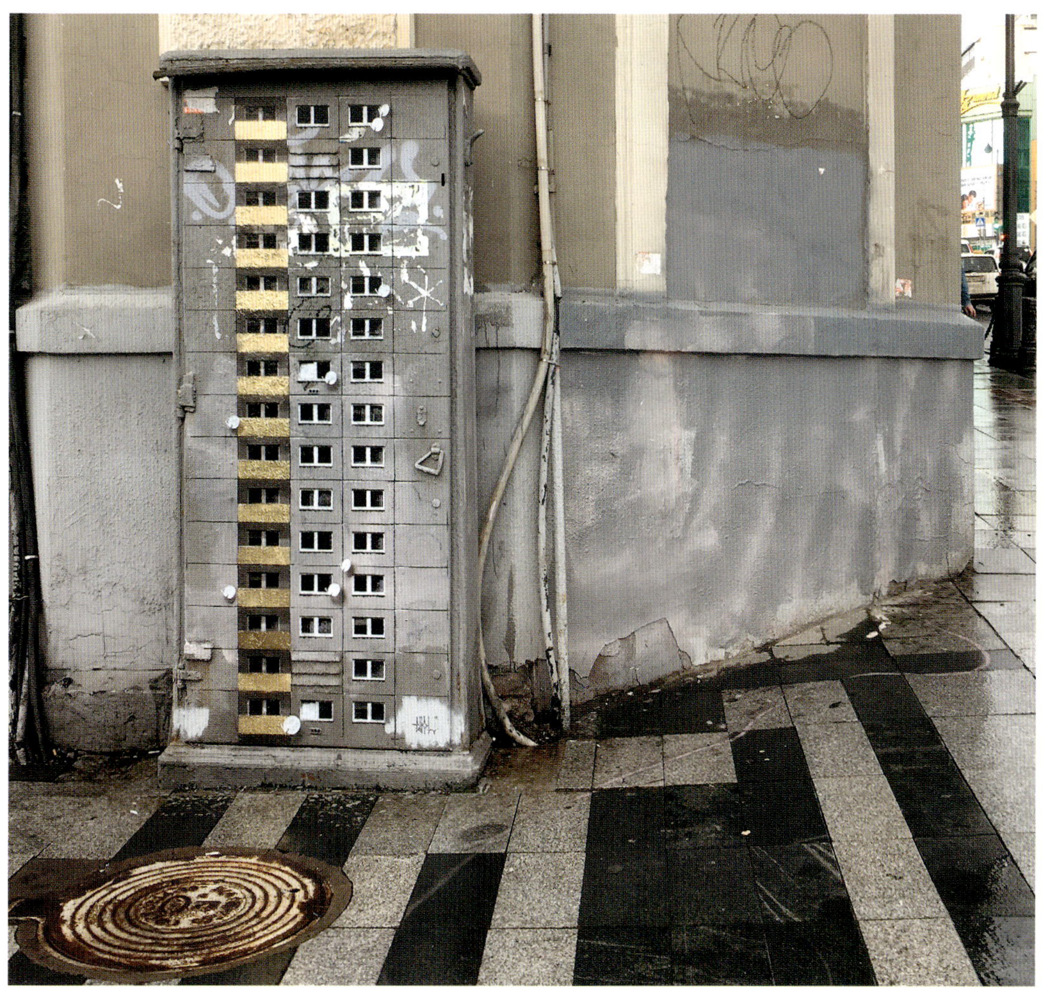

Exportware, 2012. Aerosol paint on cardboard.

Who are the artists who inspire you in your stencil work?
None, as a matter of fact. Starting from the mechanics of screenprinting, I developed and refined my technique myself. Nevertheless, this happened at a time when stencils were beginning to be reborn. Of course, some stencil artists have always been important to me. When I first began, there was an excellent site, Stencil Revolution, where you could see what was going on in the world and also discuss each other's work. In the beginning, I worked very closely with Pisa73 and we pushed each other's boundaries. Seeing Logan Hicks' work for the first time (I think I still had the nickname Workhors at the time) was a shock. It was a mural in a small gallery in Berlin. It struck me because of its size. And he was the first artist close to me that I saw using stencils with more than three or four layers. Unlike me, he praises what I would call the "flaw" of stencils, the bridges that are needed, whereas I tend to hide them in my work. Another important artist for me is Mariusz Waras (M-city), who I also met a long time ago. The size of his murals and the speed with which he executes them are incredible. But even more incredible is the way he treats his stencils or, to be honest, the way he walks on them.

What are the limits of stencils as a tool?
As you say, it's a tool. You can't drill with a hammer. So there are a lot of limits. Size is one of them. For very large surfaces, it's often better to paint freehand or use a projector as a guide. Who can carry huge stencils anyway?

At the opposite extreme, my stencils have become so detailed and the holes to be cut have become so small that the physical structure of the paper has become a problem when cutting. And if you compare the process to drawing, these constraints make you lose spontaneity.

For you, is a stencil a frame or a freedom?
Maybe both. Like I said, it's a tool. Within a given framework, it gives me a certain freedom. If I want to do something else, I use another tool.

Can you describe your studio for us?
Since my process is divided into two parts, digital and manual, I have a room for the computer and a space to paint and do all the manual activities, such as woodwork or modeling.

Apart from a large drawer with a few hundred layers and two shelves containing a hundred spray cans, paint, brushes, masking tape and other small tools, there is not much furniture. I prefer to paint the boxes flat on the floor. So I covered half of the studio floor with pressed cardboard to staple my cardboard to and prevent it from moving when I paint. Apparently even as a child I preferred to work on the floor.

And then there's this collection of hundreds of found cardboard pieces. For me, the supports are as important as what I paint: their textures, their imprints, their history . . . I collect them everywhere I go. Sometimes I send them to myself at home by mail.

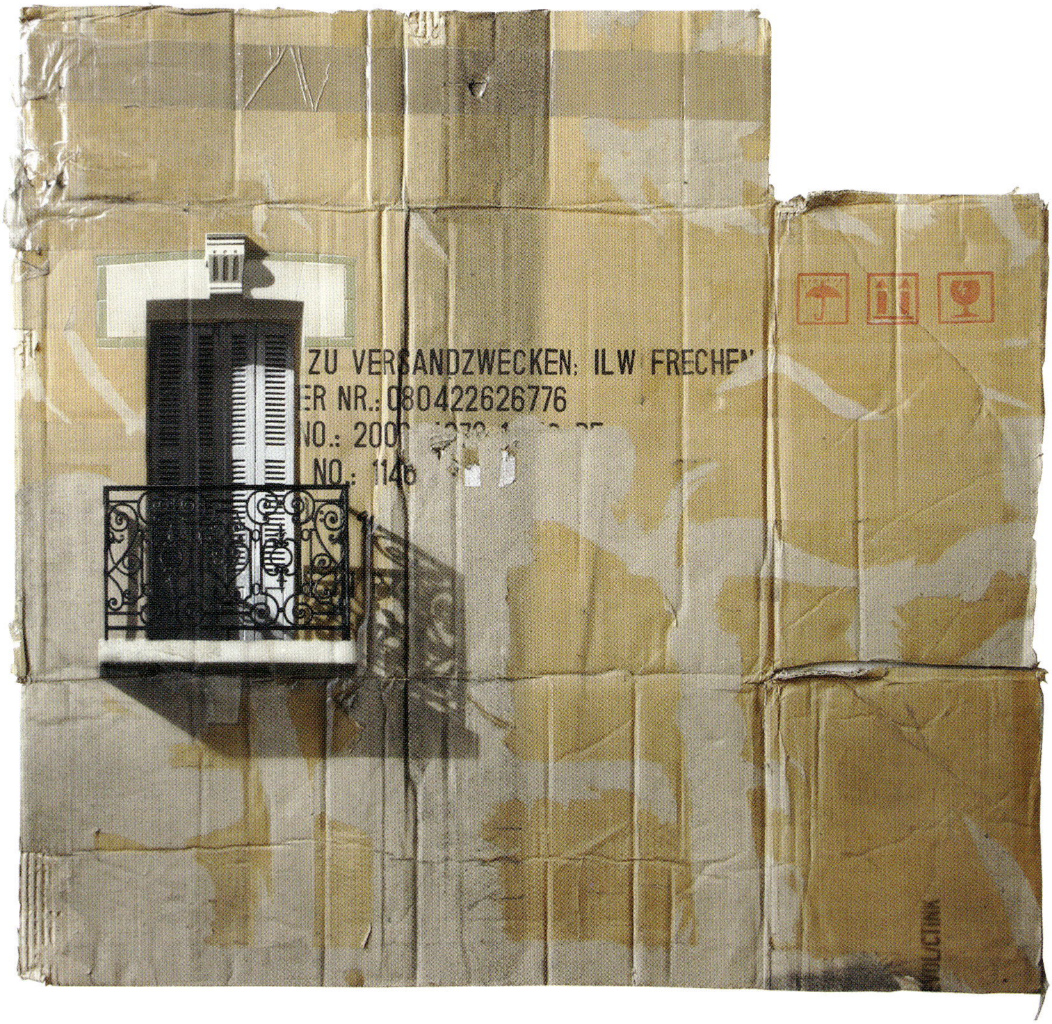

ZU VERSANDZWECKEN: ILW FRECHEN
ER NR.: 080422626776
NO.: 200
NO.: 114

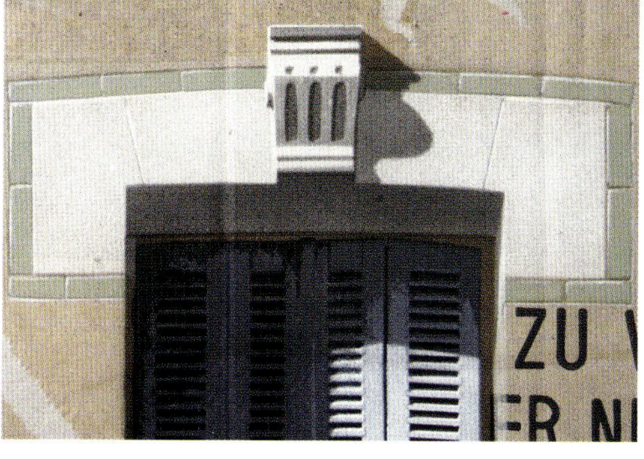
ZU

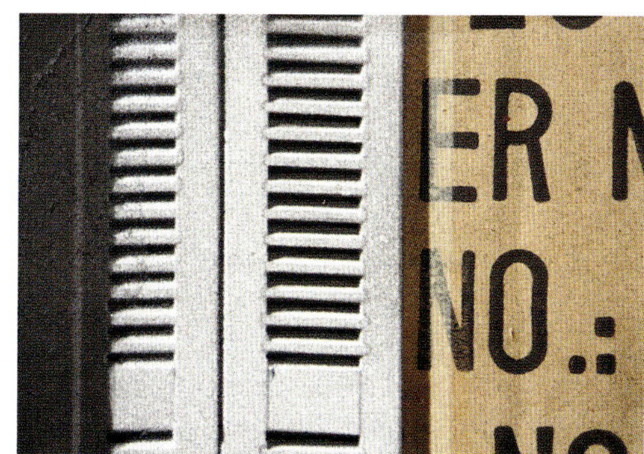
ER
NO.:

1. Add Fuel, Blackburn (UK), 2018. The use of repeating patterns makes it possible to cover large areas.

2. Banksy, Paris, 2018. Example of damask pattern.

3. Inti, Paris, 2018. Stenciled patterns on the floor of the Itinerrance gallery for the *Profane* exhibition.

PATTERNS

Because of its repetitive potential, the stencil is an ideal tool for creating patterns. This characteristic is at the very basis of its invention: from the stonecutters of ancient Egypt to wallpaper manufacturers to our grandmothers who decorated their kitchen cupboards with them, stencils have always been used to create decorative patterns by reproducing the same pattern in staggered rows, like the famous damask pattern, or more simply, the polka-dot pattern. Some graffiti artists, such as Os Gemeos or Inti, incorporate stencil patterns in their artwork. Logan Hicks has designed and produced wallpapers from patterns he created. This method of stenciling is certainly one of the most useful and accessible.

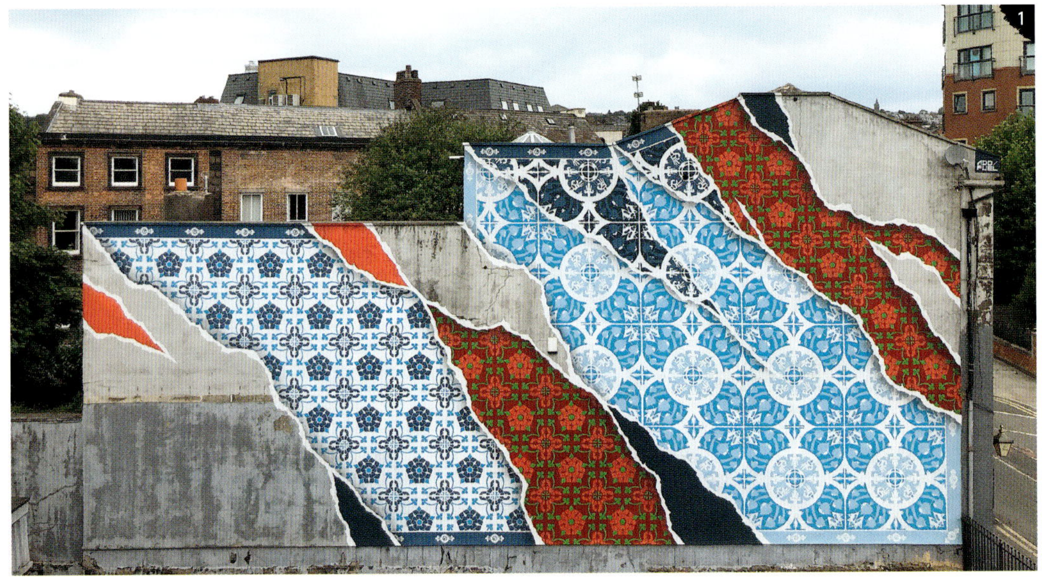
1

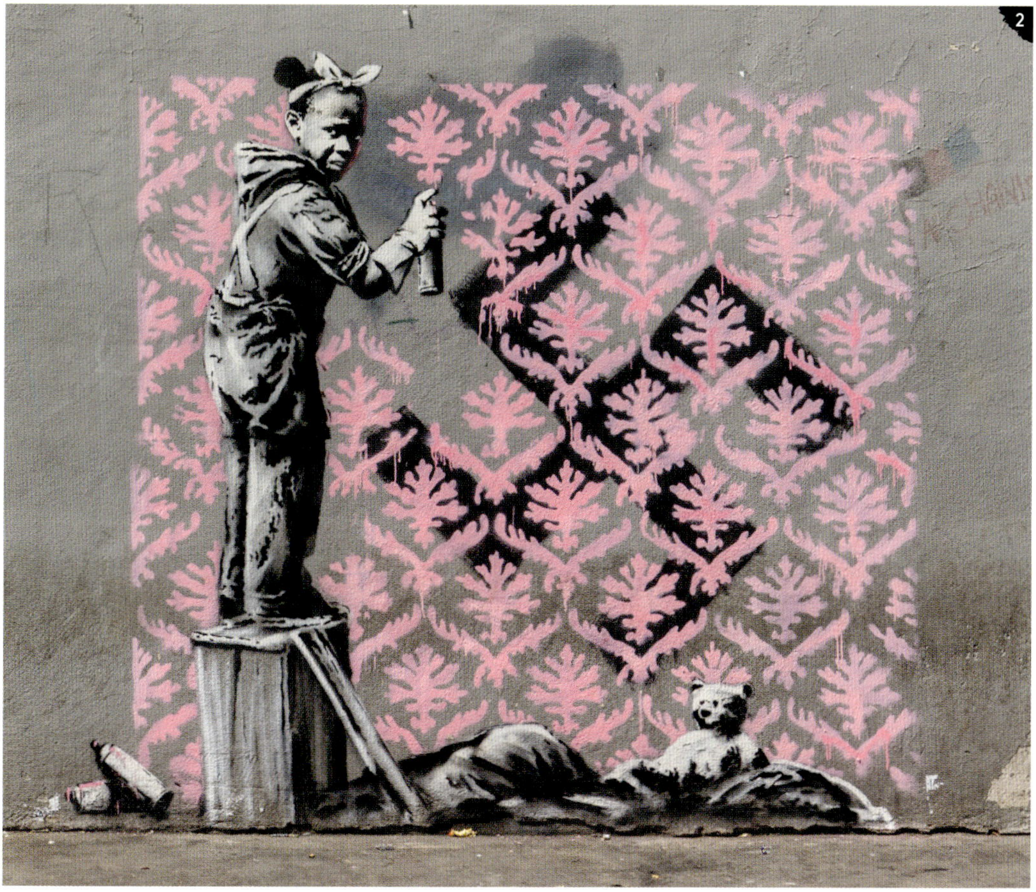

2

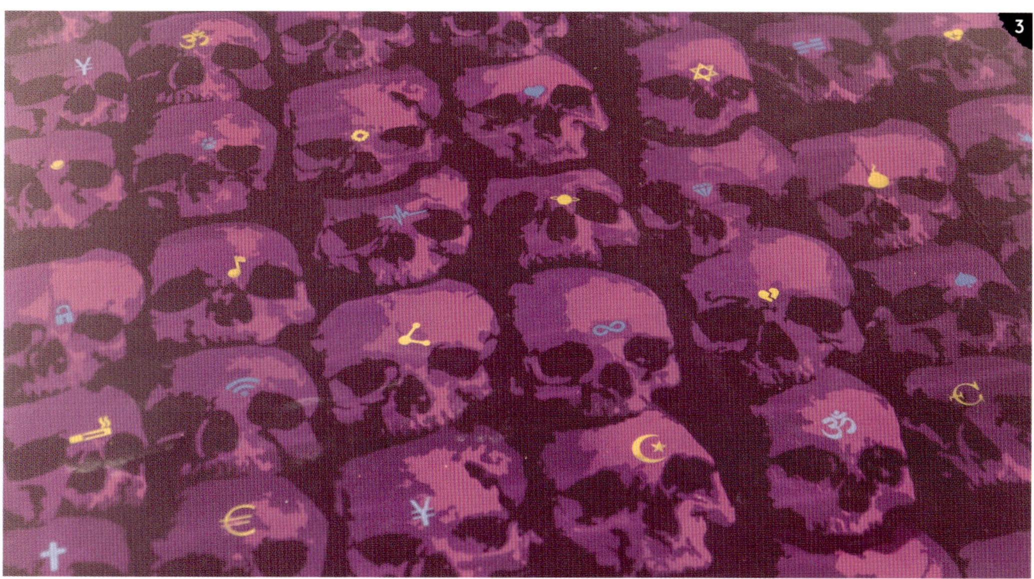

3

1. Sten & Lex, *Nevicata*, Madrid, 2015.

2. John (Poem) Edwards, *Fire and Ice*, 2017. Graffiti-type lettering and textured background done with a stencil.

3. C215, 2019. Abstract composition made from a combination of stencil-painted motifs.

ABSTRACT

Contrary to popular belief, a stencil is not a tool exclusively reserved for figurative painting. On the contrary, you can use it with complete disregard for figurative coherence, to obtain abstract rendering. A cutout doesn't necessarily need to represent something specific, or even to have a definite form. A French artist, an anarchist, certainly my favorite stencil artist and the one who has influenced me the most, has been a pioneer of abstract work since the 1980s. He uses stencils without worrying about anything other than the abstract vision of his work, which has become a Dadaist composition of incongruous forms and messages, of colors put in tension with one another. His work reflects, to me, the quintessence of stencil mastery: to paint not a stencil, but with a stencil. It is pure painting. This artist is called Epsylon Point.

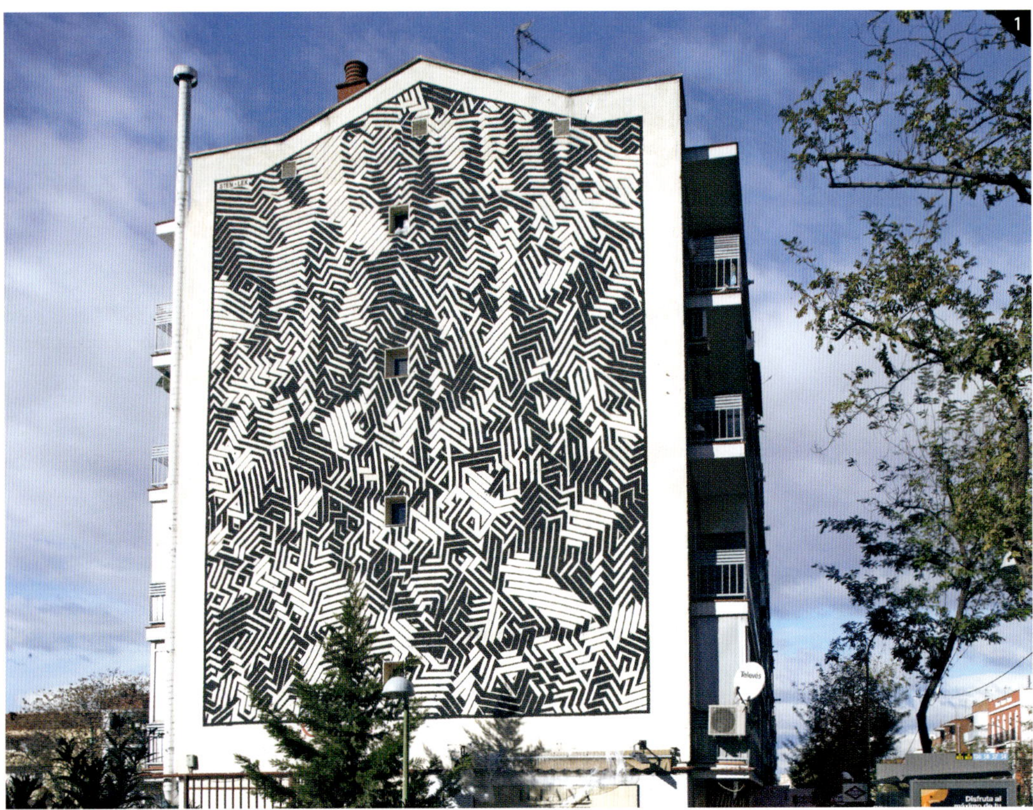
1

2

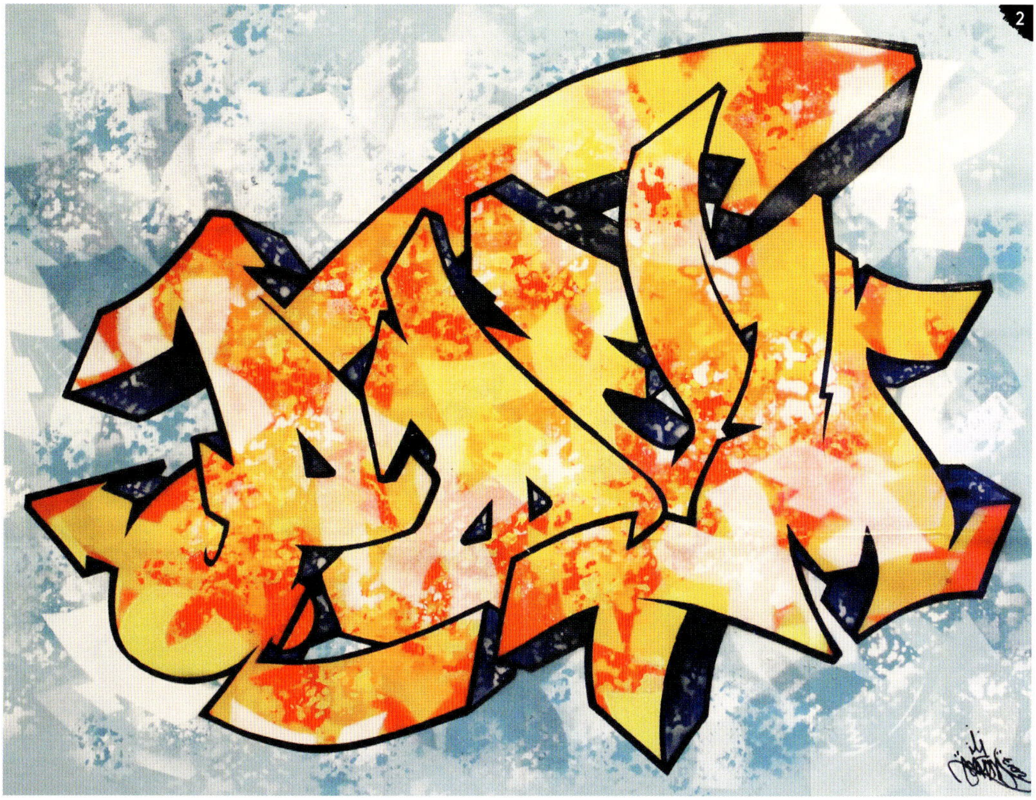

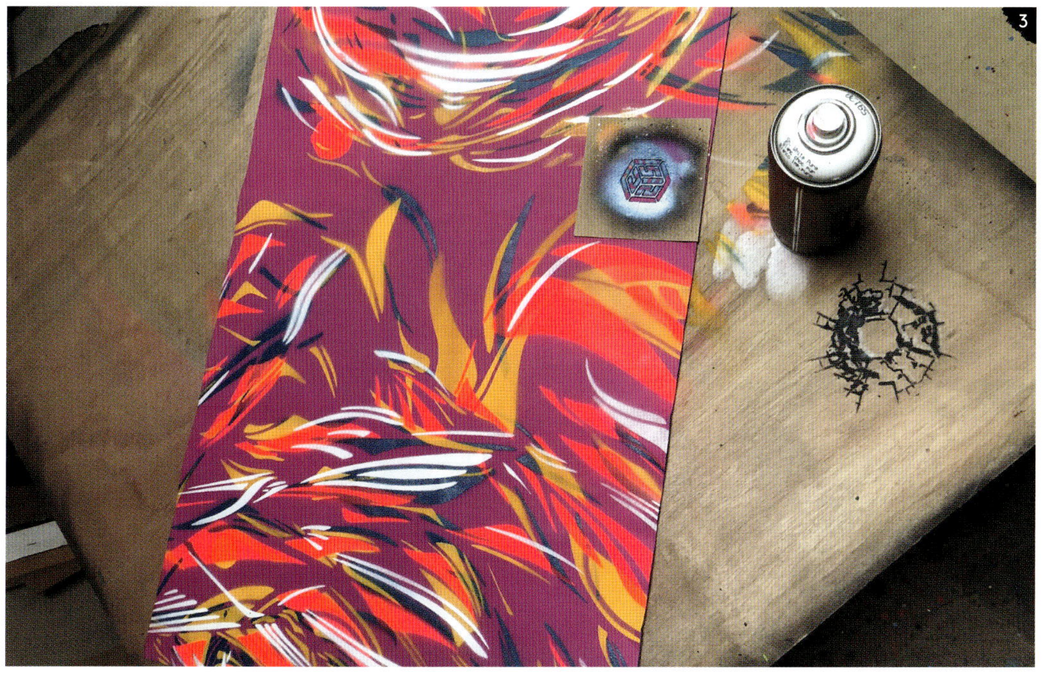

3

Les amoureux (detail), 2005. Spray paint and stencils on tarpaulin.

INTERVIEW WITH EPSYLON POINT

Coming from the anarchist movement of the 1970s and the circus universe, Epsylon Point is an unclassifiable artist. His life mixes art and performance. He has been painting in the streets since the end of the 1970s and then adopted stencil in the mid-1980s. His seemingly incoherent Dada language is a clever mix of provocation and derision.

Facebook: @EpsylonPointStencils

Why did you choose stencils rather than another painting technique?
Technically, I don't know how to draw well enough to make a portrait or an image correctly. Stenciling was a way of reproducing an image that I would never have been able to do so well by hand.

How do you make your stencils?
I take pictures, print them and place a transparent plastic film on top of them, on which I draw the shapes to be cut out later. Generally, I work on an A3 or A4 format, then I enlarge it with a photocopier to reach the necessary size because I don't have a computer. Once it's at the desired size, which at the moment is 31" x 43" (80 x 110 cm), I glue the result on 250 gsm cardboard and cut out the shapes.

I'm a purist: for me, a stencil is a single layer. Those who use several layers, it's because they don't know how to do it with just one. When there are two or three layers, with black and white, it's easy to make an eye, for example: you go around the eye with black and the center with white. Me, I make the complete circle with both levels directly on a layer.

What I like is to draw the shapes. Cutting is a pain in the ass; what counts for me is drawing.

How do you see the evolution of stencil techniques since you started out?
At the beginning, we were in a hurry to go and paint on the walls. We couldn't stay long because it was illegal, so the single stencil was indispensable. Little by little, all the art school students arrived with their computers and Photoshop, and they started to make multilayers without worrying about the time constraint that's typical of painting in the street. And they all do the same thing. I'm not talking about those who cut by hand; that's something else.

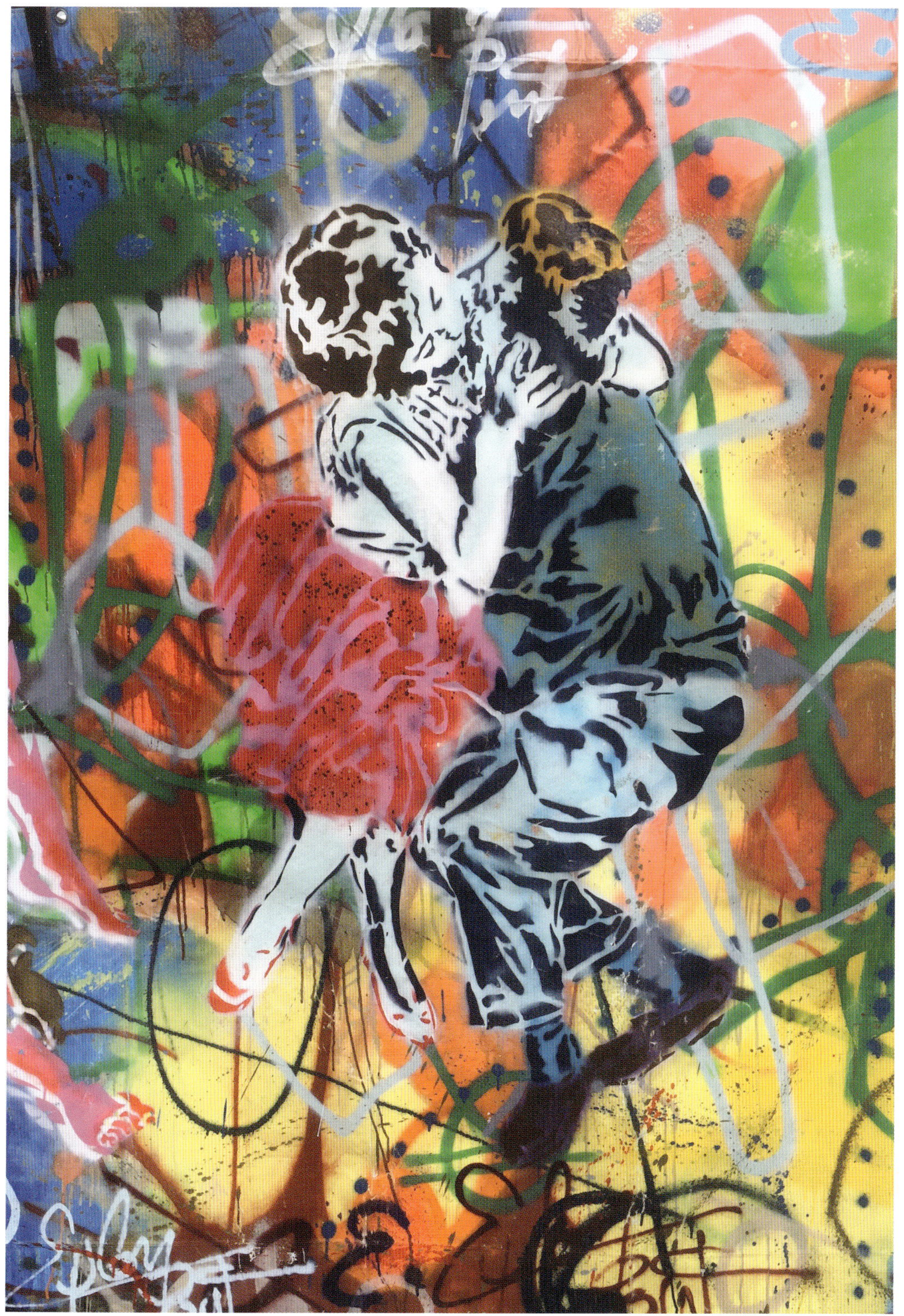

1. Cutting out in progress, 2015.

2. From 2010.

3. *Les marins génois*, 2018. Spray paint and stencils on tarpaulin.

Who are the artists who inspire you in your stencil work?

I wasn't inspired by other stencil artists; since I was among the first, I found my own way. I appreciate many artists, but they don't influence me. I work in a different way. It takes me a long time to form an opinion, but as soon as I understand something, I don't stop.

What are the limits of stencils as a tool?

The limitation is that it is simply a tool, so it all depends on the person using it. It's like a brush or anything else; you're not dependent on your tool. When you have a tool, you can do whatever you want with it, over, under, torn, etc. The stencil is not sacred in itself. I've given some away. For a long time, when I ran a school in my workshop, I allowed those who used spray cans to use my stencils to paint, and to the other artists I explained the stencils in detail. Everyone understands, or not.

Me, I paint. The stencil is just an object. I use squeegees, brushes, spray cans, I make abstract paintings and sometimes I add a stencil on top. First I paint it in white or black and then I come back in with colors. I don't set rules for myself; the paint takes care of it. For example, if I go too fast, the paint doesn't dry, so I can't get what I want. There are so many possibilities.

I am an abstract painter. Sometimes you can recognize an image in my work, but when I do it just with a line and I don't fill it in, it takes a lot of looking. What I enjoy is doing abstract painting, pink, green, a line of blue. That's what keeps me alive; the rest, I don't really give a damn.

For you, is a stencil a frame or a freedom?

It's just an object to work with; it allows me to have a line if I want it, to fly over it or not . . . It's just an object, like a brush, nothing more.

Can you describe your studio for us?

In winter, I do all my cutting in my room. I have two rooms of 33 square feet (10 square meters), I have my table and all my mess for painting—Poska and spray paint cans. For a while, I had stopped stenciling because I was fed up with it, but now I've started again.

In the spring, I go down to the social center where I live. There are two garages there, and that's where I store all my stuff. I put trestles outside and hang the painting materials in the yard. It's a lifestyle; I've been doing it for forty years.

I don't mind being poor; it's voluntary poverty. I don't chase after money, clothes, all that. The only thing I'm interested in is painting. And when I'm not doing that, I go to the multimedia library.

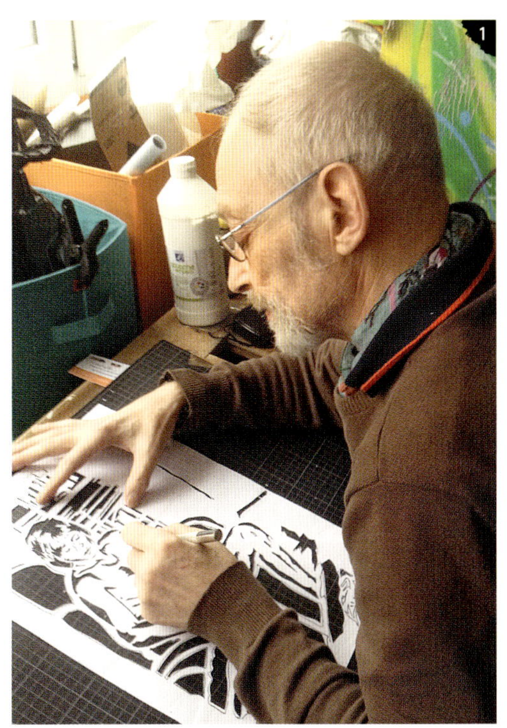

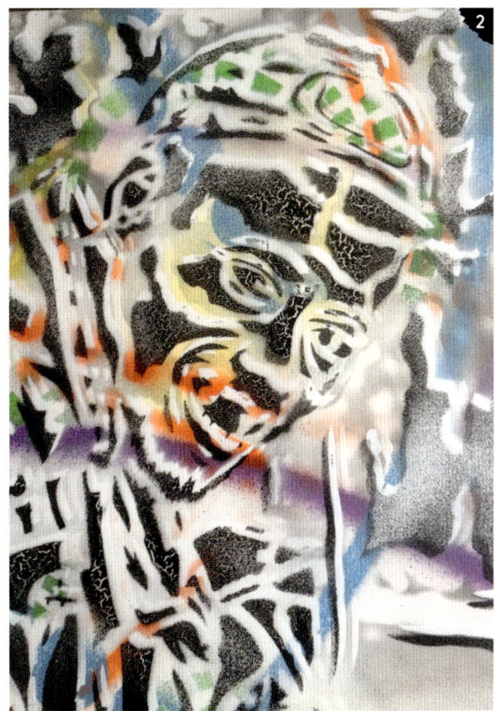

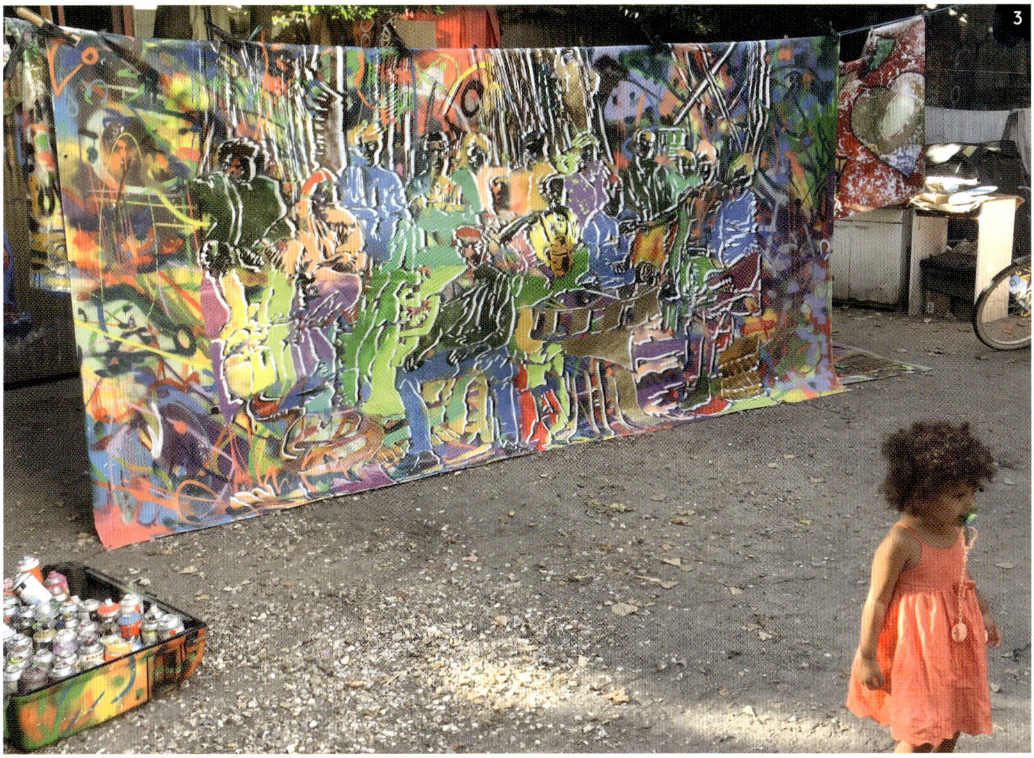

ACKNOWLEDGMENTS

Many thanks to the artists who agreed to contribute to this book, which I hope will be useful to future generations, because the history of stencil is still in its infancy. So much remains to be invented.

In this imperfect and subjective book, I wasn't able to include all the stencil artists would have liked to, including Banksy, Obey, Hao, Fremantle, Mosko, Artiste-Ouvrier, Jana & JS, BrokenCrow, John Fekner, Mr. Brainwash, Btoy, Nazza Stencil, Lucamaleonte, Martin Whatson, Smile, Penny, Zibe, Jean Bombeur, Alice Pasquini, Blek le rat, DOT DOT DOT, Stefan Winterle, Jaune, Kusek, Vexta, Fake, Fin Dac, Dotmasters, Anders, Noty, Aroz, Pure Evil, Pøbel, Dolk, Faile, Adey, Goin, Le Bateleur, RNST, MIMI the ClowN, Docteur Bergman, Nasty, Tian, KristX, LadyBug, Raf Urban, Ose, Silex, Ouroboros, Ka, BZT, Guaté Mao, Spizz . . .

. . . And there are also those that I have awkwardly forgotten or those that I don't know yet. The list is endless.

Samantha Longhi's *Stencil History X*, a collective work that I edited in 2007, has brought me so much.

I offer a special thought for Michel Longhi, who passed away in 2008, whose Paris Stencils site was the first to inventory the stencils in the city.

IMAGE CREDITS

All works and photographs are by the author, except: p. 5: Faile. Photo: Lionel Belluteau-www.unoeilquitraine.fr; p. 7 top left: photo, Patrick Colpron; p. 10: J. Monney / MC; p. 11 left: Actualité Universal; p. 11 r.: Coll. Dixmier/ KHARBINETAPABOR; p. 14 r.: Snik a.k.a Nik Ellis; p. 16 bottom: Monkey Bird. Photo: Sebastien Pons / Hans Lucas; p. 17 top: photo, Martha Cooper; p. 18: photo, Nicolas Gzeley; p. 19 left: Epsylon Point © Adagp, Paris, 2020; p. 19 r.: Aleteïa; p. 22 r.: Nemo © Adagp, Paris, 2020. Photo: Roswitha Guillemin; p. 24 top left: Snik a.k.a Nik Ellis; p. 24 bottom left: Speedy Graphito. Photo: Sarah-Mei Chan; pp. 24–25 bottom: Sten Lex; p. 26 bottom left: Speedy Graphito; pp. 26–27 top: Obey Giant Art, Inc. Photo: Lionel Belluteau-www.unoeilquitraine.fr; p. 27 top r.: Monkey Bird. Photo: Lionel Belluteau-www.unoeilquitraine.fr; p. 27 bottom–p. 32: M-city; pp. 35–39: Monkey Bird. Photo p. 35: Andrea Berlese, photos pp. 36–37: Ema Kawanago; p. 41 r.: Stinkfish; pp. 43 and 45: Studio Eyrolles. Photo: Shutterstock/Boyan Dimitrov; p. 47: Artcock; pp. 48–51: Sten Lex; pp. 53–56: Snik a.k.a Nik Ellis. Photo p. 53: Wijnand Plekker; pp. 54–55: Ian Cox; p. 56: Nika Kramer; pp. 57–62: Stew. © Adagp, Paris, 2020; p. 63 r.: Stinkfish. Photos: Anke Wiedmann; pp. 64–65 left center: Monkey Bird; pp. 70–71: Nick Walker; p. 75 top: Stinkfish; p. 75 bottom: Ben Eine Studio. Photo: OurTypes; pp. 77–80: Stinkfish. Photos pp. 78–80: Anke Wiedmann; p. 81 r. col.: C215/Mouvement ATD Quart Monde; pp. 83–85: Nick Walker; p. 86 r.: JEFAEROSOL. © Adagp, Paris, 2020; p. 88 r.: Epsylon Point. © Adagp, Paris, 2020; pp. 89–90: Speedy Graphito; p. 91 top r.: Epsylon Point. © Adagp, Paris, 2020; pp. 93–97: Add Fuel. Photo p. 93: A.B.O.; p. 98: JEFAEROSOL/Artcurial DR. © Adagp, Paris, 2020; pp. 99–100: JEFAEROSOL. © Adagp, Paris, 2020; p. 101 left: Add Fuel; p. 101 r.–p. 105: Aleteïa; p. 106 r.: Stew. © Adagp, Paris, 2020; p. 112 top: Logan Hicks; p. 112 bottom left: Stinkfish; p. 112 bottom r.: Sten Lex; pp. 114–115 top: Wrdsmth. Photo: Luna Park; p. 115 top r.: Ben Eine Studio. Photo: Hanson Images; pp. 114–115 bottom: Banksy. Photo: Luna Park; pp. 116–119: Ben Eine Studio. Photos pp. 116–117 and p. 119 top: Hanson Images, photo p. 119 bottom: Ian Cox; p. 121 top and bottom r.: © MISS TIC—Adagp/Paris, 2020; p. 121 bottom left: photo Camille Paul; pp. 122–123 left: M-city; pp. 125–129: Logan Hicks; pp. 131 and 133: Evol. © Adagp, Paris, 2020; p. 134: Add Fuel; p. 135 top: Banksy. Photo: Lionel Belluteau, www.unoeilquitraine.fr; p. 135 bottom: INTI Castro. Photo: Lionel Belluteau, www.unoeilquitraine.fr; p. 136: Sten Lex; p. 137 top: John (Poem) Edwards. Photo: Jeannette Mayol; pp. 139–141: Epsylon Point. © Adagp, Paris, 2020.

In spite of the author's best efforts, there may be some image rightsholders that we were unable to locate. Please contact the publisher with any image information so that we may correct future printings.

Other Schiffer Books on Related Subjects:

Graffiti Murals: Exploring the Impacts of Street Art,
Patrick Verel, ISBN 978-0-7643-4899-0

Detroit Graffiti, Chris Freitag, ISBN 978-0-7643-4688-0

Street Art Santiago Chile, Lord K2, ISBN 978-0-7643-4927-0

Translated from the French by Simulingua, Inc.
Originally published as *Le Manuel du Pochoir*
© Editions Eyrolles, 2020, Paris

Library of Congress Control Number: 2021942720

Type set in Botera TFE/Brown
Graphic design and layout: monsieurgerard.com
Sketch: Claire Fauvain
Editorial collaboration: Émilie Poirrier

ISBN: 978-0-7643-6327-6
Printed in India

Published by Schiffer Publishing, Ltd.
4880 Lower Valley Road
Atglen, PA 19310
Phone: (610) 593-1777; Fax: (610) 593-2002
Email: Info@schifferbooks.com
Web: www.schifferbooks.com

STENCILS & DIRECTIONS FOR USE

Here are three detachable stencils to get you started: use them freely in your own work, and practice with them before cutting your own creations. Go get your spray cans!

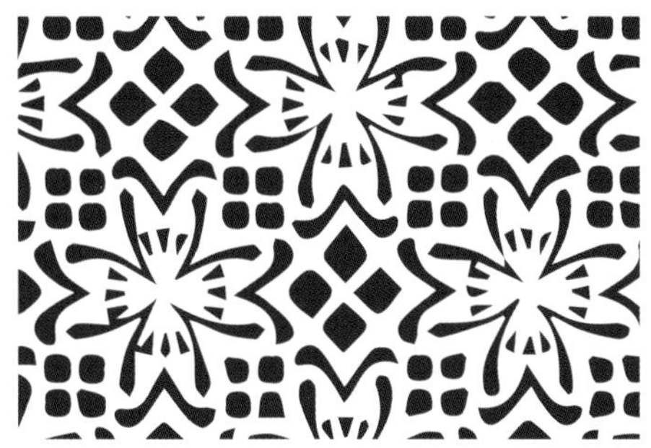

Pattern: This stencil can be painted with any color. To cover a larger area, repeat the stencil by matching up the pattern edges each time.

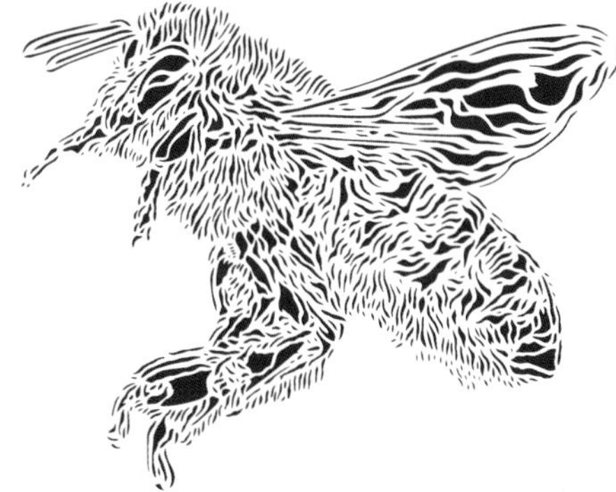

Bee: Use a dark color on a light background to paint this stencil.

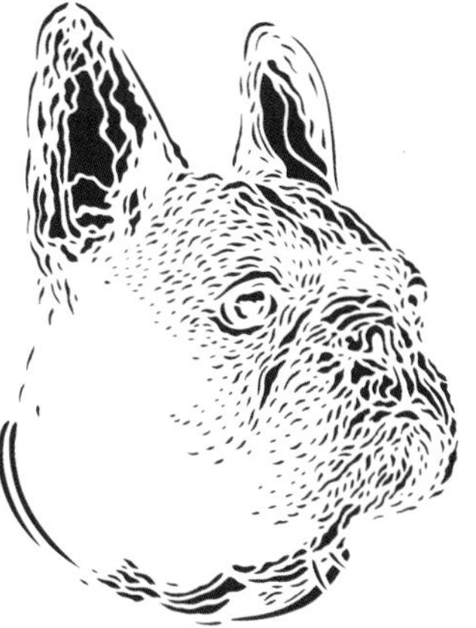

Dog: For this stencil representing my dog, use a light color on a dark background.

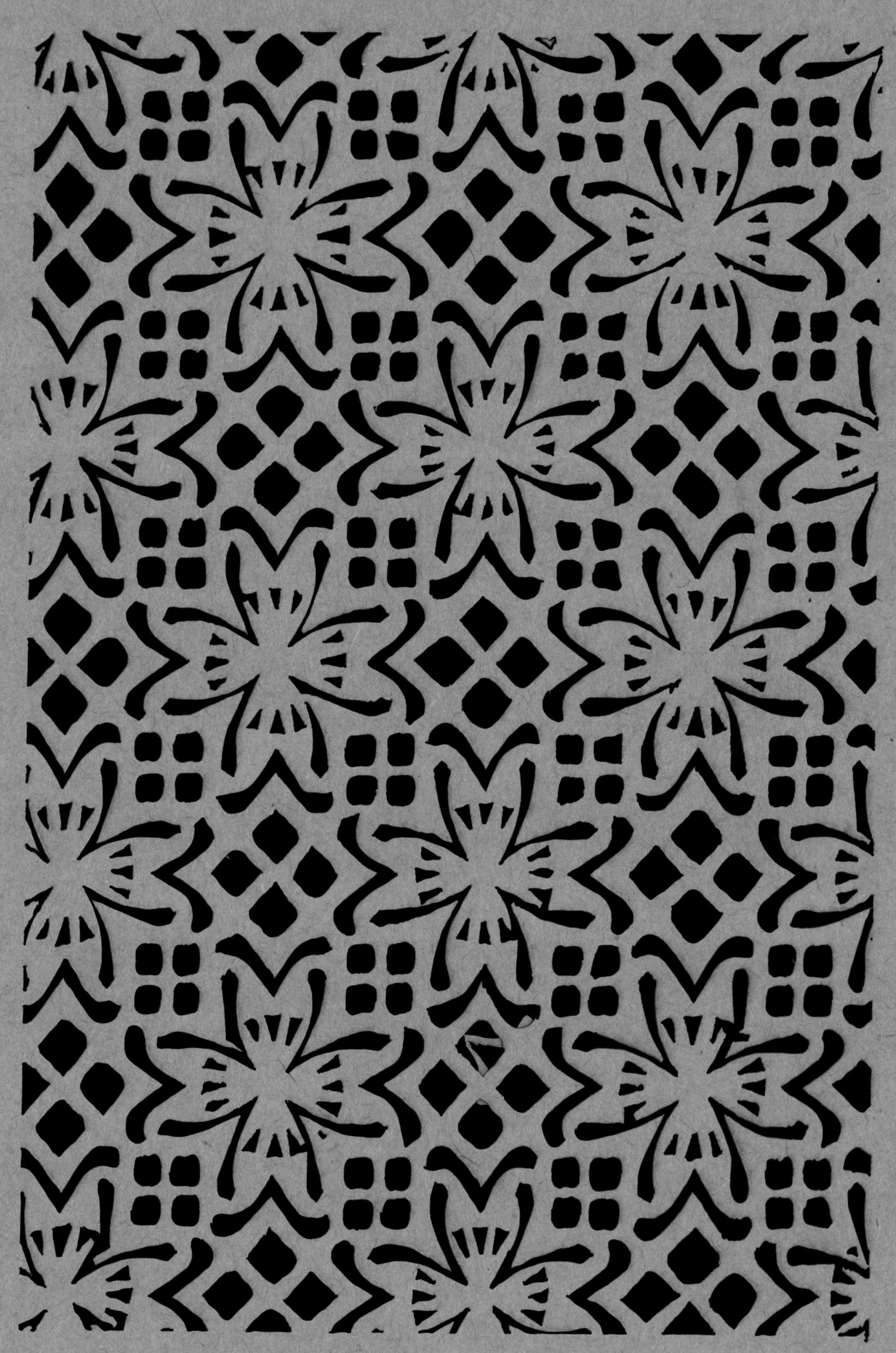

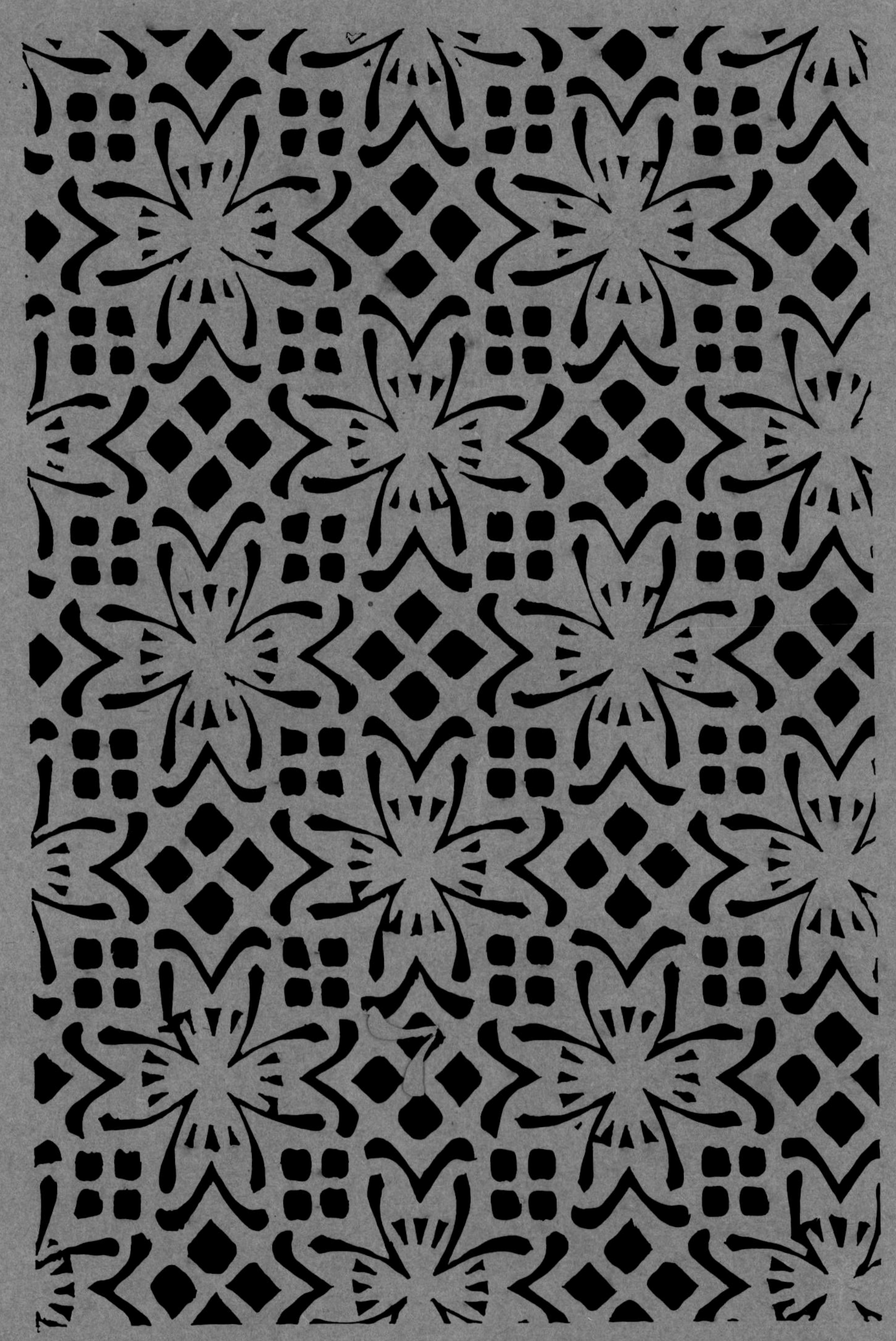

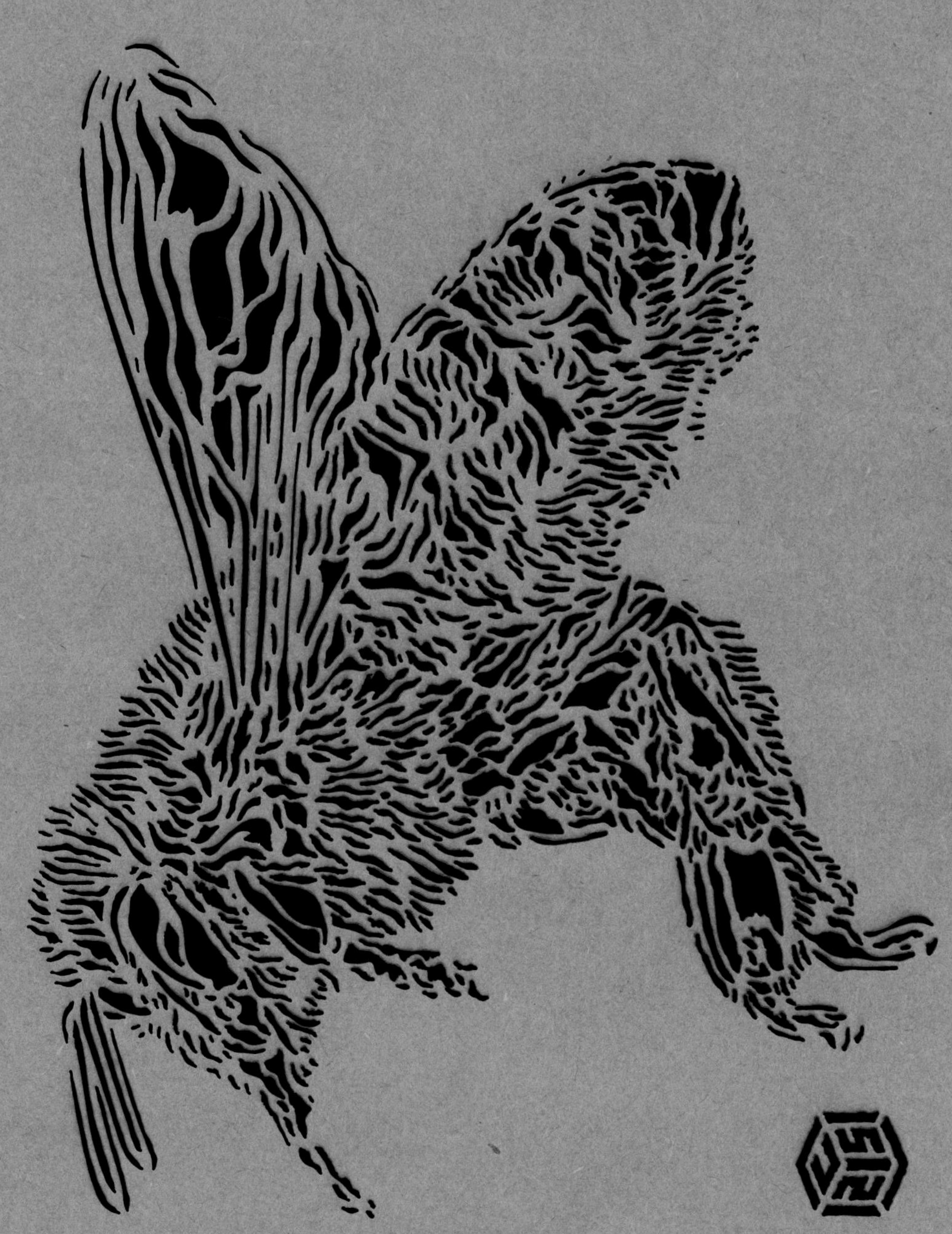

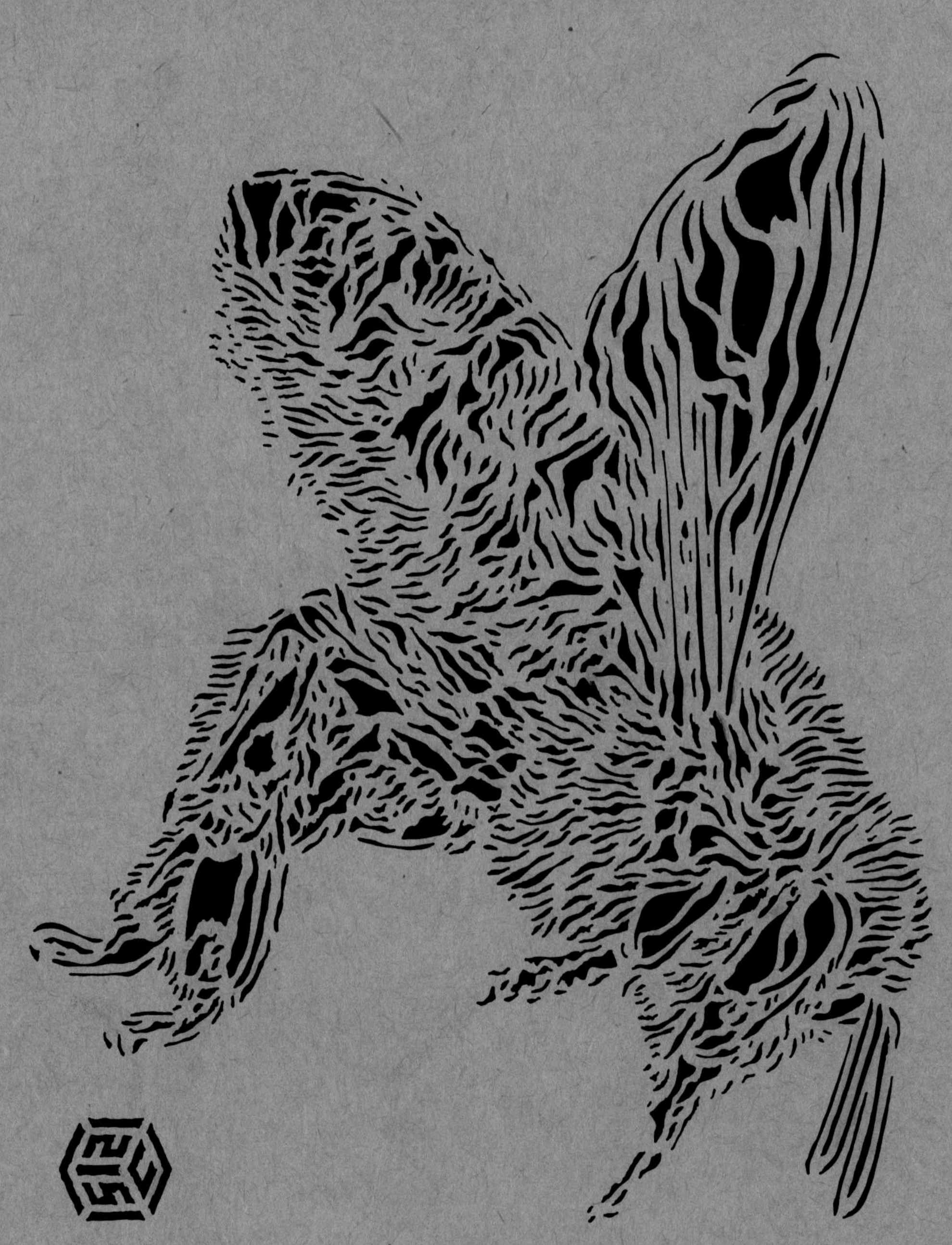

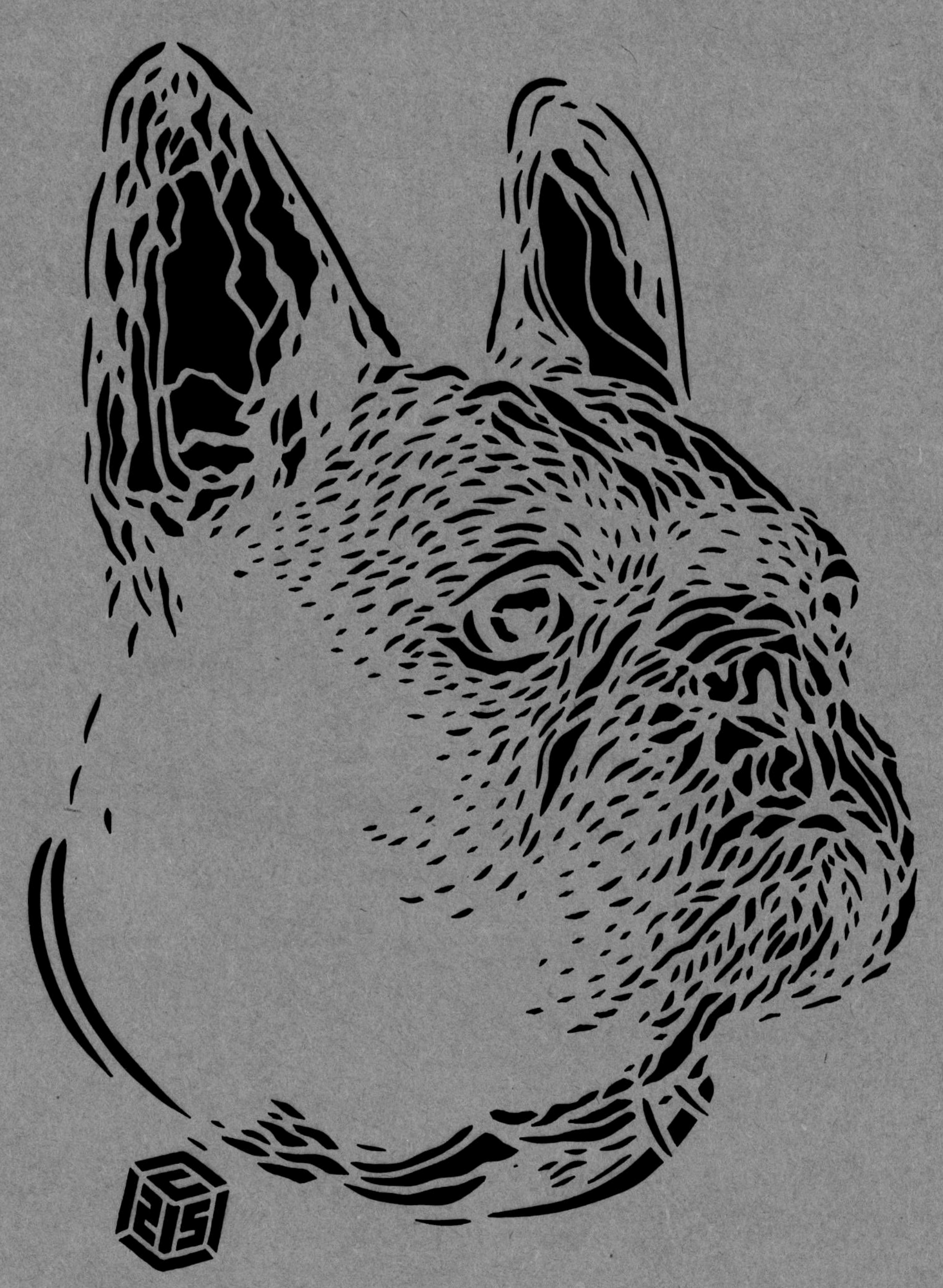

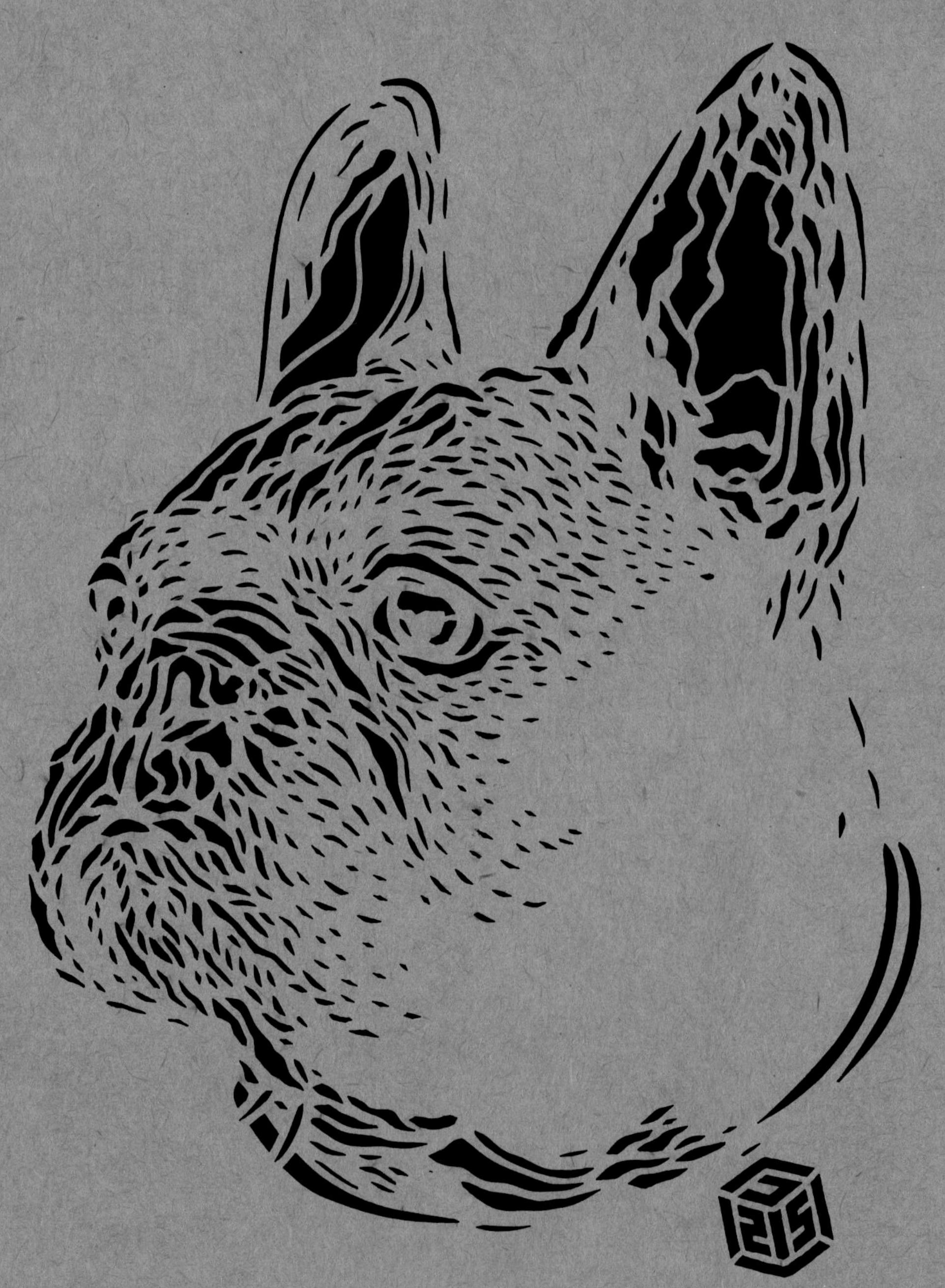